WHEN SOMEONE
YOU LOVE
IS DYING

WHEN SOMEONE YOU LOVE IS DYING

A Handbook for Counselors and Those Who Care

**Ruth Lewshenia Kopp, M.D.
with Stephen Sorenson**

Ministry
Resources
Library

Zondervan Publishing House • Grand Rapids, MI

WHEN SOMEONE YOU LOVE IS DYING
Formerly published under the title
ENCOUNTER WITH TERMINAL ILLNESS
Copyright © 1980 by The Zondervan Corporation
Grand Rapids, Michigan

MINISTRY RESOURCES LIBRARY is an imprint of Zondervan
Publishing House, 1415 Lake Drive, S.E.,
Grand Rapids, Michigan 49506

Library of Congress Cataloging in Publication Data

Kopp, Ruth Lewshenia, 1947-
    When someone you love is dying.

    1. Terminal care. 2. Death—Psychological aspects. 3. Terminal care—
Moral and religious aspects. 4. Christian life—1960-   I. Sorenson, Stephen,
joint author. II. Title. R726.8K66   248.8'6   80-10982
ISBN 0-310-41601-9

All scripture quotations, unless otherwise noted, are taken from the HOLY BIBLE:
NEW INTERNATIONAL VERSION (North American Edition). Copyright © 1978 by
The International Bible Society. Used by permission of Zondervan Bible Publish-
ers.

Designed and edited by Edward Viening

Printed in the United States of America

85 86 87 88 89 90 / 10 9 8 7 6 5 4 3

DEDICATION

This book represents a dream and a commitment: a dream of life in the face of inevitable death lived fully and courageously; a commitment to the men and women who have shared their living and dying with me, that their lives and deaths would help bring better care and more compassionate understanding to others. Therefore, I wish to dedicate this book to Hospice of Central Illinois, which is the other half of the dream, and embodies in a practical way the commitment.

CONTENTS

ACKNOWLEDGMENTS

My first and deepest debt of gratitude is to my parents, Rev. and Mrs. Constantine Lewshenia, for the way in which they taught me the Scriptures from an early age, and also taught me how to find my own answers to life's questions in God's Word. Both by direct teaching and their personal example, they made the Word of God a living and meaningful authority for all of life.

My husband, Dr. James Kopp, has continued my parents' influence and example, making the Word of God central in our home. He has continually supported me in my search for practical answers to the heart-rending issues posed in our joint practice, and has been enthusiastic in helping me share what I have learned. He has also shared with me his own quests and discoveries while facing the issues of life and death.

The patients and families who have shared their living and dying with me are too many to name, yet in my memory I can see each one, can relive the time we shared, and remember what I learned from them. I am grateful to all who generously opened their lives to me and showed me the beauty and agony and humor and horror of living with dying. Along with these people are the nurses and aides and social workers who have shared with me in the care of the terminally ill, and who have enriched my experience with their own.

Finally, I want to acknowledge my friends who encouraged and prayed to see that this book got written and published; prominent among these are Cherie Cochran, Chan Kuhn, Pete and Anita Deyneka, and my agent, Jim Johnson.

SECTION ONE

DENIAL IN TERMINAL ILLNESS

1

WHY ARE WE AFRAID TO DIE?

IN TODAY'S SOCIETY, we live in what can be called a death-denying culture. By and large, we deal with our fear of death by denying the very fact of death. For example, dying people are separated from society and placed in hospitals or nursing homes. Those who are approaching death because of their age are grouped together in retirement homes, "old people's homes," and special living areas for the elderly—far away from the rest of us.

Once dying and elderly people are segregated into identifiable groups, they are easily avoided. In many hospitals, for instance, dying individuals often are placed at the end of a corridor (away from the light, activity, and life of the nurses' station) where they "won't be disturbed" (or disturb). Children are not allowed to visit them, and family members and friends may come only during regular visiting hours, which are rarely longer than three or four hours a day. Alone most of the day and all night, the dying "patient" remains, until he dies, in strange surroundings, among strangers, without any say in what happens to him.

Even when the dying individual is not physically alone, it is unusual for anyone to be *with* him, sensing and sharing his feelings of pain, bewilderment, and anger. If the individual tries to share his feelings, he runs the risk of being totally alone. Few people will really listen to him; fewer people will give him a meaningful response. If, on the other hand, he doesn't share his feelings, he remains emotionally solitary.

As a result, the individual is alone. He usually hides his triumphs and defeats, his insights, and his feelings carefully, lest he upset, shock, or inconvenience those around him. He waits passively, allowing himself to be cared for, treated, and "worked on," and carries on little discussion because he is afraid to lose the few people who come to treat him and spend time with him.

DEATH IS SEPARATION

Death, we realize, is a one-way journey. Consequently, thinking of death in terms of separation is not new. From time to time, I think of a song that includes the words "every time we say 'good-bye' I die a little"* and realize that we tend to equate death with separation. Besides the vague fear of death itself, other aspects of dying make us hesitant and fearful. We have real, human concerns—not specifically Christian or non-Christian, spiritual or unspiritual—that affect nearly everyone, regardless of age or social status.

Physical Separation

Death is the ultimate physical separation, and it is epitomized by aloneness. Even if a dying individual avoids the frightening isolation of a hospital room at the end of the corridor by living in his own home, sleeping in his own bed, and being surrounded by family and friends, he knows that the fact of death itself will mean separation from the familiar things, places, and people that are dear to him. Death is the door leading from the known world into the unknown or, at best, partly known world beyond.

Separation of Mind and Body

In addition to physical separation from things, people, and places, we will experience a much more devastating separation at death. The "me" in each of us—the conscious, thinking part of ourselves—will be separated from our bodies. The familiar body that we each have loved, hated, and cared for all our lives will die and be left behind. Many people experience a prelude to this type of separation during their final illness. Such things as weight loss or weight gain due to disease or medication, loss of hair, changes in voice, and inability to tolerate usual activity all make our bodies seem like strangers to us and accentuate the fact that we will soon be separated from them.

Spiritual Separation From God

The final separation, or "death," according to the Bible, occurs when a man is separated from God after death. At the time of final judgment, those who have not become Christians will be finally and irrevocably separated from Him. We can be thankful that God has provided the means by which we can be spared this final spiritual death and receive eternal life through Jesus Christ.

WHY ARE WE AFRAID TO DIE?

It is important that we understand several of the reasons why we naturally fear death.

---

*Every Time We Say Good-bye, by Cole Porter. Published by Warner Bros.

Because Death Severs Our Ties to the Familiar

We have already touched on the fact that death pulls us away from familiar people, places, and things, and I believe that the analogy of a journey further illustrates this point. When we leave home to travel, even for a short length of time, we feel both the sadness of leaving and the anticipation of our trip. When we leave family behind as well as home, our mixed feelings are more pronounced. Death is a parallel to this last kind of move, for in death there is no postal service, no telephone, and no opportunity to "come back for a visit, sometime."

With this perspective in mind, is it really so strange that most of us (even as Christians) are not eager to face death? To use myself as an example, the thought of death doesn't usually fill me with anticipation and eagerness. I look forward to my own death with a heaviness and reluctance. My children are small, and I want to see them grow! My career is barely beginning, and I have exciting plans for the future that I would like to see worked out. My home is lovely and comfortable; my friends and relatives are dear to me. Right now, nothing indicates that I will not be able to see my children grow or my career plans unfold. There is no immediately forseeable day when I will no longer enjoy my friends and home. However, if someone should tell me tomorrow that my life expectancy is a matter of months rather than the thirty to fifty years I expect to enjoy, this surely would affect my attitude toward death.

Because the Time of Death Is Uncertain

Even when we know "for sure" that someone is dying, we don't know when death will come. Recently, Mrs. Clausson went into the hospital. I thought she might live a week; my husband, who is in practice with me, was convinced that she wouldn't survive the night. Almost eight weeks to the day after her admission, she died. Other people may take a sudden turn for the worse and die when everyone expected them to live. My neighbor was apparently healthy and well one day and died the next.

Death comes to people in different ways. It can be peaceful and pleasant, or it can be violent, painful, and repulsive. Some people say a calm "good-by" and just stop breathing; others die in a convulsive horror and are totally repulsive—vomiting, bleeding, etc. Terminal illness can be terribly disfiguring and cause hideous bloating or draining sores that are ugly and foul-smelling. Loss of hair, shortness of breath, dizziness, and nausea can also cause tremendous discomfort. Mental acuity may be impaired or lost completely. In short, we are afraid of what terminal illness can do to us, both physically and emotionally, for we don't know if we'll be able to tolerate our condition as we die.

Because Death Is Basically an Unknown

What happens during death cannot be understood until we experience it. People in the Bible such as Lazarus, who returned from the dead through Christ's healing power, said nothing about death. We can gain some insight into the next world by studying the Bible, but we can't know fully what it is like to die.

Current accounts of "near death" experiences, although interesting and sometimes exciting, generally serve to confuse rather than clarify the issue. Death by definition is irreversible. That is part of its mystery and a source of our fear. So the experiences of those who have been successfully resuscitated fall into a separate category. At present, we have no way of evaluating their relationship to the final experience of death.

In addition to this basic difficulty, the data about "near death" experiences has been gathered by many investigators using various methods at widely divergent intervals after their occurrence. This adds to the perplexing problem of knowing just how to evaluate the data.

FROM DEATH'S SEPARATION TO SPIRITUAL RESTORATION

Having come face to face with the devastation of death—its terrible aloneness and cruel tearing apart of families—I have come to a new appreciation of what God did in raising Christ from the dead. Christians, instead of being eternally separated from God, receive restoration to eternal life and the heavenly state God has prepared for them. Christ, who came to earth and died as a man, brings forth from the smell of decay the fragrance of eternal life and a new creation. He is able to destroy the frightening specter of aloneness that we face during our final days. He will never leave us or forsake us (Heb. 13:5), and He alone can hold our hand as we walk through the door of death. He perfectly understands the abandonment and loneliness of dying because of His experiences on the cross.

Although the Bible does not furnish us with many details about the next world, it does offer us a glimpse of what is to come. In Revelation 21:1, we read, "Then I saw a new heaven and a new earth, for the first heaven and the first earth had passed away." Best of all, the Bible promises us that the new world created by God will be free of the laws of deterioration that govern our present world. Christians will be clothed in a new body that is free from the worries of aging and death (see 1 Cor. 15:35–55). To me, a new body means no bifocals, no dentures, no arthritis. As Christians, our physical and mental powers will not decrease.

To be honest, I have in the past thought that the apostle Paul was exaggerating when he wrote in 1 Corinthians 15:19, "If only for this life we have hope in Christ, we are to be pitied more than all men." That was before I came to grips with death's awful destruction and its crippling grip of fear. Now, as I look at the shadow of death, I see the glorious, healing, hope-filled light of the Resurrection. In the Resurrection, and *only* in the Resurrection, lies an answer to our fears about death. Armed with the knowledge that Jesus Christ rose from the dead, we can at least approach death with courage, if not with open arms.

Conversely, it is only when we take a long look at death—the fearful enemy Christ has defeated—that we can begin to comprehend the greatness of His victory. I believe that knowing Christ personally can give us the courage to look honestly at death and dying, and I know that a fuller appreciation of death will enlarge our knowledge of the greatness of the salvation Christ has offered us. With this affirmation of hope, let's examine the reactions of some people who discovered that they were dying.

2

I DON'T BELIEVE IT!

WHEN AN INDIVIDUAL learns that he has a fatal illness, his initial reaction is typically, "I don't believe it!" The same disbelieving reaction occurs in close friends or family members of the person diagnosed as having the fatal illness.

DENIAL: A GREAT SAFETY VALVE

We have a great safety valve called denial, which helps us adjust to highly emotional situations by giving us time to gather our defenses so that we can cope with those situations. Initially, denial is demonstrated by such statements as, "It's not real"; "It all seems like a dream"; or "This can't *really* be happening." Denial is an extremely good defense mechanism that is commonly used in our modern culture. News of a highly emotional nature, whether good or bad, is likely to be met with initial denial. If we watch the Miss America Pageant, the Emmy Awards, the Olympics, or similar events on television, for example, we will see denial in the reactions of the winners to overwhelmingly good news.

Perhaps our favorite use of denial is in regard to death. We tend to cope with death—like we do other things we can't face—by denying its reality and focusing on remaining young and well. Youth is beauty, we think, and death is an accident that happens to other people, not to us. We live as if we will never grow old. We want to look, think, and act young, communicating to others that we are healthy and strong. After all, isn't this the *now* generation? But when all these barriers to truth are crushed before the real presence of death, our initial reaction is, "It can't be!"

In this "It can't be" response is a reflection of the first phase of denial that serves as a buffer and safety valve which cushions the impact of a sudden, emotional upheaval. Later, denial of impending death helps us develop a practical state of mind that allows our normal life to continue. However, the initial phase of denial can introduce a second phase: denial of impending death and our true physical condition. We may experience serious, life-threatening delays in seeking medical attention, may not comply with prescribed means of medical management, and may develop attitudes that impair our adjustment (and those of our families) to the drastic alterations the illness will make in our lives.

In order to understand the denial my husband and I encounter each day, it is important for me to briefly summarize our medical practice. Both my husband and I have a practice of hematology (disease of the blood) and medical oncology (drug treatment of cancer). Most of the patients we treat have diseases which give little hope for cure. They may survive for periods of a few weeks to a number of years, but most of them will die of the disease for which we treat them.

Since most of our patients are referred to us by other doctors, we know that their doctors gave them some reason for the referral. Some of the doctors are frank in telling the patients and their families that there is little hope for cure and that the treatment we offer may only give them more time to live, fewer complications, and help them feel better.

In this chapter we will primarily examine the initial denial reaction that terminally ill individuals face, and its harmful aspects. In the following chapter we will explore the second phase of denial. Let's begin by looking at the case history of a man who was forced to recognize initial denial.

THE EFFECTS OF INITIAL DENIAL

Jesse Williams, a young, active, hard-working, competent sales representative for a manufacturer of kitchen aids, was well-respected by both his employer and his customers. His territory included much of central Illinois, and he spent more than half his working time on the road.

When Jesse arrived in Bloomington, Illinois, on a spring tour of his territory, he checked into a motel and began walking down the street to a restaurant. As he walked, he felt a cramping pain in his abdomen. *I guess I've waited too long to eat dinner,* he thought as he entered the restaurant. Dinner didn't relieve his cramps, however, and Jesse found that he didn't really have much of an appetite anyway. *Surely I'll feel better tomorrow,* he told himself. He went back to the motel, called home to talk to his family, went over the next day's appointments, and went to bed.

When he awoke in the morning, he felt better and went to his 9:00 appointment. The morning schedule went fairly well, but he had no appetite for lunch. Shortly after lunch, his cramps started again, forcing him to cancel his 3:00 appointment and go back to the motel. He went out for dinner, feeling a bit better, but his appetite didn't improve.

The next morning the housekeeping service of the motel found Jesse nearly delirious with pain and fever. An ambulance took him to a hospital, and his next several days were a confused blur of pain, tests, and regular visits by nurses and doctors. About a week later, doctors moved Jesse to a Peoria, Illinois, hospital. There, he underwent an exploratory operation in which doctors discovered that he had widespread cancer of the pancreas. Following surgery, he was committed to the care of my husband.

Although both the doctors' notes on the chart and the nurses who took care of Jesse indicated that he had been told he had widespread, inoperable cancer, he didn't seem to know much about his condition. Wanting to discover how much Jesse knew, my husband went to his room.

"Mr. Williams," he said, "I understand you've been pretty sick. Can you tell me what's wrong with you?"

"Well, I'm not exactly sure," Jesse stated. "I had an operation, but the doctors didn't say what they found. I think they need to run some more tests before they know for sure."

My husband then said, "Tell me how this all started."

"You know, I really can't believe any of this," Jesse said slowly. "It's like a bad dream, and I keep thinking I'm going to wake up any moment. I was feeling so well, and work was going smoothly. I'd just started my spring tour of this territory, my sales were up, and I was in line for a promotion. Everything was fine. Then unbelievable pains started! I've never had such awful cramps. First I thought I might be hungry. Then I figured I'd gotten the 'flu,' even though I'd never had the 'flu' like that before. My oldest son graduates from high school in a little more than a month, and I can't believe that I'm here in the hospital with a bellyful of tumor. It just can't be real!"

Jesse went on to review the entire story of his illness—the increasing pain, his lack of appetite and inability to eat, the way he kept thinking that the pain would go away. After telling the story to my husband, Jesse passed through the initial denial stage and was able to talk about the surgery, his "bellyful of tumor," and the fact that any more treatment would have to wait until he had further recovered from surgery.

Partial Deafness

The first important effect of denial I've seen in my relationships with patients is that it produces a partial deafness. Although the hospital staff told Jesse that he had widespread, inoperable cancer, he was deaf to much of what he had heard. He was not unique in that respect!

At the time he is first told his diagnosis, a cancer patient (and his family) is frequently incapable of taking in the fact that a tumor is malignant, that the cancer is widespread (or sometimes that it's *not* widespread), that the surgeon wasn't able to remove all the tumor, or that further treatment is necessary or advisable. The same thing is true, respectively, for patients who have other terminal illnesses.

When an individual's denial is operative, his hearing is extremely selective and he will not hear anything he is not ready to take in. Matters such as the extent of his disease, type of treatment proposed, duration of treatment, expected effects of the treatment (good and bad), and expected long-term outlook for the disease easily elicit the deafness of denial. There seems to be less deafness for good news than for bad, but selective hearing occurs in both cases.

Although some doctors don't give their patients much information about their diagnosis or outlook, my husband and I have learned to allow for denial and its resulting deafness when we evaluate an individual's account of his illness. In addition to their denial of impending death, patients have a tendency to trigger the deaf response of denial when doctors propose the type of treatment to be used. The proposal may include description of surgery or the duration of radiation or chemotherapy, depending on the extent to which the disease has spread, and other details of treatment such as its duration, response rate, and possible side effects. Consequently, what an individual tells us may be very different from what his doctors originally told him.

Just as the cancer patients I treat do not initially hear treatment plans, expected outlook, or duration of treatment, so the individual who has had a major operation may fail to hear the details of surgery, expected period of convalescence, or restrictions on his activity. The heart patient, for example, may not initially hear any of the details regarding his diet, activity, medication, or long-term outlook. I have heard about patients recuperating from heart attacks in a coronary care unit who answered the question, "Have you ever had any heart problems?" with a resounding "No!"

To use another example, I have talked to a heart attack victim about his attack and his expected course of recovery only to have him exclaim, "No one ever told me that I had a heart attack!" We could compare this statement to the statement Jesse made earlier about never being told what was found during his surgery.

While practicing general internal medicine in outpatient clinics, I have also seen the deafness of denial time and again in people suffering from incurable high blood pressure. Since high blood pressure is a fairly common disorder, a significant number of my cancer patients also have it. Whenever I begin treating anyone for high blood pressure, I warn them that the treatment can keep their blood pressure normal as long as they take their pills, but that it will not cure them. I also tell them that they will probably have to take the medication for the rest of their lives. Yet, almost every individual I have treated for high blood pressure has asked when he could stop taking his medicine or when the hypertension would be cured. I'm not sure why people have a tendency to deny the chronic nature of high blood pressure. Perhaps the fact that it is considered an "illness" and is therefore incompatible with our ideal self—a perpetually young, athletically slim, vibrantly healthy, energetic individual—is a clue to denial.

My husband and I now assume that roughly one-third of what we tell a patient on his first visit will actually be heard by him. (Unfortunately, I still have no way of predicting which third he will hear!) Consequently, when we meet a new patient, we give him as accurate a picture as possible of his illness, his likelihood of responding to treatment, the probable length of the treatment's effectiveness, and the fact that there is little possibility for a cure. In addition, we usually mention to him that miracles do happen, but not predictably. Even though we tell our patients at least once that we are not treating them for cure, that single piece of information seems to fall on deaf ears 100 percent of the time. Many of them keep asking, "But, Doctor, isn't this going to cure me?"

The partial deafness that terminally ill patients have often causes them to receive a garbled version of what they were originally told. It is easy to see why Mr. Jones could become indignant with Dr. Smith, "who said he was just going to take that little mole off my back and ended up giving me a skin graft and a scar five inches long." In a similar situation, Mrs. Young could honestly complain, "Dr. Johnson never told me a *thing* about what he did during surgery! I only found out when I went to see Dr. Harris for these hot flashes, and he said they were a side effect of the operation."

When I first began to treat cancer patients, I held to the theory that, since the patient was the person most affected by the disease and the resulting treatment, he had a right to know what was going on. How else could he be expected to give his doctor the necessary cooperation for successful treatment? Naturally, I became righteously indignant with Dr. Jones (or Miller, or Williams, or Swanson) for not communicating with his patients when they would say, "But Dr. Jones never told me. . . ."

I finally understood when a patient told me, "But you never told me that this wouldn't cure me!" I distinctly remembered telling that same patient several weeks earlier, "This is not going to be a cure. It is a method of treatment that will allow you to live a little longer, but we can't talk about curing you." Gradually, I am learning to make allowances for the deafness of partial denial.

I met Betty Slavin while she was in the hospital recovering from a mastectomy. She had felt a small lump in her right breast about ten days earlier, and had visited her doctor immediately. As soon as he examined her, he scheduled an appointment for her with a surgeon.

"You know, Dr. Ruth," she said, "it's strange to be here in the hospital as a patient. Only a week ago I was working in the hospital gift shop, and watching people come and go. Now, here I am, a patient. It all happened so quickly! Almost before I knew it, I was in the hospital, scheduled for surgery. Of course the surgeon had told me that the lump was probably malignant, and I had half-expected it to be cancer. But when I woke up and found out that my breast was gone, well, it was so definite! For a while I felt like I was dreaming, like all this was happening to someone else. But at least the surgeon got all the cancer out."

The operation wasn't to be the end of her treatment, and I had to tell her so. "Mrs. Slavin, since we know from past experience with breast cancer that you stand a high risk of developing widespread cancer within the next five years, we recommend a year of chemotherapy for you, in hopes that we will improve your chances of having a complete cure. Although the surgeon 'got all the cancer out' as far as we can tell, it had already spread to the lymph nodes under your arm. That makes you a particularly high-risk patient."

"You mean I have to have more treatment?" Betty exclaimed. "Now? Oh, my."

I then explained the treatments. "They involve three different drugs, and you must go to your doctor weekly for an injection of two of the drugs. You will take the third drug orally every day. You should be able to go back to work in a month or two, as soon as you recover fully from the surgery. You may experience side effects, such as swelling in your arms, nausea, vomiting, and hair loss, beginning four to six weeks from the start of the treatments." After a few seconds' pause, I continued, "Mrs. Slavin, I'm going to give you a written description of the different drugs and their side effects. I know you won't remember everything I've just told you, so keep this and go over it at home. It should answer most of your questions about the treatments, but if you have other questions, please feel free to ask."

When Betty went home from the hospital, both of us were surprised and pleased to find out that she wasn't having any swelling in her arms or other distressing side effects from the mastectomy. Her strength improved almost daily. She was fitted with a breast prosthesis—the form used to take the place of the missing breast for cosmetic reasons and to help maintain normal balance—and found that her clothes fit as well as they did before the surgery.

Two weeks after she got home from the hospital, she started on chemotherapy. Three or four weeks later, she asked me, "Dr. Ruth, do you think it would be all right for me to have a permanent and get my hair tinted? I never did like white hair, and I've always done something to it."

"Well, Betty," I answered, "I think you should wait another couple of weeks before doing anything with your hair. By then you should know whether you'll have any significant hair loss with this treatment."

"Do you mean that my hair might come out?" Betty stared at me, a distressed look on her face. "I never thought of that."

"Well, it's too soon to be sure. The hair loss doesn't usually start until four to six weeks after the treatments begin. In another couple of weeks, if you haven't noticed your hair thinning, it will be safe to assume that you won't have any hair loss. Not everyone does, you know, but a woman may have enough hair loss to require wearing a wig. Of course, even if you do have some hair loss, your hair will grow back normally as soon as you finish the treatments."

Betty never did have significant hair loss. She waited a few weeks and then went ahead with a permanent and tint. Now she really looks great! She is back at work and feeling well. I didn't learn what her "deaf spot" was until she asked my advice about her hair weeks after her surgery. From all appearances, she had heard everything I told her and had adjusted well. As far as I know, this is the only time her denial made her partially deaf. But if she develops widespread cancer in the future, I expect that she will have another period of denial, and anything we tell her during that initial denial period might fall on deaf ears.

Deafness to Long-term Treatment

Perhaps the most difficult thing for the patient with a long-term illness to accept is the fact that treatment may need to continue for the rest of his life. Therefore, one of the things he is least likely to "hear" is information about his treatment. He may fix an arbitrary length of time for treatment in his mind and be sure that someone told him that the treatment would last only for that length of time. Or, he may continue to ask when he will be "all well," not having heard the fact that the treatment will control or arrest but never cure his illness. Joe Martin is a good example of someone who was deaf to his necessary treatment.

When only eighteen years old, Joe had a routine chest x-ray at the restaurant where he worked as a requirement for his job as a cook, and "spots" of various sizes showed up in his lungs. Since he could not work in the restaurant until the possibility of tuberculosis was excluded, he went to his family doctor.

"Joe," the doctor told him, "this looks more like a tumor than tuberculosis. I can establish the fact that you don't have tuberculosis so that you can go back to work, but I'd like you to go to Dr. Smith, a chest surgeon, in order to get a biopsy of the tumor and see just what it is. It will mean about a week in the hospital."

Joe didn't complain. *I can't possibly have lung cancer,* he thought. *After all, I'm only eighteen and I don't smoke. It has to be something else. When they get the biopsy, they'll find out that it's nothing serious.* But when the results came back, they showed that Joe had a rare form of cancer. There were many separate areas of malignant tumor in his lungs. Surgery, which would be impractical, couldn't cure him. Since the tumor could be treated with chemotherapy, Joe and his mother came to see me.

"The tumor is quite extensive," I told Joe, "and there's no chance of your being cured. However, we expect you to respond well to treatment. Your energy should increase, you'll be able to go back to work, and the tumor 'spots' on the chest x-ray may disappear; but even if they do, they may reappear at some future time."

I then told Joe that a complete treatment with one of the four drugs would last eight months and that at that time I would have to stop using one particular drug because of the possibility of heart damage once the minimum dose was exceeded.

During the first two days of chemotherapy treatment, Joe was in real agony, and the rest of that first week wasn't much better. All he wanted to do was lie in bed and sleep (if he could). By the end of the week, however, he had started feeling better. After two more weeks of treatment, most people wouldn't have been able to tell there was anything wrong with him.

After eight weeks of treatment, Joe was eager to have another chest x-ray taken, in order to see what the effects of the treatments had been. He was nervous about the results of the x-ray. He wanted to know what it revealed, yet he was scared that it might be bad news. After I compiled the reports, I met Joe in my office. "I've got good news for you! The tumor in your lungs is shrinking, and some of the 'spots' have even disappeared. It looks as if the treatments are going to be successful."

"That's good," Joe answered, "but are there still spots on the x-ray?"

I nodded. "Yes, but not as many."

"Do you think they'll go away, too?"

"I certainly hope so," I stated.

"If they all disappear," Joe said, a smile spreading across his face, "does that mean I'm cured? Will I get to stop treatment then?"

"Joe, even if all the spots disappear, it won't mean you're cured," I said softly. "We will have to keep you on this treatment for another six months. After that, we'll change the treatment slightly, but you still will require treatments."

Obviously Joe had been temporarily deaf when I explained that his tumor was incurable and that the treatment would have to continue indefinitely. Since the "ideal" person in our culture is young, trim, tan, energetic, and healthy, it is hard for us to accept the fact that our illnesses make that ideal impossible for us to attain. When we are healthy, we can always go on a diet or get a sun tan. But chronic disease that has no known cure automatically eliminates the possibility of being "healthy." We like to think that we are immortal—immune to human ills and to death itself. The news that we are chronically ill and will always need to take pills or receive other treatments in order to feel well is very unwelcome.

Denial, in the initial "I don't believe it" phase, is not a one-time occurrence for people with diseases such as cancer, heart disease, kidney disease, and high blood pressure, because these people can have good periods as well as setbacks. Any time there is a significant change in the disease—a setback, an improvement—or a change in the form of treatment, the patient may have an "I don't believe it" reaction.

Once a patient believes that the treatment is necessary and vital, and alters his schedule to accommodate pills, visits to the doctor's office, and laboratory tests, his treatment becomes a part of his life. Thus, any alteration in treatment is alarming and frightening, and once again the defensive aspect of denial, with its attendant loss of hearing, is brought into play.

Blindness to Symptoms

Another overwhelming result of initial denial is a blindness to symptoms and their meaning. Sometimes the blindness is directly proportional to the amount of knowledge the individual possesses about the meaning of the symptoms. Take, for example, the classic story about the slightly overweight, middle-aged male doctor who develops chest pains characteristic of a heart attack. He immediately tells his wife, who is a nurse. She looks at his pale face beaded with perspiration, listens to his labored breathing, and her own heartbeat quickens in alarm. Then they mutually agree that he has a bad case of indigestion. "It was the chili you ate for lunch," she says, and he treats himself with large doses of antacids for several hours before seeking medical attention.

When he finally arrives at the emergency room, he explains to an attendant, "Sure, I thought about my heart, but I knew it couldn't be that. My wife and I just figured that I'd eaten too much chili for lunch."

Martha Lyons was a good-humored, intelligent, earthy woman. One of her daughters is a nurse, her nephew is in medical school, and her son works as an x-ray technician in a hospital near her former home. She read extensively and knew quite a bit about cancer.

One June Martha developed a sore, red spot on her right breast. *I wonder what this is?* she thought. She felt it carefully and noticed that the soreness and the red spot were the only symptoms. *Well, that's a relief! At least it isn't a lump.*

The red spot had been the size of a nickel in June, but by Christmas it was the size of a quarter. Although the spot was sore when she first noticed it, it became extremely painful, and Martha couldn't even wear a bra. *I wonder if I should see the doctor about it?* she wondered. *If it were a lump, I'd know what to do, but this is just a spot. It is sore, though, and it does seem to be getting bigger. Well, I'll wait until after the holidays and see if it's any better.*

After the holidays, Martha had other things to do. Her second daughter, Alice, was getting married, and her youngest child, Bob, was moving away from home. It just seemed that with one thing after another, there was never time to worry about the red spot. Although when she would accidentally bump it or wear something too tight, she would notice how much bigger and how much more painful the spot had become.

By now a year had passed since Martha discovered the red spot. Alice and her new husband were coming to visit, and so was Bob. One morning, as Martha was dressing, she felt the sore spot again—it had become a habit with her—and noticed that it was no longer just a spot. There was also a lump about the size of the tip of her thumb. *I really must do something about it,* she thought, hurrying to get dressed. *As soon as the kids go home, I'll make a doctor's appointment.*

Alice and Jim went home the day before Bob was to arrive, however, leaving Martha barely enough time between the two visits to do the necessary housecleaning and shopping. Then, during Bob's stay, Martha got word that her Uncle Frank had died and that Aunt Mildred needed her. Aunt Mildred was eighty-five, slow on her feet because of arthritis, and rapidly becoming senile. Bob went to the funeral with his mother and then left to go back to his new job. Martha helped Aunt Mildred get her affairs in order and then brought her home.

Although the spot was now an open, foul-smelling ulcer the size of a tangerine, Martha still didn't make a doctor's appointment. "I knew it was probably serious," she told me later, "but how could I go into the hospital and leave Aunt Mildred at home alone? And if it was serious, I knew that I would probably have to give up caring for her and put her in a nursing home. That would have been awfully hard for me to do."

Finally, Joanie, Martha's oldest daughter and the nurse, happened to see the sore and its discharge. She made an appointment for Martha with Dr. Hendricks for the next week, moved Aunt Mildred into her own home, and began to arrange for her placement in a nursing home. She then personally escorted Martha to her first (and many of her subsequent) doctor's appointment.

I examined Martha less than two weeks later. Dr. Hendricks had drained the breast abscess and had simultaneously taken a small piece of ulcer as a biopsy specimen. The specimen turned out to be cancerous, not to anyone's surprise, and Martha then had a number of further tests—chest x-rays, bone scans, liver scans—in order to find out how widespread the cancer was. The test results showed that there was cancer in her lungs and liver, but not in her bones. That meant that Martha had an incurable case of breast cancer. No surgery—with or without radiation therapy—could remove enough of the cancer to cure her.

I advised her that her best hope was to begin chemotherapy and see if drugs could control the cancer for awhile. She agreed, and my associates and I began treating her with a four-drug combination that we use as a first-line treatment in widespread breast cancer. Although the breast ulcer healed slowly and steadily, the lung and liver cancer worsened, indicating that she was not responsive to this form of treatment.

Finally, after six weeks, I told Martha that the treatment wasn't working and that we had only one other form of treatment left to try. Martha adjusted easily to the resulting changes in treatment and routine. "Actually, this combination is easier for me to take," she told me. "Although I'm really sick on the day of treatment, I have more time to get my strength back between treatments."

Our success seemed to continue. Martha's chest x-rays and liver scans showed an improvement, and she felt great. Her appetite was terrific. "Actually, I think my appetite is too good, Dr. Ruth," she told me one afternoon. Her energy was adequate to do almost anything she wanted to do. Then one day, one of the treatments really took everything out of her. She hadn't fully recovered when it was time for the next treatment. Although we waited an extra week to treat her, she still wasn't feeling well.

The next time Martha came in, she wanted to discuss something with me. "This is it, isn't it, Dr. Ruth? I'm not getting well between treatments, and I'm weak all the time. We've reached the end of the road, haven't we?"

Of course Martha was right. I had to hospitalize her only three months later, and she never got well enough to return home. So, a little more than a year after we first discovered the cancer, Martha died.

Perhaps Martha's story would have had a different ending if she had had surgery when her tumor was "only a spot, not really a lump." Maybe she would have been one of the women who is cured by surgery alone. Or perhaps a year of preventative chemotherapy, in addition to surgery, could have cured her. Why, then, did such an intelligent, informed woman ignore such a serious condition that had such disastrous effects?

In short, Martha focused on the fact that the sore spot on her breast wasn't a lump, and her fear prevented her from seeing the symptoms. *If I go to the doctor about this spot,* Martha thought, *and if he takes it out, and if he finds out that it's cancerous, I don't know what I'll do!"* Notice all the "ifs."

When the spot became a lump, she focused on more immediate concerns—the visits of her daughter and son, and the death of Uncle Frank, which left the responsibility for Aunt Mildred up to her. In addition to the fear of the diagnosis of cancer was the fear that she wouldn't be able to continue the activities that were important to her, especially the care of Aunt Mildred. The somewhat vague fear of cancer itself became so concrete that she worried about having to place Aunt Mildred in a nursing home. There may also have been an underlying fear that she, too, would end up in a nursing home, with no one in her family to care for her. She was unable to overcome her fear and make practical arrangements to have a doctor examine her physical problem. She probably would have continued to be immobilized by fear had not her daughter intervened.

As we have already seen, a common byproduct of denial is the focusing of our attention on a peripheral issue or complaint that causes us to ignore the major problem. A patient with severe chest pain caused by heart disease may, for example, focus on the nausea caused by his pills and totally ignore the underlying heart ailment for which he is taking the pills. A cancer patient, on the other hand, may focus on a side effect of treatment or a symptom of his illness while ignoring the cancer itself. Let me illustrate.

Jennifer Dyer is an excessively demanding, careful, sixty-two-year-old who always watches her diet, exercises, and guards her health jealously. She is the one in the family who makes dental appointments (and sees to it that they are kept), gets the family to Dr. Jones for yearly physicals, and keeps the cupboard stocked with vitamins and minerals. When Dr. Jones urged her to examine her breasts regularly, Jennifer learned the technique and examined them at least once a month.

When a lump appeared in her left breast, she telephoned Dr. Jones' office immediately and told the receptionist what she had found, and Dr. Jones examined her the same week. Surgery the following week revealed a malignant tumor less than an inch in diameter. Doctors also removed two cancerous nodes under her left arm. But all in all, it looked as if Jennifer had a good chance of beating the disease. The cancer's early detection and prompt treatment gave her every opportunity to remain ahead of the cancer in the future.

Two years later, Jennifer got the "flu." She had a runny nose, fever, and a cough in September. She was still coughing in October. In November Dr. Jones said, "I don't really think it's anything to worry about, but let's get a chest x-ray anyhow. I don't like to see a cough hang on that long." The chest x-ray revealed a good reason for the cough. Jennifer had pneumonia, which probably had been helped along by a large tumor in her lung. It undoubtedly had spread from her breast cancer two years earlier. Further tests showed that the cancer had spread to her bones and liver as well.

We started Jennifer on the four-drug combination, and she did well for the first six weeks. Her cough disappeared, and our x-rays and laboratory tests showed that the tumor was disappearing. The seventh week she began complaining of chest pains. The pains seemed to be caused by the chemotherapy, since they would start five or six hours after her injection and last twenty-four to thirty-six hours. The pains were not severe or inconvenient; they could be relieved by one or two aspirin and she could continue whatever she was doing in spite of them. During the weeks in which she missed her injections, she had no chest pains.

One day Jennifer asked me, "Dr. Ruth, how many more of these treatments do I have to take?"

"I think I told you before that we will keep you on these treatments as long as you respond to them," I replied. "As long as your blood tests and chest x-rays show me that your cancer is under control, I'll keep you on these drugs."

"You mean I might be on them the rest of my life? I don't know if I can take that!"

Jennifer became more depressed and missed several treatments. When I called her to find out how she was, she told me that she had decided to stop treatment. "You know, Dr. Ruth, I think I must be allergic to those injections. Those chest pains are just too much to put up with. I can't keep on with the chemotherapy."

I persuaded her to try a variation of the treatment program, omitting one of the drugs at a time so we could see which one caused her pains. She cooperated fully, but it turned out that every one of the drugs resulted in chest pains. Concerned about the chest pains, she finally discontinued the chemotherapy altogether.

We then lost track of Jennifer and wondered how she was getting along. About four months after her last office appointment, she telephoned. "Dr. Jones told me to call you. He said that I should come back for treatments, but I don't want any more chemotherapy. Since I stopped taking the shots, my chest doesn't hurt and I don't want to start hurting again."

Dr. Jones contacted us a few hours later and told us that an x-ray he had taken of Jennifer's chest showed an alarming increase in tumor since she had stopped treatment. She was also somewhat short of breath, had almost no appetite, and had lost fifteen pounds.

Although Dr. Jones and I have talked to Jennifer about the necessity of chemotherapy in controlling her cancer, her main consideration continues to be the chest pain. She adamantly refuses to try any chemotherapy and chooses to endure the shortness of breath, loss of appetite, and tiredness caused by the progressive cancer.

Just before she dies, Jennifer may admit that the cancer is the serious problem, not the chest pains related to chemotherapy. At this point, however, she is psychologically unable to assess the relative importance of her symptoms. Her denial of the seriousness of her cancer, evidenced by her overwhelming concern with the chest pains, keeps her from making rational decisions concerning her treatment. Although the chest pains were real and painful, they were easily relieved. The cancer, on the other hand, had been kept under control by chemotherapy but began spreading rapidly as soon as chemotherapy was stopped. Focusing on the immediate, painful chest symptoms, Jennifer ignores the more subtle decreases in energy and well-being that accompany the rapid growth of her tumor.

Blind Waiting

Another form of blindness brought on by denial can be labeled the "bury your head in the sand" type. In this type, people note their symptoms in detail but elect to "wait and see if they will go away by themselves" before taking any action. This attitude makes sense in some situations, but its extremes are dangerous and foolhardy. Probably a month is the longest, safest time that anyone should wait to see if something will get better by itself. In some cases, even a month is too long.

RECOGNIZING THE REASONS BEHIND OUR BLINDNESS

Once we understand how human and at least partially realistic our fears are, we can understand why we tend to turn a blind eye to the symptoms that alert us to the fact that we may have a serious illness. It is far easier, at least at first, to deny the whole thing rather than to have to face the realities we fear most. Let's examine some of the complex reasons why we are afraid to discover the truth about our symptoms.

Our most basic fear is that something serious—heart disease, cancer, multiple sclerosis, blindness—can be wrong with us. Cancer is perhaps our most dreaded disease, for it disables, disfigures, and debilitates as well as kills. Heart disease, one of the major killers in the

United States, is only slightly less terrible, with its connotations of invalidism, curtailed activities, and restricted diet.

We also have the tendency to panic when we experience harmful symptoms, and we exaggerate the problem in our mind. When the step we should take might mean the confirmation of our worst fears, our courage falters and fails us. For example, a hard-driving businessman, who knows that he has high blood pressure, has read all about heart disease, and is fully acquainted with the warning signs of a heart attack, will continue taking Gelusil for his "indigestion" rather than acknowledge that the pain in his "stomach" is really chest pain.

We also have the tendency to wait and see if the symptoms will go away. For some reason we would rather, in the words of Hamlet, "bear those ills we have, than fly to others that we know not of." Some things that we fear do, indeed, go away with time, in part justifying our delay. After all, we reason, we would surely look like a fool running to the doctor with this complaint when waiting for a few hours (or days, or weeks) might clear the whole thing up. We are afraid of making fools of ourselves by "making a mountain out of a molehill," for we feel that worrying about something as inconsequential as a bad case of heartburn or a perfectly harmless mole will expose us to ridicule.

We also fear that we will find ourselves unable to bear the burden of a serious illness and prove not to be as strong as we had hoped we were. How will I endure the possibility of progressive loss of physical strength and ability, of pain and suffering, of parting from those I hold dear, of confinement and loss of freedom and independence? we ask ourselves. How do I know that in the final moment I will be brave? What if my "nerve" fails me and I start whimpering instead of enduring my illness with fortitude and patience as I believe mature men and women ought to bear misfortune? What if the illness uncovers my own peculiar area of cowardice, vanity, or fear, and I am not able to withstand it?

Forgetfulness

Another familiar result of initial denial is forgetfulness. Under this heading, I am including only the failure to remember specific instructions, such as which pills to take, diets to adhere to, exercises to do, or appointments to keep. This is distinctly different from cases in which an individual "forgets" such things as his diagnosis, outlook, or the description of surgery. I have chosen to call the latter the deafness of denial rather than forgetfulness. As we've seen, there is some basis for this distinction, since the individual who has heard details of pills, medication, and appointments may never recall having been told specific details about his illness and may literally not have heard them.

Coupled with the deafness that often accompanies initial denial, forgetfulness can contribute significantly to a patient's confused understanding of exactly what is wrong when coupled with vague ideas regarding such things as treatment, medication, diet, and outlook. This confusion, of course, does not enable the individual to participate fully in his treatment program as an informed, intelligent, and cooperative partner. Rather, it leaves him rather helpless and poorly informed.

Sometimes such a patient will be merely uncooperative, but at other times belligerent and rebellious. Fortunately, most physicians attempt to inform their patients about their treatment programs and incorporate them into the program as partners. It is easy to see that if there is a lack of communication on the doctor's part, total chaos can result.

Individuals with chronic illnesses who take a large number of pills daily are usually the best examples of forgetfulness. For example, a diabetic with high blood pressure and heart disease could be taking a daily dose of two pills for his heart, three pills for the diabetes, and two to four pills each of two or three different medications for his blood pressure. In addition to the nuisance of having to remember all the pills, the pills serve as constant reminders of his illness. *I am not well,* he thinks, *because I have to take pills.* It is easy for these individuals to forget to take the pills or even to say, "I was feeling so well that I didn't think I needed the pills anymore."

Most people in this group probably miss a few pills now and then. Indeed, they would have to be very compulsive to remember all their pills all the time. Most individuals in this group do manage to take their pills faithfully enough to stay well. However, I have seen people with high blood pressure or heart disease go through cycles. They come to the hospital or to their doctors' offices perturbed because they are dizzy, have headaches, or have trouble breathing. Their doctors will start them on medication and carefully explain that they must continue taking the medication if they want to continue feeling well. The patients will go home, begin feeling better, and either "forget" to take their medication or decide not to take it since they feel so well. Within several weeks, they come back to the hospital or their doctors' offices, once again complaining of dizziness, shortness of breath, or headaches.

The remarkable thing to me is that some people repeat this cycle year after year, even several times during the year. They are always genuinely perplexed when they stop feeling well, and it always surprises them that they should have continued to take their pills. This form of denial is most evident in long-term illnesses that can be kept under control by medication but for which there is no cure. It is rare in the cancer patient, who has a much shorter life expectancy as a general rule.

Ruth McReynolds, an attractive, efficient lady in her mid-fifties, was a stepmother to two grown daughters and mother to two teen-age sons. She worked for the school system, where her good judgment and common sense had won her recognition and high esteem from her colleagues and employers. To all appearances, she was successful, content, and had many useful and fulfilling years ahead of her. She had something else, however—widespread cancer. Furthermore, she was one of the large number of people whom surgery and radiation therapy could not cure.

One day, Ruth came to my office for chemotherapy. After the upheaval of tests, consultations with other doctors, more tests, and finally beginning chemotherapy treatment, Ruth settled into a new routine. Things went "back to normal," except that she had to leave work briefly on Wednesday mornings for her office appointment and chemotherapy. She had a standing appointment at 11:30. That way, she missed only forty-five minutes of her work day during the slowest period of the day.

One Wednesday, Ruth didn't show up. When I missed her, I asked the secretary to telephone her and find out what had happened. When Ruth answered, she was surprised and terribly apologetic. "I just got so caught up in what I was doing that I forgot all about it!" she exclaimed. That week, she came in on Thursday. She remembered her appointment the following week, but "forgot" the next two. Soon a pattern developed. She would make one appointment, then miss two or three. Nothing that my staff or I said had any effect; we even tried calling her the day before her appointment to remind her, only to have her say later, "The office call and telephone conversation slipped my mind entirely!"

Early in December, Ruth had missed four weeks of treatment in a row, and I was worried about her. I called her office, only to be told that she was at home, sick. That alarmed me, and when I talked with her on the phone, I became even more worried. She was coughing so badly that she could hardly talk, and she sounded very weak. "Ruth, you sound terrible," I said. "Can you get in to the office today or tomorrow and let me check you over? That cough has me worried."

"Dr. Kopp, it's just a cold; really it is. Nothing at all (cough, cough) to worry about. It'll go away soon. I don't feel sick; it's just a cough."

She must have been feeling worse than she admitted, though, to be home from work, and she did manage to come in to see me the next day. I was appalled when I saw her. She had lost at least fifteen pounds and was pale and weak; the slightest exertion made her cough. When I examined her, I could tell that she had pneumonia in both lungs. I wanted to hospitalize her right then, but she wouldn't hear of it. "Well, then, at least go home to bed," I told her. "I'll start you on antibiotics right away, and I think you'll be all right at home. But you aren't to go back to work for at least two weeks."

Not completely to my surprise, I found out that Ruth went back to work the following week as soon as she felt she could drive. The cough cleared up gradually, and she began to regain her strength and gain weight. During the time she had pneumonia, she suddenly developed a remarkable memory for her office appointments! She was there faithfully at 11:30 every Wednesday. As soon as the cough began to go away, however, her memory deteriorated. She again "got caught up in work" and forgot about her appointments.

Everyone in the office finally gave up trying to get Ruth to keep her appointments. Every three or four weeks, one of us would remind her so we saw her sporadically during her last several months. Although tired, she felt pretty well most of the time and threw herself into her work at the office and at home. One day, however, she found that she wasn't feeling as well as she had been. The next day, she could hardly get up. Although she made it to work, she had to leave in the middle of the morning and go home. Finally, she called me.

"Dr. Ruth, I have to talk to you. I don't feel well at all, and I have to see you." Her voice broke, and I could hear her crying. "When may I come in?"

"Why don't you just come to the hospital this afternoon or tomorrow morning? That way I can see you right away."

When I met her in the hospital, I knew she was dying. As we began talking, she dropped her denial of her illness and asked what lay ahead for her. We talked about treatment and together decided against any further drugs. We also talked about the short time remaining, her family, and her work. "You know, Dr. Ruth," she said, "this is going to be awfully rough for Pete. His first wife died of cancer when Lisa was just a baby. He's had a hard time of it. I'm so sorry for him." To me, this statement suddenly explained much of Ruth's denial. She had been unwilling to see her husband and family suffer because of her illness. She had denied her cancer to protect them, as much as for her own sake.

Finally we talked about Ruth herself. I knew that she had been a "loner," and I asked if she meant to go through death alone. Bravely, but almost hopelessly, she said, "I guess so." At that point, I told her that I would be with her as long as I could and then shared with her that she didn't have to be alone. "There is One who can be with you all the way," I said, knowing by her response that she immediately knew what I meant.

"I know," she said, "My dad is in heaven." We talked a little longer, and before I had to leave I knew that she had received the peace that only God could give. Ruth was no longer alone.

She had only a few weeks left, and everyone noticed the difference that God was making in her life. Her peace became a source of strength and comfort to her family. There were still things she left undone, for the time between the admission of her condition and her death was too short to do everything, and she was too sick to prepare her family completely for the time when she would not be with them. Still, she had made the most important preparation; she had provided a way for a reunion in heaven and had left her family with a testimony of the reality of Christ, who will not leave anyone alone, even in the valley of death.

Ruth was one of the few cancer patients I've known who maintained initial denial through most of the course of her illness. Although I have emphasized her forgetfulness, she was also blind to symptoms and their meaning and had a good deal of "deafness." Her denial, which was strong and persistent, was able to shield her and her family from the grim reality of her disease until just a few weeks before her death.

Shopping for Another Diagnosis

A person who persists in maintaining initial denial during the course of his disease will also look for support. Unwilling to believe that things can be "that bad," he will try to find someone to tell him that the doctor is wrong. This can take the form of a frantic pilgrimage from doctor to doctor and from medical center to medical center to find someone who will give him a more favorable, hopeful diagnosis. It can take the form of a desperate belief that God will heal, which causes him to travel from one revival to another, from faith healer to faith healer. This need for support also provides a person with the basis for turning to quack remedies, special diets, and other "cures" reported in the press.

There are many reasons for changing doctors, visiting major medical centers, and in general "shopping around" for a diagnosis and a treatment program. I encourage people to look for a second opinion and to try to find a type of treatment and doctor they can trust. If the best doctor is a Christian, so much the better. Denial is only one element in this picture, and not always the main one. However, when an individual has seen two or three specialists in the same field and has received essentially the same verdict from all of them, the continued search for "another opinion" probably reflects denial rather than a search for a cure. We will examine this point more thoroughly in a later chapter.

It should be evident by now that denial effectively allows us to put off facing unpalatable facts. Unfortunately, the delays incurred by going from place to place and doctor to doctor or those brought about by "waiting for this to go away" may be costly in terms of precious time lost. Delay, induced by denial, may mean the difference between a curable disease and a treatable disease; it may provide the opportunity for cancer to spread or for high blood pressure to produce heart damage or a stroke. How high a price are we willing to pay for the luxury of absorbing bad news slowly? How can we keep from being robbed of precious time and irreplaceable opportunities by our denial?

The apostle Paul was faced with an "incurable" condition that he asked God to heal on three separate occasions. God didn't heal him, but He did promise to give Paul sufficient grace to live with the condition and used his weakness to reveal His power (see 2 Cor. 12:8, 9). We, too, can use our weaknesses as stepping stones to finding God's power, and we can use our inadequacies as a means of experiencing God's sufficiency.

3

THE IMPORTANCE OF "NOT YET" DENIAL

INITIAL DENIAL, as we saw in chapter 2, tends to be a mixed blessing. While giving the individual time to gather his resources to face an emotional upheaval, it can also encourage costly, time-consuming procrastination in treatment that can have disastrous effects. So, denial needs to be handled in such a way that the terminally ill individual receives the best possible treatment as early as possible without undue emotional trauma.

Yet, during the course of a terminal illness, there is more to denial than just the initial phase. During the phase of initial denial, the individual has not yet faced the fact that his days are numbered. Once he recognizes this fact and the true meaning of his diagnosis, his denial is less extreme. Instead of thinking, *I can't believe this is real,* he tends to think, *Yes, it's real, but not yet.*

BENEFITS OF "NOT YET" DENIAL

At this point, it is important for us to realize that it is not harmful for the individual to assume the defense of "not yet" denial after passing through initial denial and adjusting to the nature and seriousness of his terminal illness.

The "not yet" phase of denial during the course of an individual's fatal illness is an entirely normal, appropriate, and functional progression, not a regression. After all, no one can really tell the sick individual when he will die, and he wants to be able to fully live all his life to the actual moment of death. As far as I can tell, "not yet" denial is the only functional attitude to maintain during the course of terminal illness and needs to be kept intact if the terminally ill person is to function as well as possible for the rest of his life. The failure to progress into the normal state of "not yet" denial can be as much a problem as an extended period of initial denial. A serious breach in the individual's denial defense generally renders him powerless in the grips of severe depression and a sense of life's uselessness.

The "not yet" phase of denial allows the terminally ill individual to go on living and to enjoy the time he has left. This type of denial is even necessary when the course of the illness has stabilized (as in the case of cancer or leukemia patients) or when the illness is in remission (a complete disappearance of all signs and symptoms, which is usually temporary). During this time, the individual and members of his family need to "act as if there were nothing at all wrong" with him. Most of his time should be spent in the business of everyday life—his work, his interests, his friends. For him to sit around all day brooding about his illness and waiting to die would be inappropriate and harmful. The "not yet" phase of denial allows him to lead a meaningful, useful life as long as possible, for it eases the burden of continually facing the reality of his mortality and the predictability of his own death.

Most of the people I treat who are either in a complete or partial remission function with a healthy dose of denial. After the initial reaction to a relapse, even terminally ill individuals maintain a prevailing attitude of "not yet" denial. Most of these patients go back to work for as long as they are physically capable. They plan parties, remodel houses, get married, change jobs, plant gardens, plan vacations, and make future dates and appointments. "Business as usual" is their way of life. Again, the majority act as if nothing were wrong with them.

In greater or lesser intensity, the "not yet" phase of denial is consistently present throughout the course of a terminal illness. Times of stress during the course of an illness—changes in treatment, relapses, major decisions such as selling a house or going into business—tend to evoke a stronger form of "not yet" denial that is reminiscent of initial denial. During this time, the extreme features seen in initial denial such as deafness, blindness to symptoms, and faulty memory are most likely to appear.

When "Not Yet" Denial Fails

When I first met Paula Geissler, a young housewife and mother in her mid-thirties, she had a fairly advanced case of Hodgkin's disease. Sick, and afraid that she was dying, Paula began a new treatment. Within a few days, she started regaining strength. In less than a week, she left the hospital and went home where she continued to improve.

Soon she was able to resume her normal household duties. She began baking for school parties, taking her six-year-old daughter, Cindy, to various school activities, and singing in the church choir. Her disease was well under control, and Paula began planning a big family reunion at Easter. Cindy was doing well in school; her husband, Dan, had just gotten a promotion at work. In short, everything looked great. As part of the preparation for the reunion, she and Dan were having the kitchen remodeled. She had hated her old kitchen, and Dan's promotion made the remodeling possible. Her life was full.

During this time, Paula came into our office for a routine checkup and chemotherapy appointment. Although her appetite was good, her weight was stable, and there were absolutely no signs of disease anywhere, Paula was in tears! "Paula, what's wrong?" I asked. "Why are you crying? Everything seems to be just fine."

"Dr. Ruth, I don't know what's happening to me," she replied. "I've been feeling well, and I know that the Hodgkin's disease is under control, but I'm just so depressed. I don't feel like doing anything at all. It's all I can do to get out of bed in the morning and get Cindy off to school. The house is too much bother to clean. I can't think of anything to fix for meals. I pick up a book and stare at the same page for minutes on end and then can't even remember what the book is about. What's the use of doing anything?"

"Can you think of anything in your life that has changed recently?" I asked.

"Well, I've wanted to remodel the kitchen, as you know, and we're finally ready to go ahead. But I can't help wondering if I will ever get a chance to enjoy it. All the time I'm looking at wallpaper, cabinets, and floor plans, I keep wondering, *Who am I fixing the kitchen for? Who will Dan bring in to keep house in my new kitchen when I'm gone?* I get so upset that I can hardly see. When I look at Cindy, I feel like pushing her away from me and saying, 'Save your love for your new mother. Don't get too close to me. I'm going to die.' Dr. Ruth, what's wrong with me?"

Paula's "not yet" denial had failed. Probably the large project of remodeling the kitchen had reminded her of the uncertainty of her future, and she was temporarily unable to cope. Realistically, she wondered whether she would be around to see the project finished and be able to enjoy its results. These considerations then affected other aspects of her life—her housekeeping, her relationship with her daughter, her interest in the world around her, her ability to get up in the morning. Her ability to function as a wife and mother was severely impaired as long as her denial was ineffective. We talked about the problem for quite a while, and Paula left the office determined to enjoy life again.

When I saw Paula the following month, her eyes were sparkling, and there was a bounce in her step. When I asked her about the kitchen, she bubbled excitedly about wallpaper and cabinets, floor coverings and curtains. She had recovered her "not yet" denial and through it had found the ability to go on living.

"Not Yet" Denial Should Be a Family Affair

Denial is necessary not only to the patient. It must also be functional in his friends and family, or his personal and family life will be severely crippled.

Sam Tucker, who had a lymphoma, was in complete remission and on a limited period of maintenance treatment. I always liked to talk with Sam. With his pleasant manners and immaculate dress, he seemed sensible in his outlook on his disease—aware of its seriousness but adjusting to it with a sense of humor and the determination to be well. His wife, though, had never come into the office, and I was a bit curious about her.

About six months after Sam started treatment, my secretary told me that his wife was on the telephone and wanted to talk to me about him. When I picked up the receiver, she told me hysterically that she was sure Sam was dying. "He doesn't tell you everything, Doctor. I'm sure he's hiding things from me, too. Every time I ask him how he's doing, he just says 'fine' and doesn't want to discuss it. Tell me the truth, Doctor. How is Sam? How long does he have to live? I don't want to be protected; I want to know!"

"Mrs. Tucker," I answered, "the last time I saw Sam, a little more than a week ago, he was fine. He is in a complete remission, which means that there is no sign of the lymphoma anywhere. He could stay in remission for years. There is even a slim chance that he could be completely cured. What has happened in the last week that has you worried?"

Mrs. Tucker then told me that Sam had a bad cold. "He has a slight fever, a cough and sore throat, and a runny nose. I want him to call you, but he refuses. 'If my temperature really gets high, I'll call, but I'm sure it's just a cold.'" At that point, Mrs. Tucker had become hysterical and had called me herself.

When Sam came in a few days later, I asked him about the cold. "Oh, that," he said, grinning. "It wasn't anything, just a head cold. My temperature never got above 100 degrees. I bet my wife called you."

Obviously Sam was playing things down and his wife was probably exaggerating, but which story was closer to the truth? I let things go for a few more weeks, talking to Mrs. Tucker regularly on the phone and seeing Sam every other week. Finally I felt that I could talk with Sam about the situation. "You know, you and your wife have very different ideas about your illness," I said to him. "I'm caught between wondering whether things are as bad as she makes out or if they are as fine as you say. Frankly, I suspect that they are somewhere in-between."

"Dr. Ruth," Sam said, "She's really starting to get to me. When I get home from your office, she wants a word-by-word account of my visit. 'What did the doctor say?' she asks. 'What did you say? Did you tell him about your cough? How was your blood count?' I tell her that everything's just fine, but she isn't satisfied. Even when she talks to you, it doesn't help for long. She's so depressed. She cries all the time now, and sometimes I catch her looking at me with a heartbroken expression on her face. I can't get her to go out with her friends. She won't go anywhere with me, not even to a movie or out to dinner. The housework gets done only half-heartedly. I figure she's already got me dead and buried!"

It was obvious that Mrs. Tucker's lack of "not yet" denial was hurting her ability to function and was also alienating Sam. True, he had a malignancy and it would probably prove to be fatal. But he wasn't "dead and buried" yet, and she was poisoning the time they had left together with her depression. Although she had grasped the meaning and implications of Sam's diagnosis of lymphoma, she had omitted the consideration that for most of the time Sam had left, he would feel well, go to work, and lead a normal life. He was not an invalid with one foot in the grave, but a strong, able-bodied, early middle-aged man.

Mrs. Tucker's "not yet" denial may have failed for a number of reasons. She may have been unwilling to let her hopes rise, only to have them crushed again. She may have found the uncertainty of the future intolerable or have acted from a sense of guilt for not being the "perfect wife" and for "letting" Sam become ill. Her actions may have been based on a desire to care for Sam and to protect him from his illness. There was also an underlying mistrust, a feeling that both Sam and I were not telling her the truth. Any or all of these factors can enter into the picture when "not yet" denial fails.

The failure of "not yet" denial could easily have ruined the Tuckers' marriage. Facing a crying wife who has him "already dead and buried" is small inducement for a man to go home! Not one of us really relishes the role of spectator at his own funeral. Perhaps less obviously, Mrs. Tucker's reaction to her husband's illness affected her ability to function in the same way that Paula reacted to her illness when her "not yet" denial failed. Mrs. Tucker was immobilized in a state of grief and depression, unable to carry on the normal activities of her life.

After I realized what was happening, I urged Mrs. Tucker to come in with her husband when he received treatments and to discuss the situation with both of us at the same time. Gradually, she began to accept Sam's illness and became thankful for the time they had together. Their involvement with friends increased, and the joy they once had in their marriage returned.

"Not yet" denial, then, is an emotional buffer. It is a practical frame of mind that allows normal life to continue throughout the course of a fatal illness. It should fill in time between periods of adjustment to different points in the illness and between the times when the necessary preparations for death are being accomplished. In its best form, "not yet" denial allows the dying individual to live life to the fullest.

4

RESPONSES TO DENIAL

INAPPROPRIATE DENIAL can be very difficult to live with, whether the denial is in the one who is ill (possibly causing him to treat his illness in an unwise fashion) or in the family (making it impossible for the dying individual to have meaningful conversations with the family and thus prepare himself and them for his death). In order to determine which response to denial is appropriate in a given situation, let's examine a few case histories and evaluate the common responses as to their effectiveness.

Larry Johnson had been fighting cancer for eight of his twenty-seven years, and for five of those years he was winning. Now, hospitalized and needing continual care and medication, Larry couldn't go home again. There was no way he could receive adequate care at home. But he wasn't a "quitter," and he intended to keep fighting as long as there was a breath in his body. His wife, Judy, was with him almost constantly, and his parents and sisters visited daily.

One day, while making rounds, I stopped in Larry's room. "Hey, do you need anything?"

"Only to get home as soon as possible," Larry replied. "Just get me strong enough to get home."

Before I could say anything, Judy patted his hand and answered, "Don't fret, honey. Dr. Kopp will have you as good as new in no time. Why, I'll bet you'll be able to come home in a couple of days."

Larry looked at Judy and then at me. "I really am stronger, you know," he stated. "I can go without oxygen most of the time now, and I've been up and walking to the bathroom." Although he was close to death, he still clung to his hope of going home. Judy quickly supported Larry, responding to his denial with a denial of her own.

Richard Moore had numerous polyps in his large bowel and he knew that cancer of the colon could soon develop. Richard's doctor, Dr. Morrison, had checked him regularly, had taken x-rays of his colon, and had given him proctoscopic examinations every six months for two years. But when Richard began having cramping abdominal pain and diarrhea, he was sure that he had the "flu." Three days later, the diarrhea stopped and he began vomiting uncontrollably. Finally, doubled over in pain, he telephoned Dr. Morrison in desperation. "I can't keep a thing down, and the pain is so bad that I break out in a cold sweat."

"Come to the hospital right away," Dr. Morrison said. He met Richard at the door to the emergency room and examined him as soon as he was admitted. "Richard, you're going to need surgery."

Dismayed and surprised, Richard lay in bed after surgery. *I've been praying and claiming healing from God,* he thought, *so why do I have cancer of the colon? I was so sure I'd be healed.*

As Richard lay in bed, thinking, Dr. Morrison walked into the room. "I got everything cancerous I could see," he said, "but that isn't a guarantee you're cured. It will be four or five years before we know for sure, and there's still a chance the cancer will recur."

Richard went home and did well for almost a year. Then he got the "flu" again—cramps, diarrhea, vomiting. Again, he waited, sure that the sickness would pass. *God has cured me of cancer,* he told himself. *It can't be that! It mustn't be that!* After several days, Richard was no better. In desperation he again called Dr. Morrison and was admitted to the hospital. Again he went to surgery as an emergency patient and again the doctor discovered cancer.

HOW SHOULD YOU RESPOND TO ANOTHER'S DENIAL?

Responding With Denial

The easiest way to respond to someone who is "playing ostrich" is to join the game, like Judy did. If the terminally ill individual thinks he's getting well, humor him. Go along with his plans and dreams for the future. Pretend, at least for awhile, that the situation is all a bad dream.

Generally speaking, it is appropriate to respond to denial with denial if the individual's denial is functional (of the "not yet" type). The individual cannot face the fact of his own death twenty-four hours a day. He needs a respite from it, a respite easily gained through denial. On the other hand, if your response supports behavior that is harmful to the individual, it is inappropriate.

Responding by Being Noncommittal

When an individual's denial seems inappropriate, it is probably best to approach him with a noncommittal attitude, rather than to try to force him to "come to his senses." By having a "no comment" attitude, you can convey the message that the individual doesn't have to maintain his facade of denial for your sake.

To illustrate a noncommittal attitude, let us imagine that Peter Harris—a jovial, hearty, sixty-two-year-old with high blood pressure, chronic heart failure, and a mild degree of asthma—is being treated by Dr. Michaels. Dr. Michaels finally has Peter's problems under control and has specified that Peter is to take five blood pressure pills and two heart pills every day.

One morning, Mrs. Harris notices that the pill bottles are nearly empty. "I'll stop by the pharmacy while I'm out shopping," she calls out, "and get your refills on your medicine."

"Alma, I get awfully sick of taking all those pills every day," Peter replies. "I'm feeling fine now, anyway. I think I'll just stop taking the pills."

"But Dr. Michaels warned you that if you stopped taking the medicine, you would develop problems and could even have a stroke."

"Oh, Dr. Michaels is just being an old mother hen," Peter states loudly. "Besides, he probably has an agreement with that pharmacist. I say I feel well, and I'm not going to stand for being stuffed full of pills like an invalid."

In this situation, it is not appropriate for Alma to support her husband's denial, nor is it appropriate for her to rant and rave about the importance of his taking the pills. Probably the most prudent thing for her to do is to get the prescriptions refilled and say nothing more to him about it. Peter may then find it possible to continue taking the pills without having an emotional reaction to being "treated like an invalid."

Following Richard's colon surgery (p. 43), I also used a noncommittal approach in his treatment. When I met with him a week after his surgery, he said, "Dr. Ruth, I know that God has cured me of cancer. If He means to do it through chemotherapy, that's okay with me. Or He might use another way. But I know He has healed me."

"We don't know what God has in store for you or for me," I answered gently. "But as you and I both trust and follow Him, we can believe that He has led us together. He has the ability to heal you completely or only grant you temporary healing in the form of a remission. Your healing is all in His hands. I must use my medical judgment, and that means starting chemotherapy now. I think we can take that as God's will for now and leave the future in His hands." Although I didn't endorse Richard's belief in his healing, neither did I challenge it. After all, I didn't know whether or not God would heal him. Maybe He would!

Responding With a Challenge

Sometimes you may find it impossible to support someone else's denial. Everything inside you screams, *No, no, no! Can't you see that you're not getting any better? Can't you tell?* In such a situation you can sometimes swallow your feelings and remain quiet. At other times, however, you will have to challenge the individual and say something similar to what I said to Larry (p. 43).

As I stood in the room, talking with Larry and Judy and witnessing their mutual denial, I couldn't bring myself to say, "Well, we'll get you home as soon as we can," and walk out. Everything inside me rebelled against that. So I sat down beside Larry's bed. "Larry," I asked, "have you thought about the possibility that you might not go home? I'm not saying you won't but what *if?*"

Larry didn't say anything for a few seconds. Then he whispered, "Yes, I've thought about it. I'm as ready as I can be." Tears came to his eyes, and the three of us sat in silence for several minutes. Then I stood up slowly and left the room, leaving Larry and Judy alone until they were ready for a follow-up discussion.

If you gently challenge an individual's denial when you have time to follow it through, it will generally not be harmful. In fact, the challenge will prove especially helpful in differentiating between initial denial and functional "not yet" denial. Stern admonitions to "face the facts" will not even faze the individual involved in initial denial, for he will not be reached by facts or questions. An individual who hears the challenge, on the other hand, is probably ready to face the possibility of dropping his denial. As in the noncommittal response, you can convey the message, "You don't have to play ostrich for me. I'm willing to face facts and talk about them, too, if that's what you want."

It is important to remember that you should not challenge an attitude of denial and then automatically walk out of the room. Whenever possible, discuss the issue before allowing the conversation to shift to another topic, or stop the discussion altogether and follow up your "challenge" with further discussion in the near future.

Responding With a "Wait and See" Attitude

After I challenged Judy and Larry's denial, Judy followed me down the hallway. Crying and shaking with anger, she exclaimed, "What do you mean by saying that he won't go home? He's *got* to get well! He's just *got* to! I know he's better today than he was yesterday and that in a few more days I'll be able to take him home."

I answered Judy's denial using a fourth response to denial. I led her to a sofa, and we both sat down. I let her go on for awhile about the ways in which she could tell that Larry was getting better. Then I told her, "I'm glad that Larry seems better to you. You know, I'm not always right. Maybe he will go home. But I can't guarantee that. There is still the possibility that he won't. Let's wait several days and see how he is."

Through the years, I have learned to use the "wait and see" response whenever a terminally ill individual says, "God has healed me." If God has healed, it will be evident in time. If He has not healed, there will be time enough to face that later.

Challenging statements made by a terminally ill individual in denial only results in anger and hostility. Yet, agreeing to something that is obviously untrue can be harmful and, for me at least, unpleasant. The "wait and see" response gives me and the patient time to deal with the situation. It prevents me from angrily defending my authority and prevents the individual from hostilely defending his position. The "wait and see" response is honest and does not "put down" the other person for his beliefs or statements. In time, the terminally ill patient may be ready to let go of his denial or I may be ready to accept his denial as his method of coping with the situation.

Responding by Withdrawal

The last common response to denial is withdrawal from or avoidance of the person who is denying. When we can't bring ourselves to go along with his denial, we feel uncomfortable. Since we don't like to feel uncomfortable, we start avoiding that person. When we are forced to be with him, we keep the conversation light and superficial and make excuses to keep the visit brief.

Richard Moore's sister, Fran, for example, had always been close to him. When the cancer developed, she took it hard, spending days and nights crying. "Why?" she kept asking. "Why Richard? It isn't fair for him to have cancer. He's always been so careful. He never drank or smoked. He has always watched his weight and exercised regularly. Why him?"

When Richard started talking about being healed, it worried Fran. She wanted desperately to believe him, but she couldn't. On the other hand, she didn't want to shake his faith or depress him. During the year following his first operation, she watched him improve steadily. Finally she began to tell herself, *After all, Richard has a lot of faith. If anyone should be healed, it should be Richard.* When he had gone for eight months without problems or evidence of new disease, Fran, too, became convinced that he had been healed.

Then Richard's cancer recurred. "How can this happen?" Fran cried out as we were talking in my office. "How can he have cancer again? He was so sure he was healed! I even believed in his healing. And now this. It's gone just the way Dr. Morrison feared it would. I don't see how Richard can ignore it any more. It's gotten so I can hardly bear to be with him. I can't see him lying there weak and in pain from surgery, telling me how God has healed him. I just can't take it!"

Finally, Fran began seeing Richard for only ten or fifteen minutes on her way home from work, instead of going to the hospital to spend the evening with him. Before long she was visiting two, or at most three, times a week rather than seeing him every day. They had less and less to talk about, and even the short, infrequent visits became a strain.

Withdrawal is probably the least satisfactory method of responding to denial. It leads to alienation and blocks communication, as in the case of Richard and Fran. However, there are times when it may be the only response you can make and still retain your own psychological and emotional integrity. If withdrawal becomes necessary, you shouldn't go too far away, and you should try to remain open to re-establishing the relationship as soon as the emotional climate passes.

Regardless of which response to denial you believe is the most appropriate, these important points will make the denial easier to tolerate:

(1) Don't push the individual or try to force him into realizing the true nature of the situation. If you find the denial intolerable, find a third person (minister, nurse, doctor) with whom you can discuss the situation.

(2) Remember the deafness of denial. Be prepared to write down information that may be needed at a later date. Such information will be useful in dealing with your own denial as well. Be alert to notice that things have been heard incompletely or not at all, and be ready to repeat information as often as necessary.

As the one who accompanies the patient on his visits to the doctor, write down information the doctor (nurse, secretary) gives you, check with the informant for accuracy, and keep the notes handy for future reference.

As a spouse, child, parent, or close friend of the ill individual who is not accompanying him to his medical appointments, be alert to the fact that the individual may not be hearing things correctly. If you have any doubts about "what the doctor said," make an attempt to check with the doctor before reacting to the information.

(3) Be aware that denial can make an individual forgetful. If you are in a position to do so, make forgetting a difficult thing. For example, offer to drive the individual to his doctor's appointments and be sure you get the appointment card for the next time so that you can be responsible for getting him there. A simple matter of each evening counting out the right pills for the following day and leaving them on the breakfast table can help prevent him from forgetting his medicine. You can also devise other "tricks" to jog the memory that will work equally well for yourself.

(4) When the denial takes the form of a denial of symptoms, the family and friends of the sick individual may prepare a list of questions

and problems to send to the doctor with the individual. This helps the doctor get a more complete picture of how the person is doing. Off-hand, I can think of several women whose daughters send in a list of concerns with them, some men and women whose husbands and wives make a list of the problems that seem worrisome, and one young man who always has a list of questions from his mother.

(5) The last thing I want to say about denial is that "things are not always what they seem to be." Many dying individuals, as well as their loved ones, become involved in a game that I choose to call, "Let's Spare Him." The rules are as follows: Player A is the patient. He knows he is seriously ill and, in fact, is dying. There are important things he'd like to say to his wife and children, but he "knows" they don't realize how bad things are and decides to spare them the agony of knowing that he is dying. Player B is the wife (husband) who knows that her husband is dying. In fact, the doctor has taken her into his confidence, and she knows the time is short. She would like to ask her husband many questions about such things as family finances, the children, and his parents. However, she believes that he doesn't know how bad it is and that he'd lose heart and maybe even die sooner if she tells him. So she decides to spare him her questions and struggles through bravely. Players C, D, and E are children and friends who would like to tell A how much he has meant to them and say some of the things they never got around to saying. Afraid that if he knows how bad things are it will make his condition worse, they decide to spare him. Besides, B and the doctor have agreed that A knows nothing at all about his true ·condition.

You can see that everyone—minister, doctors, nurses, roommates —can all become involved in this game. On the surface, it looks like mass denial of the illness. Underneath, all the players may actually be in any of the other stages one encounters in the course of a terminal illness. If you think you may be involved in a game of "Let's Spare Him," it is safe to probe gently to find out if others involved are pretending denial too. Rather than going along enthusiastically with plans for the future and predictions of the time A will be well, adopt a noncommittal attitude or introduce a pause into the conversation. Remember that it is very difficult to force an individual in initial denial out of that phase. There is little danger you will give him a traumatic shock if you handle things with compassion and patience. Instead of rushing to reassure him that things are going well when he asks, "Did the doctor say anything about how I'm doing?" offer him an opportunity to tell you how he thinks things are going. "What did he tell you?" you might ask. "What do you think that means? Do you feel that things are going well?" This approach will open up the opportunity for him to talk. If that's what he's looking for, he will gladly avail himself of the opportunity. When we recall that aloneness is a large part of the horror of dying, we begin to see the importance of concerned listeners to the dying individual (and his family and friends). The ability to talk about the aspects of illness that are most feared and disliked eases the burden of the illness.

---- 5 ----

CHRISTIANS' RESPONSES TO DENIAL

THOSE OF US WHO are Christians are often bombarded with a barrage of attitudes and assumptions that are antithetical to biblical teaching, for we do not live in a vacuum but in a society that has developed basically non-Christian values and standards. The worship of youth's exuberance and physical prowess and the accompanying denial of death and the shunning of illness are examples of the cultural phenomena with which we have to cope. Often these false attitudes and assumptions subtly and insidiously become part of our thinking.

It is true that, as Christians, we have many resources to help us meet the problems of terminal illness and death. Yet we too are human and we quail at the prospect of suffering, pain, and death. Our bodies are mixed blessings, for the physical joys they make possible are offset by physical suffering. They can lift us up and pull us down. When we are in good health and feel well, it is easy for us to be on top of things emotionally and spiritually. Ill health and suffering, on the other hand, can produce discouragement, denial, and despair.

How can Christians living in physical bodies in a basically non-Christian culture cope with this? What do we do when the strain becomes too much and we fall into the pitfalls of denial and despair? What part does denial play in the terminal illness we face as Christians? What does the Christian faith have to offer us in dealing with the problem of denial? I think that the example of one of my former patients, George Harris, will answer several of these questions.

George Harris was born into a Christian home, brought up in church and Sunday school, and was familiar with the Bible and Christian doctrine. He had just turned twenty-two when my husband and I met him. Having graduated from a Christian college a year earlier, he was working for a prominent business in town.

Nearly six weeks before we met him, George had noticed a swollen "gland" on the left side of his neck. At first he paid no attention to it. Instead of becoming smaller, however, the gland had become larger,

51

harder, and finally painful. At that point, George made an appointment with Dr. Johnson, his family doctor.

Dr. Johnson examined George and took a close look at the lump, which was three inches long and about an inch and a half wide. It didn't appear to be a boil, and George didn't have a sore throat. Dr. Johnson gave George a quick physical examination and asked detailed questions about any other symptoms or problems George might have had. "There are no other problems as far as I know," George stated. "The swelling I've had in my neck for nearly six weeks is the only thing out of the ordinary."

"Well," Dr. Johnson answered, "in that case I think you may have Hodgkin's disease. You're the right age, and there seem to be no other abnormalities present that could cause that type of swelling." To confirm the diagnosis, Dr. Johnson scheduled a surgical biopsy, which would be followed by tests to determine the extent of the disease.

Much to the chagrin of everyone involved, the tissue diagnosis from the biopsy revealed malignant cells that originated from one of George's testicles. Dr. Johnson then did a genital examination and discovered that the left testicle was about the size of a small orange, three to five times the normal size. "How long has your testicle been swollen, George?" Dr. Johnson asked.

"I didn't even know that it was swollen," George replied. Apparently he was as surprised as everyone else to learn the source of his problem. Due to the tumor's location and its size at the time of discovery, George must have noticed it earlier. Therefore, his surprise concerning the tumor must be interpreted as denial in that he was blind to the symptoms and their implications.

With the diagnosis of testicular cancer, the doctors had to perform new tests, and George's outlook became less hopeful. The new test results indicated that George's cancer had already spread to his liver, neck, and lymph nodes in the chest. It was definitely too late for George to be totally cured through surgery. Although in rare cases chemotherapy has cured people with this type of cancer, George's tumor was too widespread. We started him on a combination of chemotherapeutic agents, explaining to him that we could slow down the cancer's progress but a cure in his case would be nothing short of a miracle.

The first six months of treatment went well. The chemotherapy seemed to be reversing the tumor's growth, and George was adjusting well to the changes in his schedule and had few problems with the treatments. So it came as a big surprise to us when he began missing office appointments. First, he made an unexpected trip out of town to visit friends and "just happened" to be gone when he was due for a treatment. Then he missed an appointment because of car trouble. When his next treatment was due, he told us he had a cold and wanted to wait a few weeks. His erratic schedule of treatments continued for eight or nine months.

During that time George was feeling well. Although he had been told he had cancer, he couldn't believe it. He had a good appetite, had no pain, continued working regularly, and became active in the young adults' group at church. He had a steady girl friend and was popular among his friends and acquaintances. As he told me later, "I kept thinking that it had to be a bad dream and pretty soon I'd wake up and find that this had all been a dreadful mistake! How could I believe that I had cancer when I felt so well? I could do almost anything at all, certainly anything that I wanted or needed to do. I wasn't tired. I didn't have an ache or a pain anywhere. I seemed to be walking along in a nightmare, and felt that at any moment I was going to wake up.

"Then what you said about having a relapse hit me, Dr. Kopp. I'd sit down to breakfast and find out that I wasn't hungry. I'd go to work and be exhausted by noon. I started coughing, and I couldn't walk up a flight of stairs without having to stop and catch my breath. That was a good thing for me, though, because I finally knew for sure that I had cancer and that if I didn't get in there and fight it, I'd be finished."

We helped George "get in there and fight it." A different type of chemotherapy bought him another four and a half months of relatively good health. This time the chemotherapy made him sick, and he had to be hospitalized five days out of every month in order to be treated. Still, it was working, and we were all grateful. George never felt that five days in the hospital was too high a price to pay for three weeks of relatively good health.

Toward the end of his illness, George and I had a number of conversations about his spiritual faith. "You know, I've always been able to quote that verse about all things working together for good," he told me. "I'm not sure I ever believed it until now. When you first told me I had cancer and that it was incurable, I was really mad at God. I sort of dared Him to take my cancer and work it into good! I even insisted that He take care of me without the chemotherapy. Then I told Him I'd go ahead and take chemotherapy, but only if He'd keep me from getting sick. I know that I wasn't responsible in keeping appointments when I first got sick. Maybe things would be different if I had gone to a doctor sooner or if I had come to you for regular treatments. I don't know. Now, I'm just tired of running away from things. God hasn't done any of the things I asked for, but now I can trust Him. He knew what was happening even from the beginning, and I don't believe He'll let me die a day too soon. If the treatments help, that's because God has made them effective; if they don't, well, that's His business, too."

George was a "model" patient during the last few months of his life. He was at peace with himself and with God. I never heard him regretting the past or being bitter about his future. He cooperated with all of us who cared for him and had few complaints. He seemed to draw on unlimited strength and endured the sickness and suffering of the terminal phase of his illness with hardiness and fortitude. Shortly after his twenty-fourth birthday, he died.

During the last several months of his life, George had been able to use the resources of strength and encouragement God supplied him. Why, then, did he go through a long period of initial denial, tragically delaying treatment?

It's not hard to imagine that George—young, athletic, handsome—was afraid that something was terribly wrong when his testicle first began to grow. It's even easier to realize how he could keep putting off the doctor's appointment, waiting "just another day or two" to see if the swelling would go away. Perhaps there were days when the testicle seemed to be better and nearly normal in size. Maybe George was afraid he would not have the courage or strength to face a serious illness. Perhaps the thought of surgery that might rob him of his ability to father a child and impair his sexual functioning was too threatening for his male ego to face. Certainly the career and job implications of a diagnosis such as cancer must have crossed his mind. All these fears combined kept him blind to the true significance of his condition even to the extent that he could not remember that his testicle was larger than normal.

Where was George's faith when his denial kept him so tragically blind during the early stages of his illness? He was no different from anyone else at that time, for his preoccupation with the "what ifs" blinded him to the facts. Although God has promised to supply all our needs, He hasn't guaranteed He will answer all our "what if" questions. His supply of grace is designed to meet the real crises we face, not the imagined troubles of tomorrow! George's faith came through with flying colors when he finally put it (and God) to the test. He faced the truth of his illness and found God sufficient to see him through. But, as in so many other aspects of life, as long as he ran from the problem he was unable to appropriate God's grace in facing his crisis. Once he stopped running, he found that God was with him in illness and trial, providing the strength and endurance he had been afraid he would not find.

Later, as the cancer progressed, George had to fight against bitterness and anger that he expressed partly through not keeping his appointments. In his anger George demanded healing from God, dared God to touch his body, and made an attempt to bargain with Him in a number of ways. ("God, if You will make sure I don't get sick, I'll go ahead with the treatments. If I prove my faith in You by stopping chemotherapy, You've got to heal me!") It is both interesting and comforting to know that in the end George found peace and acceptance with God. He was free from self-reproach and the endless feeling of "if only I had . . . ." He was able to forgive himself for his delay and denial.

Although his attitude during the terminal phase of his illness may seem like fatalism, to me it represents a real grasp of God's sovereignty. God truly knew in advance all things, including George's denial and consequent delay in treatment, and allowed them to happen nevertheless. The success of his treatment, or its failure, also lay in God's hands. God did not let George die a day too soon or a day too late. By trusting in God, George was able to face his death with hope and the knowledge that God was working His will through his situation.

FAITH HEALING

As we consider the uniquely Christian aspects of denial and the confrontation of terminal illness, it is impossible to avoid the issue of faith healing. This is a particularly sticky issue, and all pronouncements in this area are subject to extremism and misinterpretation. In spite of these dangers and the issue's highly emotional nature, a few things need to be emphasized about faith healing.

God Heals

Sometimes God heals instantaneously, without any medical intervention. More often (at least in my own experience), He gives a miraculous response to accepted medical therapy. Divine healing is not always permanent. Sometimes a miraculous remission occurs, only to be followed by a relapse and death. I personally believe that all our responses to medical and surgical treatment can be ultimately credited to God, as Maker and Sustainer. He created our bodies with their intricate workings and capabilities to fight disease and to respond to treatment.

God Allows Suffering

Although I certainly don't believe that God derives pleasure from seeing His children (or anyone else) suffer, I cannot say that suffering is never in His permissive will for anyone. He definitely allows illness, pain, and suffering to exist. He does not heal everyone who asks for healing, and those He does heal are not often the ones I would nominate for healing on the basis of faith, prominence in Christian work, or purity of life. Those who prove the quality of their faith by refusing all medical attention and by clinging to the unswerving belief that God alone will heal them are as likely to die of cancer or another disease as anyone else. No less impressive is the faith of those who submit to all prescribed medical treatment cheerfully, in the belief that God can use any instrument He will to heal. Yet, among these people are also found nonresponders to therapy whose illness proves to be fatal. Faith doesn't seem to be a crucial issue in the matter of healing. Some people who are blatantly skeptical of God's ability to heal are healed.

TYPES OF BELIEF IN DIVINE HEALING

Belief in divine healing can easily mask deep-rooted and long-lasting initial denial. People with this form of belief in faith healing insist that God *will* heal them and confidently exclude the possibility that He may choose not to intervene in their particular case. In effect, they say, "This illness is not all that bad. After all, God will heal me and I won't die!" But such a response is a form of denial, for it desperately appeals for a reversal of the "fatal" verdict.

Another form of belief in divine healing stems from a faith in God's ability to heal coupled with a humility that's willing to accept a yes or no answer from God. The person's desire for healing is no less intense, and his belief in God's power is just as firm. However, instead of the insistent "You've *got* to heal me, God!" the cry is "Lord, have mercy!" Job expressed this belief when he said, "Though he slay me, yet will I hope in him" (Job 13:15). This type of belief in divine healing is not a form of denial. The individual faces the awful nature of his illness knowing that unless God intervenes he will die. Healing is seen, not as just due, but rather as a gracious act of God's mercy.

With few exceptions, people who have cancer believe in miracles. This is also true for those with other forms of fatal illness. Part of this belief stems from the disbelief in our own mortality. *This disease couldn't really kill me*, each person thinks. In this state of mind, we tend to see ourselves as the exception, not the rule. *If 90 percent of the patients with the kind of tumor I have will die within the year*, we think, *I'm sure that I'll be numbered among the other 10 percent*.

As Christians, we tend to believe that, although God has not healed many others, we will be one of those He chooses to touch. We believe that our faith, our prayers, and our pleading will prevail where that of others has failed. Spiritual pride in our own faith and presumption of our understanding of the total situation and God's complete will are real dangers here. The temptation is even greater when we pray for the healing of someone dear to us, for then the question of selfish motives is less evident and the matter of spiritual pride is ignored in our eagerness to serve others through our prayers and faith.

This is not to say that we should not pray, even beg, for our own healing. I certainly do not intend to discourage the fervent prayers of believers for each other. Just because there is a danger of spiritual pride and selfish motives, we should not abandon the issue of divine healing. Though faith is not the only—or even the most crucial—factor in the matter of healing, that doesn't mean we should throw out our belief in God's ability to heal. However, we ought to be alert to the attitude toward healing that is really a guise for denial, at the same time respecting the fact that God does heal and that healing is a legitimate request we can make of Him.

Following is an example of misguided belief in healing. Bill and Bertha Miller were well-known citizens of Carlock, Illinois, a small town near us. They ran a Christian bookstore and had an outreach to many people through its ministry. In addition, Bertha taught three weekly women's Bible studies and Bill was on the board of elders at their church. Two of their children were married and living in town. Bill, Jr., was learning the bookstore business from his dad and gave his parents much help and companionship. Judy, their youngest, was living at home and attending school at a nearby junior college. To all appearances, the Millers had everything to live for—a good business, a happy family, an active position of Christian service. Yet, cancer entered this "ideal" situation and created chaos.

One morning, Bertha woke up with intense pain in her stomach. She had been having a lot of stomach pain lately, but this was the worst she had ever experienced. It took her breath away and made her break out in a cold sweat. *I guess I'd better get to the doctor soon,* she thought. *Maybe I'll go tomorrow. If I just sit still here for a minute or two, maybe the pain will go away. I'd hate to miss the Bible study this morning.* She sat on the sofa, and the pain eased. She began feeling almost normal, although the pain had left her a bit dizzy and weak. *I'll make the Bible study after all,* she thought. Suddenly she became violently nauseated and barely made it to the bathroom in time. *I must telephone Marianne to tell her I won't be coming.* As she started to stand up, she lost consciousness.

When Bertha didn't show up for Bible study, Marianne called her house to see what was wrong. She didn't get an answer and finally called Bill at the store to find out where Bertha was. Bill was concerned. Although Bertha hadn't complained much, her facial expressions from time to time had made him think that she was in severe pain. Her appetite hadn't been good, either, and he thought she was losing weight. When Marianne called him, he rushed right home and found Bertha lying unconscious on the bathroom floor. She was pale, and the toilet bowl was full of blood. There were traces of blood on her mouth and hands, too; evidently she had vomited the blood and then fainted.

Bill rushed her to the hospital emergency room. Because she had lost so much blood, her condition was serious. Hospital personnel quickly gave her a blood transfusion and took a number of x-rays. Soon it became clear that the suspected bleeding ulcer was not an ordinary ulcer but an ulcerated, malignant tumor of the stomach.

Until she lost consciousness under the anaesthetic on the operating table, Bertha prayed, hoping that the tumor would turn out to be benign in spite of all indications to the contrary. Bill stood by her, steadfastly refusing to talk about the possibility of cancer and answering all her doubts with the assurance that the Lord would take care of her and heal her. The surgery was successful; most of her stomach and apparently all of the tumor were removed at the same time. Examination of the tissue showed that it was cancerous, however.

Initially this diagnosis was a big blow to Bertha. Then she began to think, *Why should I stop believing that God can heal me? Now that the tumor has been proven to be cancerous, my healing will be more of a miracle. If the tumor had turned out to be benign, it would just have been attributed to the "margin of error" in a diagnosis. This way, everyone will have to admit that God has healed me.* She and Bill clung to the belief that God would heal her, never allowing themselves to think of the alternative.

Although there was no evidence at the time of surgery that the cancer had spread outside the stomach, several routine tests were performed. These revealed that Bertha's liver and lungs also contained tumor, indicating that her cancer was widespread. There was no longer any medical hope for a cure. Once again, Bertha accepted this fact with the idea that her healing in a medically hopeless case would bring more honor to God.

My husband and I began treating Bertha at this point, and we advised her that the only promising form of treatment for her incurable cancer was still experimental. "We can get the drug for you," I told her, "and with it you will have a fair chance of arresting the disease for anywhere from several months to a year or two. Of course," I added, "there is virtually no chance that the drug will cure you."

During Bertha's hospitalization, her Bible study groups and home church began to pray for her healing. She was flooded with cards and notes of encouragement from concerned friends and acquaintances. Many of these people assured her that they, too, "knew" that God was going to heal her. People were in and out of her hospital room long after visiting hours were over, and soon she was being urged to go to Mayo Clinic for a second opinion and a "new" form of treatment.

When the Millers asked us about going to Mayo Clinic, we told them that doctors there were treating stomach cancer in basically the same way we were. They, too, were using the experimental drug we had described to Bertha. However, since the Millers needed to feel comfortable with the diagnosis and treatment recommendations, we agreed that if a visit to Mayo Clinic would set their minds at ease, they should go.

As soon as Bertha felt up to traveling, Bill took her to Mayo Clinic. Friends continued to pray for her and write letters. The doctors at the clinic had the same opinion we had. "There is no hope for a cure," they said, "but drug treatment might arrest the disease for awhile." They recommended that Bertha return home and begin chemotherapy as soon as possible so that she would have the best chance of responding to treatment.

When the Millers returned home, they received a warm and loving response from their church and Bible study groups. People they scarcely knew dropped by the house to see Bertha or stopped Bill at the store to tell him they were praying for her. Their comfort and encouragement to the Millers was inestimable! Many continually assured them that Bertha would be healed and urged them to "keep their faith strong" and "not doubt."

Bill and Bertha felt that it would show a lack of faith to make arrangements for the possibility that Bertha might not be healed. They tried to keep from mentioning the negative aspects of her illness; she emphasized her strength and well-being, pushed away all thoughts of her recurrent nausea, nagging backache, and increasing inability to do anything at all around the house. She continued to refuse our suggestions that she begin chemotherapy treatment.

Before long, friends were urging the Millers to go to M. D. Anderson Hospital in Houston, Texas. "It can't hurt. Maybe they have something new and different." The Millers went to Houston; the diagnosis, opinions, and recommendations were once again the same. Perhaps there was just a bit more insistence this time that Bertha should begin treatment immediately.

The cancer was beginning to take its toll. Bertha had been losing weight steadily; her lack of appetite had turned into continual nausea. The nagging ache in her back became a throbbing roar of pain with the slightest exertion. Soon she found that standing for even five minutes was enough to put her in bed for the rest of the day. Bertha once again came to us, and tests showed that cancerous tumor had spread to the bones in her back and was causing the intense pain. We urged her to begin radiation therapy for the radiation would almost certainly relieve the back pain. Again, we asked her to consider chemotherapy, in hopes that the disease could be arrested. Bertha, still clinging stubbornly to the belief that God would heal her, began to consider radiation treatments. However, the people in her church intervened again. They had heard that a clinic in California was using a new "wonder drug" and were sure that it was the Lord's will for her to go to California. Concerned friends even bought Bertha's plane ticket and arranged to care for her home and the business while the Millers were gone!

When Bertha returned from California, she was little more than skin and bones. Every movement required an extreme effort; pain was her constant companion. She had little appetite, and what little she was able to eat frequently produced violent nausea and vomiting. We felt that the end was near. Her friends continued to urge her to "claim healing." Bill was continually reproached for not having enough faith. If he attempted to make practical arrangements for her hospitalization or for her imminent death, friends berated him for not "believing."

Bertha finally was hospitalized. Weak, her pain barely controlled by large doses of narcotics, she seemed ready to give up the fight and prepare for her own death, but no one near her would support her in this effort. She finally died, while family and friends prayed for her healing. She never had a chance to say farewell or to prepare for death.

Through this unfortunate instance, we can learn a number of things. First, the denial of people who are important to us exerts a powerful influence. If those whom we love and depend on deny our illness, our own inclinations toward denial are reinforced. If we encounter an overwhelming amount of denial in those around us, it is much more difficult for us to work through the initial denial and accept the reality of our illness. Conversely, a patient's strong initial denial can influence family and loved ones to maintain their own denial.

Second, this situation amply illustrates the attitude of denial that can be present in people's belief in faith healing. Bertha's friends, for example, used their belief in healing to buttress their denial. According to my observation, the effect that this type of belief has in healing is equivalent to saying, "Anyone who has enough faith *will* be healed." It ignores the fact that many good Christians who believe in God and in His healing power do get sick and die. It also puts the burden of "faith" on the sick individual and his family. This type of faith is almost a self-hypnosis, for it states, "I will get well; I am getting well; I am well," and refuses to take external signs and symptoms of the illness into account. The person who admits that he doesn't feel as well as he did yesterday is "expressing unbelief" or "confessing illness," thus confirming both spiritual and physical illness.

We can see that this type of belief in faith healing puts enormous pressure on an individual to meet the fact of his illness, and its signs and symptoms, with denial. "Confess health and you will have health" is the basic belief. So, in spite of excruciating back pain, violent nausea, and a splitting headache, a person will "confess" that he feels well!

This type of denial tends to be more confusing because it is not all negative. Our psychological attitude toward terminal illness does influence the way we feel; our outlook does play a part in our recovery or lack of recovery. In fact, the difference between a positive outlook and outright denial is often evident only in degree. If a person has an underlying acceptance of his condition and recognizes such negative factors as pain, poor appetite, and weakness, then his deliberate choice to focus on the positive can be very healthy. If, however, his focus on the positive is an attempt to hide from the negative and so effectually deny its very existence, the focus can be detrimental.

Any scripturally sound approach to healing must include the admission that God's ways are not our ways, nor are our thoughts His thoughts (see Isa. 55:8, 9). It must allow for the fact that illness, death, and suffering are a part of God's permissive will for this world and that no human being has been exempt from them, including God's Son.

Before asking God to heal a terminally ill person, we must admit that the situation is indeed desperate, that the illness is real and terminal. Then God's touch can be asked for, not on the basis of our faith, our hope, our knowledge of Scripture, or on any ground other than His gracious mercy. We must allow for the possibility that His will may not include healing now, or ever, on this earth. This decision must be left to His wisdom and judgment. Our request for healing should be just that—a request and not a demand.

God does heal—with or without medicine, temporarily or permanently, gradually or instantaneously. There is no formula, however, and I doubt that we will ever fully understand His decision to heal in one case and not heal in another.

WE ARE RESPONSIBLE FOR OTHERS

As Christians, we are dependent on one another and responsible for each other. As members of one body, we are members of each other. We are not alone, for we have Christian family, friends, or acquaintances. A parent can assume responsibility for a child, for example, and a child can do the same for a parent. A friend can help out a friend. The command to bear one another's burdens in Galatians 6:2 applies to the practical problem of denial just as it does to the more spiritual issues to which the verse is readily applied. Often someone close to us can help us counteract the blindness of our denial and combat its deafness. Sometimes a gentle push in the right direction can help a friend or loved one overcome his denial enough to motivate him to do the rational thing about an alarming or annoying symptom.

While on vacation one summer, Donald Young noticed a mole on his left shoulder. Because he swam often, he noticed that the mole gradually became darker. Toward the end of the summer it developed an angry red border. Noticing it from time to time, Don thought, *As soon as school starts, I'll go to the doctor.*

However, when school started Don was caught up in registration, buying books, and getting settled into the fall semester. There always seemed to be something more important than having a doctor check the mole. Once he stopped in at the college health center, but many people were waiting to see the doctor and he had a class in twenty minutes. So he left, planning to go back another day.

"Another day" just didn't arrive. First he was involved in a tough geometry class and spent several weeks getting straightened out in it. Then came tryouts for the men's glee club and college choir. After that it was time for midterms. Don noticed the mole from time to time, when dressing or undressing, but it didn't bother him. Usually he thought of seeing the doctor early in the morning or late at night, when it was impossible to do anything about it.

When Don went home for Thanksgiving vacation, his mother saw the mole for the first time when he was wandering around the house without a shirt on. "How long has that been there?" she demanded.

Don shrugged his shoulders. "Six or eight weeks, I guess. Maybe a bit longer. I'm going to do something about it as soon as I get back to school. I don't really think it's anything to worry about, though."

"Has it always looked so black? How long has it been red around the edges like that? I think you should see a doctor right away."

"Aw, Mom, why do you have to make a fuss? I'll see about it as soon as I get back to school."

Mrs. Young persisted, however, and made an appointment for Don with a dermatologist. He removed the mole, which turned out to be a form of skin cancer. Further surgery and extensive testing revealed that the cancer had not spread into the adjacent skin. Don's outlook is optimistic, thanks to the fact that his mother realized the mole was potentially malignant. The dangerous aspect of Don's denial was averted by his mother's awareness and intervention.

WE ARE RESPONSIBLE TO OURSELVES

Our responsibility to and for each other must not, however, override our legitimate concern and responsibility for our own bodies. After admonishing us to bear each other's burdens, the apostle Paul goes on to say, "Each one should carry his own load" (Gal. 6:5). There is a balance between our independence—with its individual responsibility for ourselves before God—and our existence in the interdependent Christian community, the body of Christ.

The sayings, "Christ first, others second, self last" and "Joy means Jesus, others, and you, in that order," are not always applicable, at least not in the ways in which we are prone to apply them. "Others," in such forms as business meetings, people in our carpool, committee members, luncheon dates, church meetings, and cookie baking partners do not always have priority over yourself.

Some activities and commitments are necessary in order to maintain our physical and emotional health. Certainly if we wait for a "convenient" time to make a doctor's appointment, the appointment is not likely to be made and less likely to be kept. For there are always urgent demands on our time. Yet the preservation of our physical and emotional health is a prerequisite for effective functioning in relationship to others! Unless we see to it that our own needs are met, we will soon be in a position where we are unable to perceive or meet the needs of those around us. The balance between bearing the burdens of others and bearing our own burdens must be maintained.

SPECIAL PROBLEMS AND SOLUTIONS

Spiritual Rationalization

There is a real danger that we will rationalize our denial and put a "spiritual" face on it. We can convince ourselves and others, for example, that we are so busy doing "the Lord's work" that we have no time to think about our physical needs. When our "putting others first" results in physical and emotional illness, we need to reevaluate our priorities and our stewardship responsibility before God toward our own physical and emotional health. We may find that our human denial has adopted a spiritual guise of "humility" or "self-denial." Once this type of denial is unmasked, we will soon recognize that it springs from a variety of fears, anxieties, and human needs.

Fear of Cowardice

Part of the fear of the diagnosis of cancer (or any other serious, life-threatening illness) is, as we examined earlier, a fear that we will lose our nerve and disgrace ourselves in a cowardly reaction to the diagnosis of terminal illness.

In my experience this fear is largely unfounded. Of those whose denial caused considerable delay in their receiving treatment, not one had "gone to pieces" when faced with the actual diagnosis. They universally showed remarkable courage in facing the diagnosis and developed a fighting spirit and a sturdy sense of humor.

If we are Christians, we can take heart in knowing that God has given us frequently underestimated, human resources of courage and endurance that we haven't yet tapped, including the support and communion of fellow Christians. We never need to live more than one moment at a time. If we can avoid borrowing trouble, we will generally find that the resources at our disposal are sufficient from moment to moment. Even the worst hours are only a succession of minutes, and almost anyone can live through a minute of discomfort, pain, or suffering.

When we live each moment as it comes, we can, as Christians, draw on our own strength and look to God for His promises concerning the resources at our disposal. We must remember that we have more than our own strength to rely on; we are promised the presence of Christ. Almost beyond imagining, Christ has shared our sorrows and has made a way for us to know His sustaining power in the midst of trouble. He has promised to strengthen us always, under all circumstances, so that we can endure all things (see Isa. 40:31). He has promised to supply all our needs, including our need for courage and fortitude in the face of adversity (see Phil. 4:13, 19). He has also promised to give us His peace in times of distress (see John 14:27).

With God's resources at our disposal, long-term, initial denial does not need to be a problem for us. We have God the Father at our right hand, Christ and the Holy Spirit beside us, and heaven before us. Through God's help, we can cope with denial. We can move forward to deal with the issues at hand as we practice God's presence in our lives and rely on His promises.

SECTION TWO

THE PATIENT AND HIS DOCTOR

6

SELECTING AN IDEAL DOCTOR

How can I possibly choose the right doctor when there are so many to choose from? How can I find one I can trust? These are two questions that you as a terminally ill person or as a friend or family member of a terminally ill person must face when you choose a doctor. In selecting a doctor who will be capable of working in your particular situation, the choices may be difficult.

Although you may get recommendations from various places, the final decision is up to you. It is wise to take your family's feelings and preferences into account, but don't sacrifice your confidence in or your rapport with a doctor to your family's preferences. Remember, although you are the one who has to get along with your doctor, your family will be much more at ease if you have a doctor to whom they can relate and whom they can trust.

Getting the name of a doctor who is reputed to be competent in his field is, however, only part of the problem. Next on the list of priorities is deciding whether you can get along with him (or her). This is particularly true in cases where there is more than one doctor in your area who is medically competent to treat you. Of course, if there is only one cardiologist, endocrinologist, or hematologist in a fifty to one hundred mile radius, you have little choice.

How to Select a Doctor

Ask Others

1. Your family doctor. If you already have access to a doctor whom you trust, such as a family doctor, you can generally ask his advice in selecting another doctor. His recommendation about the competence of a colleague should carry more weight than that of your next-door neighbor. For example, if you are moving and need a family doctor in your new location, ask your doctor if he knows someone there or if he can get you the name of a doctor there from someone else he knows. Your family doctor can recommend a surgeon; your obstetrician can recommend a pediatrician; your internist can give you the name of a

dermatologist. You can also get suggestions from a doctor you know socially or one who is a friend of the family.

2. Your friends. Once you find that you have a particular illness, Aunt Minnie across the street, the neighbor over your back fence, the elderly gentleman who always greets you at church, a woman in your wife's bridge club, and others may have the same diagnosis or know someone else who has it. You can then find out who is treating them and what they like and don't like about their doctor. Ask questions that will help you find out how well you, personally, would get along with that doctor. Then reserve judgment until you have seen the doctor a time or two and can decide for yourself how well you like him.

The best way to see if you can get along with Dr. Jones is to find out his reputation in the community. There are some doctors of whom you will hear nothing but good; there are others about whom you hear the opposite. Although this kind of reputation has little bearing on the doctor's medical abilities, it is a reliable indicator of his public relations skills and his bedside manner. It tends to be a fair judge of the doctor's human (as opposed to professional) qualities.

3. Hospital employees. You may try to discover who takes care of the doctors' wives, husbands, children, and parents in your community. Unfortunately, this type of information is not generally available, and only such people as nurses, medical students, and hospital employees who have some entrance into the medical community can find this out. With a bit of effort, however, I believe that the average person can probably pick up some of this information. Although you may not have an entrance into the medical community, perhaps a friend or relative has this type of connection.

This method is probably the most reliable in picking out extremes in doctors. Those who are extremely good or extremely bad will be talked about, while doctors who are average or slightly above or below average won't receive much attention.

4. Medical centers. Another possibility particularly applicable to the cancer patient is that of calling one of the major medical centers in the country known for its research facilities and asking its staff to recommend a doctor in your community. Many major research centers will see patients on referral from doctors located in a wide area. Staff members will evaluate the patients, advise them about treatments, and return them to the referring doctors for follow-up care. In this manner, the doctors at the research centers become acquainted with doctors in the surrounding communities and are in a position to make recommendations. Obviously, this method of gaining information is not always applicable. You may live in an area that has no doctor known to the research center. (This doesn't mean that no doctor in your area can treat you. It just means that the center near you doesn't know of anyone.)

If you choose this route, be sure that you know your specific diagnosis in as much detail as possible. The word "cancer," for instance, is too vague. "Cancer of the colon that has spread to the liver and lung" would be far better. When calling the research center, be sure to ask for the right department. The adult cancer patient, for example, would ask for the adult medical oncology department.

Once you get through to the department, tell the person you reach that you need the name of a doctor near you and ask if the staff member(s) knows someone in your area he could recommend. The individual who answers the phone may not have this information. In that case, ask that your request be given to an appropriate individual and leave your name, diagnosis, and telephone number so that your call can be returned.

5. University hospitals. Most university hospitals associated with medical schools function as referral centers and as such can probably give you information about doctors who refer patients to them. This is not a guaranteed way of finding a competent doctor in your field of interest, but it's worth a try, particularly in the case of serious or rare diseases with complicated treatments.

6. Other organizations. Other organizations can also provide you with information. For example, the American Heart Association could send you a list of cardiologists in your area; the Cancer Society could tell you who is practicing hematology and oncology; the Kidney Foundation could provide you with a list of doctors practicing in the subspecialty of nephrology.

Board Examinations

I would also like to say that board examinations given in various specialties will give you the best standards currently available for medical competence. These examinations certify doctors in such broad specialties as surgery, internal medicine, pediatrics, family practice, pathology, radiology, obstetrics, and gynecology. In addition, subspecialty examinations cover such areas as urology, pediatric cardiology, pediatric endocrinology, adult cardiology, medical and surgical oncology, radiation therapy, plastic surgery, etc.

Board certification is important, since it tells you that a particular doctor has completed the required training in the field and has taken and passed the board examinations. The boards tell you that the doctor has had special training in your area of interest and has been judged competent in that area by acknowledged experts in that field.

To find out which doctors have taken and passed the board examinations in the area in which they are practicing, telephone their offices and ask. Or, you can contact the local medical association, requesting a list of "board certified" doctors in your area of interest.

Board Eligibility

Board eligibility is slightly different from board certification. Although the doctor in question has met the requirements of residency training and course work in his specialty area, he has not yet passed the board examinations. For example, a board certified internist has had three years of internal medicine residency with an exposure to the major subspecialties of internal medicine during that time and has taken and passed the board examinations in internal medicine. A board eligible internist, on the other hand, has met the residency requirements but has not yet passed the examinations. He may have attempted the examinations and failed, or he may not yet have taken them. If he fails to take and pass the examinations within a limited period of time after finishing his residency training, he will lose his board eligibility.

Since there are competent doctors in all specialty areas who are neither board certified or board eligible, you will have to discover their reputation in the medical community, since there is no other way you can learn of their abilities. Doctors in this group may have gained expertise through practical, clinical experience rather than through approved residency training programs, thus making them ineligible for board examinations. They may have had their training in another country and are unable to transfer their credentials.

Set Guidelines

You won't find a perfect doctor, even with the best advice in the world, recommendations from friends, and diligent research into professional competence. The best doctors make errors of judgment and fumble technical procedures from time to time; the most compassionate doctors can become tired, rude, short-tempered, or inattentive. I believe that professional competence is the most important factor in choosing a doctor, especially in the matter of a serious, life-threatening illness, and I'm willing to sacrifice a lot in the way of bedside manner in exchange for confidence in a doctor's medical knowledge and sound judgment. However, your interactions in the doctor-patient relationship can affect your attitude and comfort, so it is crucial that you do everything possible to make the relationship open, flexible, and comfortable for yourself as well as for the doctor.

Fortunately, there are some guidelines to help in selecting a doctor you can trust and who will help you or your loved ones be as comfortable as possible during terminal illness. Both in choosing a doctor and in establishing a relationship with him once you've found him, keep in mind what you need from him. Arrange the following requirements according to your own priorities and make sure you get the most important requirements satisfied first.

Your Doctor Should Assume Responsibility

First and foremost, your doctor should assume full responsibility for making decisions about your treatment. After all, this is the reason you need a doctor! You must choose a doctor who has been appropriately and specially trained to make diagnoses and decisions in the field of medicine that concerns you and who has access to medical history, current research data, standards of accepted therapy, and a multitude of other factors that constitute the basis for sound medical decision-making. You will give him your story, which he must supplement with necessary laboratory tests, x-ray studies, and so on. He will have access to other doctors, both in your own community and across the country, for advice and consultation. It will be his responsibility to say, "This, in my opinion, is the best treatment that medical science can offer in your case."

He will consult your wishes concerning hospitalization, home care, and further treatment, but he will never leave you with the whole burden of making these decisions. He should take your feelings and preferences, fears and misgivings, into account, but he should still give you his decision in the form of a definite recommendation of a specific form of treatment. Only if two or more different courses of action are totally equivalent in terms of their advantages and disadvantages should he give you a choice among options. Even in this situation, once the treatment has been decided on, he should confirm it by saying, "I think that this is the right thing for you."

Although your doctor will keep your desires in mind, he will not allow them to override his best medical judgment. Treatment decisions have great emotional potential. If it seems to you that your doctor has been unduly swayed by your feelings and those of your family, this can leave you with grave doubts about his competency. You may then wonder, *Have I really gotten the best available treatment, or did I talk the doctor into doing something less than the best for me?* This will lead to self-blame, accusations of family members, guilt, and anger. This can turn the family into warring, accusing parties, preventing the members from giving each other the emotional support and comfort they need. These negative emotions can be particularly destructive after the death of the patient during the grief period. If the doctor assumes the responsibility for treatment decisions, family members may blame him, but they will at least be able to avoid much of the guilt and anger within the family circle.

On the other hand, if you refuse to follow your doctor's advice and his recommendations for treatment, you cannot expect him to force you to do what is best for you. He should inform you of the consequences of not following his advice (as well as he can predict them) and the expected results if you go along with his recommendations. Should he be willing to continue caring for you in spite of your refusal to accept his judgment regarding the best possible treatment, he should be willing to be supportive and not have an "I told you so" attitude if you develop the problems he predicted. He will, instead, help you face your problems at that point, wasting little effort or time on regrets. I'd like to reiterate that I personally believe the doctor's medical competence takes precedence over all other considerations. The doctor's ability to keep me adequately informed would be second on my list.

Your Doctor Should Believe in Your Treatment

An important prerequisite for your doctor is that he believes your illness is treatable. For example, you may have an internist or general practitioner who believes that all cancer is hopeless. If you then develop cancer, you should insist on a second opinion about treatment before you accept his pronouncement that there is no hope. Your doctor's basic attitude toward cancer will influence his care of you. He will not be inclined to keep up with the literature on cancer treatment, for example, if he believes that "patients with cancer all die anyhow, so why bother?" I have heard this from highly respected doctors in an "enlightened" medical community.

Perhaps you have a severely disabling heart condition, and your family doctor is the type who believes that "a little hard work never hurt anyone." Besides making you uncomfortable for not being able to work hard, he might compromise your health by encouraging you to do more than your heart can take.

In situations such as the ones above, probably the safest and wisest choice is to look for another doctor who will take responsibility for treating your illness. Of course, not all kinds of terminal illness are treatable, and a doctor who claims to be able to treat "anything at all" is highly suspect. However, even in the event of an untreatable illness, your doctor should give you the benefit of withholding judgment until he has carefully evaluated you and all your records. He should approach your problem with an open mind and be willing to find some factor or combination of factors that will make you a candidate for therapy. If these factors are not present, he will then tell you regretfully that he knows of no treatment for your disease at present.

Your Doctor Should Be Willing to Care for You

Granted that there is a treatment for your illness, is your doctor willing to undertake it? Does he feel competent and confident in this treatment area, or is he uncertain? Even if there is no specific treatment for your serious illness, there is still the question of finding a doctor to care for you throughout the course of the illness. He must be willing to advise you about diet and activity, prescribe pain medications, and in general do all that is necessary to keep you functioning comfortably. If the doctor you have seems unwilling or very reluctant to give you the kind of care you need, you might do well to look for another doctor.

My personal bias is that most ailments can be adequately treated by a practitioner in or near your home community. However, if you have a rare or unusual disease, you should be referred to a research center and placed under the direction of doctors there. This is both for the benefit of the patient and for medical knowledge. While doctors who are most familiar with a rare disease are treating an individual, the data accumulated from the patient's history will be used to broaden the understanding of the disease process and its response to treatment.

Your Doctor Should Recognize the Importance of Teamwork

The ideal doctor will make you feel that you are an integral part of the team treating your illness. Instead of saying, "Leave everything to me; I'll take care of you!" he will alert you to things you can do for yourself and give you an opportunity to do them. He will realize your need to have some control over your own life and care and will not rob you of your independence.

Your Doctor Should Be Sensitive to Your Personhood

The ideal doctor doesn't give the impression he is always in a hurry. No matter how pressing his commitments, he will sense when you are dissatisfied or questioning and will either take time to help you understand what is going on or arrange to talk to you some other time. He is willing to discuss your illness with you and is able to use terms you can understand without making you feel he is talking down to you.

The small details that are important to your comfort will be important to him. He will be willing to take time to discuss your diet, the view that you have from your window, how you can handle your work in such a way that it won't overtire or unnecessarily frustrate you, the side effects of your medication and how they can be minimized, and how you can best tell Grandma how sick you are. He will also do his utmost to see that you can spend as much of your time as possible in the way you choose, without prolonging your hospital stays or scheduling overly frequent office appointments. He will allow you the options of travel or vacations and will help you arrange your medical care while you're away. He will take your feelings into account and will not dismiss you from the hospital when you or your family feel that your resources at home are insufficient to cope with your illness.

Your doctor should approach you as a unique individual, not just as one of many cases. Your comfort, your peace of mind, and your outlook on life will be as important to him as your blood tests and x-rays. For this reason, he will talk to you, not over your head. He will not stand at the foot of your bed and discuss your case with the nurses or medical students, referring to you as "he," "she," or even "Mrs. Jones." Rather, he will talk to you during his visit, explain things to the nurses, medical students, and residents as necessary but include you as a participant in the discussion. You will feel that, in his eyes, you are a person, not a disease, hospital room number, or "case."

Your Doctor Should Be Honest

Although the ideal doctor will not destroy your hope, neither will he nourish false encouragement. He will be honest when things are bad. Gently and with kindness, he will urge you to face the crises when they come. He will not continue to offer you treatment plan after treatment plan when the reasonable expectations of your benefit from them are nonexistent. He himself will be willing to face the fact that you are no longer responsive to treatment and will give you support and encouragement in facing this truth.

Although he cannot tell you precisely how much time you have left or exactly what your personal response to treatment will be, he will give you an idea of what usually happens to people with your diagnosis. He will give you a general idea of the disease you have, its usual progress, and the different methods of treating it. He will be able to help you understand the ways in which your illness differs from that of other patients with the same diagnosis and in what ways it is the same. He will be able and willing to give you an explanation for his choice of treatment in your particular case, based on his explanation of what's wrong with you. He will be honest about the types of side effects that usually are produced by the medicines he prescribes for you. If serious and alarming side effects occur even rarely, he will mention them to you. In all of this, he will emphasize the encouraging signs in your case and help you maintain a hopeful attitude.

Your Doctor Should Be Communicative

Another essential characteristic in a doctor who will care for you during a life-threatening and probably fatal illness is the ability to communicate. I will speak later of methods you can use to improve the quality of these communications.

I am convinced that most doctors love to talk. It is just a matter of finding the right key to get them started! In my own experience, the more recent medical school graduates (from 1960 on) are more concerned with keeping you informed and less protective of their own dignity and authority. However, the outstanding doctors in any community—whatever their age or medical school class—are those who are most approachable and easiest to talk with. A communicative doctor won't shut you up but will listen to your concerns and attempt to answer your questions as honestly and completely as he can when you speak to him concerning relapse, deterioration, and death.

When you ask questions he can't answer, he will be honest with you. If there is information on the subject that he doesn't have on hand, he will look it up for you. If there are no answers to the questions you are asking, he will tell you. He is not afraid to say, "I don't know" or "I'll have to look that up for you." He will be willing to refer you to another doctor or research center if he feels it is in your best interests. If you request a second opinion, he will cooperate in getting your records together and arranging an appointment for you. (This is not necessarily true if you choose to have six or seven additional opinions; there is a limit to his patience as well!)

He will not be afraid to tell you and your family about your illness. He will insist on explaining things. He will not create a rift in the family by telling you one thing and your family something different, nor will he be party to a conspiracy to hide information from you or your family. Although he may reserve certain details of information for himself until he is able to see just what they mean in the overall picture, he will never deliberately mislead you regarding your outlook and future expectations. Being aware of the enormous stress and anxiety produced by uncertainty, he will talk to you from time to time, updating the information you have and keeping you informed about your progress.

The way he will tell you things may be as important as the actual information he conveys. Bad news will seem more tolerable if he takes you into a room, closes the door, and sits down to talk with you. The same news can have a much more devastating impact if he asks his nurse to call you or if he tells you himself in a brief phone call. If he has good news and is obviously happy for you, it will add to your own elation. There are scores of little ways he can communicate his care for you, not just interest in your disease, and can make you feel like a worthwhile individual.

Your Doctor Should Be Emotionally Supportive

Ideally, your doctor should be able to give you some emotional support, in addition to your medical care and the information you require. Some of the reassurance and support you need will be automatically provided if your communication is open and adequate. Knowing that you can be free about the way you feel and that you don't need to "put on a front" for him will also relieve you of emotional stress.

I wish that the majority of the doctors I know met the lofty standards of compassion and caring that I've set down, even half the time. I wish, too, that I could be more consistent in this area. The truth is that time, fatigue, and personality all get in the way of my being consistently compassionate, caring, and nurturing with all my patients, and I know this is true of other doctors as well. I'm not even sure that it is fair to your doctor to ask him to pour himself into your care to this extent, for it is certainly not realistic. Even with the most perfect doctor, you will need to find some emotional support elsewhere. Even "ideal" doctors take vacations, get sick, or go to meetings and are unavailable to be compassionate and caring every time you need them. With the average doctor, you can expect to get part of your emotional support from him, but not all you may need.

With this perspective in mind, I can also say that your doctor can give you much in the way of emotional support. He can exhibit a sensitivity and compassion that makes you feel he really shares your suffering. He can bolster your sagging hopes with well-timed words of encouragement. If your doctor chooses to make the effort, he can do much to dispel self-doubt and guilt by complimenting you and your family on the things you are doing right.

Your Doctor Should Be Open-minded

You will feel free to ask the ideal doctor about treatments you have read about, diets, exercises, and other matters of concern without fearing he will laugh at you or scold you. He will try to give you an honest answer to your questions and will consider your suggestions about treatment. He has an air of confidence and maturity, mixed with a willingness to learn and an awareness of his own limitations. He is not an arrogant "know-it-all."

Your Doctor Should Maintain a Sense of Humor

The "ideal" doctor will exhibit an appropriate, tension-breaking sense of humor. One of my patients related that she had complained to a doctor friend of hers about the hair loss she had suffered as a side effect of chemotherapy. Instead of sympathizing with her, he bent his head down toward her, revealing a shiny, bald dome, and said, "Well, now you know how I feel!"

Your Doctor Should Be Reassuring

The ideal doctor is reassuring. Although he will not give you false hopes, he will never completely destroy the hope you do have. He will never brutally and brusquely state, "This is the end." He may say, "It looks bad," or even, "I'm afraid this is all I can do for you now," but he will admit he could be wrong and that there is a chance, however slim, of your pulling through the crisis.

Instead of patting you on the head and telling you, "Don't worry about that," he will give you some signs to look for that will indicate you are doing as well as can be expected. He will be willing to tell you the types of symptoms he feels are important enough to report to him. Regardless of the hopelessness of the situation, he will not abandon you. Even when he has no further treatment to offer, he will continue to care for your comfort and continue to examine you. His manner will convey the message, "However bad it gets, we're in it together, and who knows? We might just make it!"

Your Doctor Should Always Keep Medical Costs in Mind

The ideal doctor is aware of the costs of medical care and will, within the limits imposed by his medical judgment, try to keep your expenses to a minimum. He will keep your finances in mind and, realizing that money worries can hinder your recovery, refer you to community resources or social workers who can help you receive available financial aid. He will never sacrifice your care to financial concerns, but he will be aware of your financial burden and be willing to help you find assistance.

Your Doctor Should Be Family-oriented

The ideal doctor does not object to having the family accompany the patient on an office visit, nor to having family members stay in the hospital room while he is talking to the patient. Although he may request that the number of family members be limited to one or two and may ask them to leave the room during part of his examination, he will welcome family interest in the patient's well-being and be eager to include them in his plans for the care of the patient. He will not hurry his explanations, but will allow time for questions and try to make sure that the family members as well as the patient understand what is going on.

Your Doctor Should Possess a Christian Belief

Although the ideal doctor is competent and able to meet your particular needs, if he is a Christian so much the better. As a Christian, he is in close touch with the Great Physician, trusting not only his own medical judgment and up-to-date knowledge, but also depending on God's leading from day to day. He is not ashamed to ask God for direction in his decisions. He will pray about you, for you, and with you (if you wish), and will acknowledge God's help in all he does.

A Christian doctor can add untold warmth to your relationship by telling you that he's praying for you, taking time to share his faith with you, and even praying aloud with you in times of crisis. This can help strengthen your own faith and also increase your confidence in the doctor. Due to the fact that he has had experience with your illness and has known others with your problems, he may be a good source for specific Scripture that applies to your situation or for secular and Christian literature that has helped others.

Summary

Unfortunately, the ideal doctor as described above is a rare find! Add to this fact the humanness of your doctor, and you will find that the relationship you have with him will not be consistently smooth and comfortable. However, there are things you can do to assure that your relationship with him is as close to ideal as possible, even though your doctor is less than perfect and circumstances will not always be favorable. These are discussed in the next two chapters.

7

IT'S UP TO YOU, NOW

To a large degree, you as the patient (or family member) set the tone of your relationship with your doctor. If you expect to be included in the team that is caring for your medical needs, don't just sit back and wait for that to happen. By now, you should have a clear idea of the type of relationship you want with your doctor and what you expect of him. Now you must examine the questions, What do I expect of myself? What does my doctor expect of me?

Guidelines to Becoming the "Ideal" Patient

Bearing in mind that there is really no such thing as an "ideal" patient, I would like to share with you a composite sketch of my ideal, adult patient. Obviously the "ideal" patient who is in a relationship with the "ideal" doctor will encounter few problems. In real life, ideal patients are not quite so rare as ideal doctors, but no one becomes an ideal patient automatically. In order to lay the groundwork for a smooth doctor/patient relationship, you must be committed to maintaining your part of the bargain.

Realize that there will be times when you couldn't feel less ideal! Sometimes you get the feeling that you and your doctor *almost* have a good relationship, but you're just slightly out of step with each other. What do you do then? The following characteristics of the "ideal" patient will help you to function in the most effective ways.

Exhibit Intelligent Interest in Your Own Health

Perhaps surprisingly, my first characteristic of an ideal patient is the exhibiting of an intelligent interest in his own health coupled with a willingness to do his part in caring for himself. Although he is considerate of the doctor and his feelings, his own health is more important to him than the doctor's convenience. So, he doesn't have an inflated sense of the worth of his doctor's time and is willing to "bother" him with symptoms that worry him.

The ideal patient must try to understand enough of his own illness to usually tell which symptoms are important in his particular case and which are probably safe to ignore. When he is in doubt, he will call his doctor.

If he has a fever on Friday that climbs to 104 degrees by night and is accompanied by drenching sweat and shaking chills, he won't "wait to see if it will go away by itself." He may apologize for "bothering" the doctor on the weekend or in the middle of the night, but he certainly should call. A patient who knows that he has heart trouble and who experiences chest pains or frightening shortness of breath in the middle of the night, for example, shouldn't wait until morning to call.

If he develops a new pain, a rash, increased nausea, dizzy spells, shortness of breath, or a persistent cough, he will let his doctor know. This doesn't mean he will give him minute-by-minute descriptions of his feelings, physical discomfort, diet, and exercise; it does mean he will promptly report any alarming changes in the way he feels or in his routine.

I do, of course, appreciate people who show a genuine consideration for me and don't call during my time off except in the case of an emergency. But I would rather answer nine false alarms and catch a genuine emergency in the tenth call than not be bothered at all. This viewpoint is partly my own, but many doctors I know also share this view.

Learn Your Diagnosis and Medications

Although it may not be easy, the ideal patient who is confronted with a life-threatening illness behaves in a responsible manner. He does not dismiss all explanations by saying, "I can't understand all these medical terms. They are impossible to pronounce and even harder to spell." Rather, he writes them down and eventually learns his diagnosis and the names of his medications. He gains a general idea of what the medications are supposed to do and what their common side effects are.

It is particularly important for the ideal patient to know the exact diagnosis of his condition and the names and doses of his medications. In our mobile society, it is possible that he could become sick away from home and be taken to an emergency room in another city. He will get speedier and more appropriate care if he knows what his illness is called and what medicines he is taking. This principle also applies if he moves to a new location.

It is also a good thing for him to note the most common side effects of his medicine and any danger signs he needs to watch for. These danger signs could either signal overdosage with the medicine or a change in his underlying illness. He must not be afraid to ask, "How do you spell that?" when he encounters difficult terms and names. Some medicines have a number of different brand names, and he may be confused if the pharmacist starts supplying him with the same drug put out by a different company under a different name. He should ask the doctor if this could happen or, if he's given a bottle of pills with a different name than he's used to on the label, he could ask the pharmacist if it's the same thing.

Become Somewhat Familiar With Your Tests

The ideal patient asks for explanations of his condition, the results of tests taken, and the treatments he is receiving. He is interested in the outcome of the laboratory and x-ray studies his doctor orders and has a rough idea of why they are being done.

When he doesn't understand some aspect of his tests, the ideal patient asks questions. He doesn't go to his best friend and say, "That doctor never tells me anything" until he has let the doctor know that he wants more information than he has been given. If his explanations and terms are too technical, the ideal patient will say, "I'm sorry, Doctor, but I didn't understand that. Could you go over it again, please?" When the patient thinks he understands the doctor, he repeats in his own terms what he was told so that the doctor can catch any serious gaps in communication.

It isn't really necessary for the patient to keep an exhaustive summary of his laboratory and x-ray studies. Some people are more comfortable with less detailed explanations of the tests they've had, while others prefer to know exactly what was done when, where, and why. If he is one of the latter, he should keep a notebook as he goes along. He must not ask the doctor to fill him in after six months with a detailed report of every test he has had and what it showed. If he wants reports of previous work, he should check with the secretary and find out how his doctor usually handles this type of situation.

List Important Phone Numbers

The ideal patient keeps a list of such important phone numbers as the doctor's office, hospital emergency room, doctor's home and/or answering service, and community agencies his doctor recommends as a source of help for him.

Assume Responsibility for Treatment

The ideal patient assumes his share of responsibility in his treatment program. He remembers his office appointments, makes sure that the ordered x-rays and laboratory studies are done, and takes his medicine as directed (noticing when he needs refills). He takes notes of things he needs to remember, keeps his appointment card in a place where he will see it, and cancels and reschedules appointments or tests when conflicts arise.

He realizes that his relationship to his doctor is not one of an infant to his mother but rather the relationship of two responsible adults. He won't expect the doctor to cajole, threaten, or beg him to do the things that are good for him. He doesn't expect him to pry pertinent information out of him, piece by juicy piece! If he has symptoms or problems he believes his doctor should know about, he will arrange them in an orderly fashion in his mind or write them down and tell him about them as clearly and concisely as possible. He will make an honest attempt to stick to his prescribed diet, required exercise, limitations on activity, or prescribed medications.

As we noted earlier, the ideal patient knows his own situation and treatments well enough to notice if there is any change in them. If there is any change in the routine, he feels free enough to call it to his doctor's attention and find out whether it is intentional rather than accidental. He also keeps track of routine tests and when they fall due, and he jogs the doctor's memory in case he forgets.

When I ask the ideal patient about his preferences in such areas as whether he prefers to be cared for at home or at the hospital, or if he wants a doctor nearer his home to take over part of his care, he expresses his preferences. He doesn't answer, "You're the doctor. I'll do whatever you say." He will also tell me when he feels that the results of his treatment are not worth the side effects he is suffering. When he would like to stop treatment altogether, he will let me know. If he wants to try anything that is available, regardless of how small the chance is that it will benefit him, he'll let me know that, too.

Respect Your Doctor's Opinions

The ideal patient will not accept medical information taken from a daily newspaper, *The Reader's Digest, The Ladies Home Journal,* or other periodicals or books in an unquestioning manner. Although he will listen to neighbors, friends and family members who have had a similar condition (or know someone who has), he will not consider them to be automatic authorities on his medical problem and its treatment. Before he accepts their truths, he will check their information with his doctor. If he wonders why the doctor didn't prescribe "Aunt Mabel's little white pills" for him, he will ask him, listen to his explanation, and accept it.

If he has questions about the side effects of his medications or thinks that an annoying symptom could be the result of his medications, he doesn't just stop taking the medications altogether. First, he will discuss the symptom with his doctor. If he chooses to ignore his advice, he will tell him what he is doing. He will not increase or decrease the dosage of his medications on his own, but tells the doctor if he feels it should be done. In short, he is willing to accept the doctor's explanations and decisions and will exhibit enough trust in his medical judgment to allow him to make the recommendations for his treatment.

Don't Ask Impossible Questions

The ideal patient doesn't ask such impossible questions as, "If I had been given this drug two years ago, would there have been a chance for a cure?" or "Did Dr. Karleoff do the right thing for me back in 1958?" Questions such as these have no good answers (although they are asked with good intent); other questions have no answers whatsoever. If the ideal patient happens to ask that type of question, he will accept his doctor's answer when he tells him that such speculation is fruitless and leads nowhere. He won't, for example, try to pin the doctor down to a specific date for his funeral; he will realize that he can only give him an estimate of the length of survival of the average patient in his condition and that such an estimate is dependent on many known and unknown variables. He won't expect him to guarantee that he will respond to the recommended treatment. He won't ask him to guarantee the side effects he will (or won't) experience. If he does ask a question about his length of survival, the way he can expect to feel, or his response to treatment, he will accept the fact that his doctor can only give him the reported, average survival time, the percentage of people who have responded to treatment in other doctors' experiences, and the side effects that are most and least common in his experience. He will understand that, as a unique individual, he must wait and see what his personal responses and reactions are.

Don't Pressure Your Doctor to Judge Another Doctor

The ideal patient doesn't ask his doctor to breach medical etiquette by passing judgment on a fellow doctor on the basis of anecdotal and/or unconfirmed information. He respects that doctor's right not to single out one surgeon, pediatrician, obstetrician, or internist as the "very best" in the community, realizing that his personal preferences also reflect the bias of his personality and may not correspond to the patient's needs or preferences.

He also realizes that his doctor may ask him to continue seeing his family doctor for treatment of such things as blood pressure, heart disease, and headaches. He knows that the specialist's preference for having his family doctor handle his general medical problems is not due to an unwillingness or inability to handle such problems himself but is based on the fact that he is only one person. The more general problems he attempts to handle, the less energy and attention he has in caring for patients in his own specialty area. Conversely, he will accept the fact that his family doctor may ask a specialist to be responsible for certain aspects of treatment and diagnosis.

Be Cooperative in Referrals

The ideal patient understands when his doctor feels a need for consultation with another expert in another discipline—a neurologist, radiation therapist, orthopedic surgeon, etc.—and is cooperative in this matter. He respects the doctor's assessment of his own capabilities and limitations and does not ask him to take on the responsibility for judgments or decisions that he is not trained or qualified to make. The patient recognizes that his choice of specialty is an outgrowth of his self-knowledge and personality, and he is willing to allow the doctor to restrict himself to his specialty. He also realizes that a limited field of responsibility allows the doctor (and his colleagues) time and energy to achieve an in-depth grasp of his own field.

Don't Use Your Doctor As a Pawn

The ideal patient doesn't try to use his doctor as an arbiter in family disputes, as a co-conspirator against his family and friends, or as a judge in his quarrel with another doctor, hospital, nurse, social worker, etc. He generally doesn't ask him to act as a go-between for him and his spouse, parents, or children, but there are, of course, exceptions to this rule.

Show Genuine Feelings

The ideal patient doesn't try to live up to an inhuman standard of "perfect acceptance" or "complete adjustment" to his illness, treatment, or diagnosis, and he feels no need to put on a good front for his doctor. When he needs help in coping with things, he'll admit it. He is free to express sadness, discouragement, exuberance, joy, or frustration. If he feels like crying, he cries. When he seems depressed and his doctor asks, "Is anything wrong?" he answers honestly instead of forcing a brave smile and saying, "No, everything's OK." He also knows that he has the right to either discuss his depression with his doctor or to deal with it in another way, based on what seems best to him. By the same token, he doesn't expect his doctor to be his mother, pastor, priest, social worker, psychiatrist, dietician, or physical therapist, and he is not hurt or insulted when the doctor suggests consultation with one of the above individuals.

Look to Others Besides Your Doctor for Emotional Support

No matter how much emotional support a doctor can give the ideal patient, he should look around for additional sources of strength and comfort. One good prospect for a source of strength and comfort is his pastor or his pastor's wife. Either of them should have access to Scripture and literature that can be of help to him. Both probably have more experience in helping individuals face critical situations than anyone else except a professional counselor or doctor. If the ideal patient's pastor and his wife are mature Christians, they have access to the wisdom and knowledge available in Christ Jesus and have experience in drawing on these resources.

Individuals who have a measure of Christian maturity and have learned from similar crises in their own lives are excellent resources to turn to for advice and sympathy. Although these individuals are usually older, sometimes a teenager or young adult will show remarkable insight and sensitivity and be able to offer much help. A nurse, secretary, laboratory technician, or other individual working in the ideal patient's doctor's office may have a special gift for comforting and advising. Someone employed in the hospital may also have a talent for this sort of work.

Of course, the ideal patient's own family is a good place for him to look for emotional support. His wife (or husband), mother, father, aunt, uncle, brother, sister, and/or cousin may be in a perfect position to help him. Often these individuals are able to give him physical and material help as well. The same thing applies to his Christian friends.

As we see, there are a number of people to whom the ideal patient can turn for emotional support. He will not ask any one of them to be everything he needs, turning instead to two or three he can lean on. He must not be afraid to admit his need, remembering that God has not put us in the world alone but in families. As we each learn to depend on each other, we will receive the strength God supplies to us.

Be Willing to Work Toward a Good Relationship With Your Doctor

Most of all, the ideal patient is willing to work at keeping his relationship with his doctor at its best. He realizes, for example, that the doctor is human and he makes allowances for his humanity. When he makes a mistake, he can be understanding; when he is hurried, cross, impatient, or behind schedule, he can forgive him. He knows what is important to him and will insist on it; he also knows on what issues he can afford to give in. He realizes that he, too, is human and accepts his own humanity with grace and good humor. When he is mistaken or in the wrong, he apologizes and accepts forgiveness.

In the following chapter, we will build on what we have learned about the "ideal" doctor and the "ideal" patient to better understand how both of them can work together effectively.

8

THE IDEAL PATIENT/DOCTOR RELATIONSHIP

RECENTLY, A GROWING emphasis has been placed on consumers' rights. In the health professions, the trend has been to stress the fact that the body being x-rayed, tested, dissected, and medicated belongs to the "consumer"—the patient—and not to the doctor. From this step, it logically follows that patients have a right to know what's going on with their bodies and should be granted a say in the type of treatment they undergo.

Insofar as this viewpoint has prompted people to take an intelligent interest in their medical care and to learn more about their bodies and what's wrong (and right) with them, the emphasis is good. The fact that people are insisting on being included as active members of their health care team rather than merely being bodies that are acted upon is extremely beneficial.

Unfortunately, there is just a small step from the premise "It is my body, so I should know what's going on" to the belief "Since it is my body, I know better than anyone else what is going on and am best able to decide what is right for me."

There are, therefore, two extremes. On one hand, the dictatorial, lordly, and august doctor who makes all the decisions. These decisions are passed down through the proper chain of command to the passive patient, who never dares to question the decision or the reasons behind it. At the other extreme is the well-read, well-informed patient who reserves the right to pass judgment on all aspects of his care. The physician is at best the patient's pal, at worst merely a "health care provider" whose every move and decision must be explained and approved before the patient will concur.

There must be some middle ground between these poles! There can be a workable relationship between patient and doctor that takes into account the patient's feelings and intelligence while still recognizing the doctor's specialized knowledge and informed judgment. Doctor and patient should be capable of respecting each other and allowing each to use his expertise (the doctor in medical matters, the patient in his own personal considerations) in order to contribute to the best possible care for the individual.

This type of relationship requires at least a minimum of mutual trust. The patient must believe that the doctor has the knowledge to make wise decisions; the doctor must trust the patient with enough information for him to follow orders intelligently and willingly.

IMPORTANT PRINCIPLES IN THE DOCTOR/PATIENT RELATIONSHIP

Allow Your Doctor to Make Decisions

Certain responsibilities and judgments in your medical care should lie totally with your doctor. There are two reasons for this. First, there are medical situations in which you as a layman can't acquire adequate information to make sound decisions. Second, there is a great emotional burden in many decisions that can cause tremendous strain in your family if your doctor doesn't assume responsibility for them.

If you have chosen (to the best of your ability) a doctor whose qualifications make him an authority in the treatment of your disease, you should be able to trust his recommendations concerning treatment. If, however, you (or someone close to you) are strongly interested in a particular treatment, you should have the option to pursue it. If your doctor doesn't believe it will be dangerous to you and that your becoming involved in it will not compromise the care he has recommended, it is probably safe. If you choose to disregard your doctor's advice in this area, you cannot expect him to be responsible for what happens to you, nor can you expect him to continue treating you.

Any decision that will arouse anger and/or guilt in the family, or any accusation from you or your family, is best made by the doctor. He is not a member of the family circle, and directing negative emotions toward him helps preserve the family circle. The doctor carries an authority with both family and patient; they may object to his decisions, but they will most likely obey him. Anger and blame directed toward the doctor do not have the same devastating effect on the doctor/patient relationship that they do on family relationships, since the emotional reactions are usually temporary. Of course, permanent anger and blame directed toward your doctor destroys the trust you have in him and disrupts the relationship. Even so, a doctor is easier to replace than a family member!

Realize that Some Decisions Deal With Emotionally Packed Issues

Decisions concerning highly emotional issues generally include the question of hospitalization versus home care, changes in therapy, and the decision to continue or discontinue treatment.

For instance, when your hospitalization is necessary for medical or psychological reasons, either you or your family may object to it. In this case, your doctor should assume responsibility for the decision. Often you and your family will have ambivalent feelings in this situation. You may be reluctant to leave home, yet long for the peace and quiet of a hospital. Your family wants to keep you home but is feeling greatly overburdened with the demands of your care. Your doctor, who tends to be less involved emotionally, is able to see the picture more clearly and can make a reasonable decision.

The issue of discontinuing treatment can cause much guilt and bitterness during the terminal phase of illness and in the initial grief period after death. If the doctor, gently but firmly, continues to reassure you that all reasonable treatment has been given and that there is nothing further that would be of benefit, your guilt and bitterness can be minimized (even though there probably will still be some).

The doctor should definitely take the side effects—nausea, fatigue, shortness of breath—into consideration and weigh them against the benefits of treatment when making a decision to continue or discontinue treatment. He should also consider patient and family preferences. Once the doctor has received everyone's input and the medical information he needs, the decision is medical and lies with him.

Similarly, you and your family are responsible for deciding whether or not you need another opinion or a referral. Again, if you trust your doctor, his opinion will carry much weight. If he believes that a referral isn't necessary, this might be enough for you. If you have any doubts, however, you should insist on a second opinion but not necessarily a third, fourth, or fifth.

If you feel the need for another opinion and your doctor is reluctant or downright unwilling to refer you, what should you do? Most doctors will eventually yield to consistent pressure from you and your family. If your doctor remains unwilling to make arrangements for you to see another doctor, he must at least release your records to you, your representative, or a requesting doctor (with your permission). If you plan to visit a well-known diagnostic or research clinic, such as the Mayo Clinic, obtain copies of your records from your doctor and take the records with you. In fact, as a rule it is better to request the records and take them with you than it is to trust the mails.

In the event that you are seeking a third, fourth, or fifth opinion, I personally believe that your doctor is justified in refusing to make the arrangements for you. However, he still should make you a copy of your records to take with you (for which he is justified in charging a copying fee). If you intend to contact every medical center and every doctor who might be able to offer you hope for a cure (the "no stone unturned" approach), you should keep a copy for your records that you can duplicate when you hear of another place to investigate.

How to Improve Communication With Your Doctor

You Must Be Open to Learning

First, as we discussed in the chapter on the ideal patient, you must think of yourself as an intelligent, mature adult. Although you don't have an M.D. degree, you should be able to understand enough about your body and its functions so that you can understand your illness. If you approach the doctor thinking that you'll never understand anything he tells you, chances are you won't. This, in turn, will frustrate the doctor, and he will become less and less open in discussing your ailments and treatment with you. Expect to be told and to understand what you are told.

Realize That Family Communication Is the Family's Responsibility

You and your family are responsible for your own communications. Don't expect the doctor to act as a go-between for you and your family. You may ask for his help and advice in this area, but keeping family communication open is a family responsibility.

Encourage a Necessary Family/Doctor Relationship

It is important for your doctor to be willing to talk to your family about your situation, but be considerate of him. I do *not* mean that your doctor must be willing to talk to every member of your family, giving them a detailed, weekly explanation of what's going on. He will probably not be willing to talk to *each* individual member of your family even in times of crisis. (Multiply 500 patients by 4 family members per patient, then multiply that figure by 15 minutes per conference, and you'll realize that your doctor doesn't have time to do that and continue practicing medicine!)

However, there will be times when you will not feel capable of relaying explanations from the doctor to your family. Maybe you didn't quite understand the explanation. Maybe you are afraid that your emotions are distorting your hearing and that you are perceiving a twisted version of what your doctor actually said. In this event, ask the family to pick a representative to talk to the doctor. This person can then accompany you to the doctor's office or talk to the doctor on the telephone. The doctor should be willing to talk to one family representative in addition to the patient. The family representative should always be courteous. If he reaches the doctor by telephone at a very busy time, he should leave a telephone number and ask to have his call returned when the doctor has time to talk. If the family member goes to see the doctor personally, it is best to make an appointment in advance so that the doctor can set aside some time to talk.

Although family communication with your doctor is most necessary at such crisis times as changes of therapy, new tests, hospitaliza-tion, or relapse—times when you are most likely to be reacting in denial and thus not hearing straight—try to have a family member present during most of your routine visits with the doctor. I've found that this tends to decrease the number of misunderstandings that arise and also enhances communication in most families.

Prepare Questions

You may find it helpful to do some "homework" before your doc-tor's appointments. If your doctor seems reluctant to talk to you about your illness, prepare for your appointments by figuring out what you need to know and forming a few, well-phrased, intelligent questions. For example, you might ask, "Why do you call my tumor breast cancer when my breast was removed two years ago and the tumor is in the lung now?" or, "Can you explain to me what you mean by the term 'heart attack' in my condition? Can you tell me how I will recover from it and give me some idea of the recovery time involved?"

If you have well-phrased questions written down, you won't be groping for words in the doctor's office. He will be more inclined to listen to you, and he will probably answer your questions on the level on which you ask them. Although some doctors really don't want to give patients information, many more are eager and willing teachers. All you have to do is ask them. Don't complain, "My doctor never tells me anything," without at least *trying* to ask him!

If you ask questions and receive answers but are unable to under-stand the answers, be tactful. Tell your doctor that you don't quite understand what he's saying and ask him if he can rephrase it. Try repeating what he's said to you in your own words, to make sure you are hearing it correctly.

If you have prepared your questions and the doctor is obviously in a hurry, tell him that you have questions and ask the ones that are urgent. Limit yourself to questions that really won't wait. Then ask him when it would be convenient for you to talk with him to get an-swers to your other questions. Be polite, but firm, and set up a definite appointment time when you will be able to talk with him.

Learn What's Important

Some of the important basic information you need from your doc-tor involves what he wants you to tell him. Although the "ideal" doctor will listen to your problems and complaints without begrudging you the time it takes, time is still important. At a certain point, he is going to stop listening and go on with his work. You need to know which of your complaints are important and which you can safely ignore. You won't always be right, but having your doctor lay down some guidelines at the beginning of your association will keep you alert to the critical issues and help you give the doctor the information he needs in the most abbreviated form possible.

Plan for the Emergency

You also need to know how your doctor expects you to handle unexpected emergencies. Should you call him at home, regardless of the time? Should you go straight to the hospital emergency room and have the emergency room doctor call him? Should you come straight to his office if the emergency happens during office hours? A clear understanding of his preferences in this matter can save both of you much time and frustration.

Take Notes

When your doctor is explaining things to you, take notes. Later, if the same question or a similar one is bothering you, refer to your notes first. If you still aren't sure of the answer, don't ask the same question you asked before. Rather, rephrase it. "Doctor," you might say, "you said that my high blood pressure was causing heart damage. Is my blood pressure still high, and is it still harming my heart?" In this way, he will know that you paid attention when he was explaining things to you, and he'll know just what part of his explanation needs to be clarified or updated. Although your doctor seems to be patient as you ask him the same questions week after week, he's sure to feel that you aren't really interested in his answers since they never seem to make any impression on you! Of course, he may not even attempt to hide his impatience and will not be eager to continue explaining things to you.

WHAT TO DO WHEN DOCTOR/PATIENT COMMUNICATION FAILS

Sometimes every attempt you make to get your doctor to talk with you is frustrated. He refuses to take your questions seriously. He keeps postponing your time to talk, telling you each time you see him, "Can you keep your questions until next time? I'm in an awful hurry today." When he does give you an answer, it's entirely in a medical language that he seems incapable of or unwilling to translate. Although you still believe that his training and competence make him the best qualified doctor to care for you and you don't want to change doctors, you walk around in a fog, wondering what's going on. Is there anything you can do to improve this situation?

Confront Your Doctor When Necessary

Some doctors will not give you any emotional support and may, in fact, leave you feeling emotionally black and blue after you've seen them. If your doctor is consistently brusque, rude, and thick-skinned in his dealings with you and/or your family, try confronting him with your observation.

Tell him kindly, but firmly, that you feel battered psychologically after a visit with him, or that you feel that his treatment of your family is cruel and insensitive. Be as tactful and brief as possible. When you offer your criticism, include specific examples of the type of treatment you mean. Try to mention some other aspects of his care that you appreciate and admire, such as, "You have a reputation for being the best doctor available for treating kidney ailments, and I haven't felt as well in years as I have since you began treating me."

If your doctor has other patients who don't have the same problem with him, talk with them and see if you can learn a better way of relating to him. The gap in communication may be something small that could easily be changed once you become aware of it.

Choose a Go-between

Try to find someone in your immediate family to serve as a go-between for you. Maybe the doctor feels at ease with your husband, your wife, your son, or your cousin. Someone who works in a medical field himself would be an excellent candidate for a go-between. Medical students, resident doctors, and other doctors are the most likely to get answers, followed by dentists, nurses, and medical technologists. The role of a go-between can sometimes be handled just as effectively by a family member or friend with authority in another professional area—a clergyman, prominent businessman, etc. (Don't ask your family lawyer, however. That will only make your doctor nervous!)

Asking a doctor in your family to be your contact with your own doctor can be touchy, because your doctor may feel that his medical judgment is being questioned or his authority threatened. On the other hand, professional etiquette makes it almost mandatory for him to talk to another doctor who approaches him as a concerned friend or family member. The initial contact is practically guaranteed.

Once an individual has agreed to be a go-between, ask him to take the initiative in getting information from your doctor. Of course, it goes almost without saying that your go-between should approach the situation tactfully. If he jumps in with both feet, accusing the doctor of poor communication, it will make his task more difficult or even impossible. If he can handle the initial contact without arrogance, belligerence, or hostility, he can form a firm bond with your doctor and provide an effective channel for information.

If You Must, Switch Doctors

The most drastic means of coping with a less-than-ideal doctor is to change doctors. If your doctor is totally unable to satisfy your need for information—regardless of any method you use to improve the communication—this may be your wisest course of action. You will need to weigh the communication problem carefully, particularly in the event that the doctor involved is the best qualified doctor for you. If his medical competence is unmatched by anyone else available, I think you should make every effort to get along with him. There is, however, a point where the communication breakdown is severe enough to impair the quality of the care you are getting. In that case, it might be best to look for another doctor.

If you can find no way of establishing a comfortable relationship with your doctor, ask him to refer you to someone else. Express appreciation for his care and his judgment, but tell him that you need more emotional support than his busy schedule allows. Ask if some other doctor could give you the same care he is. If there isn't, ask if there is someone who could care for you under his direction. If he is unwilling even to do this for you, find another doctor on your own and ask to have your records transferred to him. Switching doctors should be your last recourse and should not be undertaken lightly if you already have a doctor in whom you have confidence.

SECTION THREE

TERMINAL ILLNESS AND THE FAMILY

9

THE IMPORTANCE OF COMMUNICATING THE DIAGNOSIS

I BELIEVE THAT a dying individual has the right to be told, in meaningful terms, that he has a serious and probably fatal illness. He should know his diagnosis and have a fairly good idea of its implications so that he can deal with the facts as he sees fit.

For instance, the dying individual needs to have some idea that his time is limited. An individual who has not been told of his imminent death or unpredictable future is robbed of the opportunity to prepare for his death and make the best of his remaining time. As long as he believes that his death is in the distant future, he may avoid making preparations. If he is expected to take medicine and/or receive treatments, he needs to understand why the medicine and/or treatment is necessary in order for him to cooperate fully.

Few people cannot handle the knowledge of their terminal condition. I have found that those who cannot handle such knowledge invariably have a history of being unable to handle crisis situations. They may have been, or may currently be, under psychiatric care. Even so, such individuals should be told the truth in a carefully edited fashion.

Young children and mentally retarded or senile adults who have a poor sense of time and a limited understanding of death still need to have an idea of their illness. They can understand pain, confinement to their home or bed, and changes in their daily lives caused by terminal illness. They can also understand, in part, what it means to be separated from loved ones, important places, and things. Doctors, family members, or friends should not presume that these individuals do not need to prepare for death and shouldn't deny them the opportunity to make their preparations.

THE PATIENT HAS A RIGHT TO KNOW

Although it is important for the terminally ill individual to know his diagnosis in order to understand his treatment and prepare for death, he also has a "right to know" so that he can handle the crisis in his own way.

In my opinion, no one has enough information to judge accurately what is "best" for a terminally ill individual. Although there are cases in which the doctor, family, and friends must do their best to choose for another, the individual has a right to face his own crisis and to deal with it in his own way. In a matter of life and death, each of us has things we must take care of and things we want to do.

Furthermore, the terminally ill individual is entitled to test himself—to know his own strengths and weaknesses—and to discover the help and encouragement that God can and will provide. Therefore, I believe strongly that we do not have a right (much less an obligation) to shield others from situations in which they can learn much about themselves and experience firsthand the goodness and sufficiency of God. To attempt to order the lives of others is to usurp the prerogative of God. And, while we often are unhappy with the way He orders His universe, most of us, in the last analysis, wouldn't really want His job! Firsthand experience of His power and sufficiency in trials is the fertile ground in which our trust in Him grows. Our witness of His support in trials also strengthens and encourages others in their faith in God.

TRUSTING RELATIONSHIPS ARE BUILT ON TRUTH

An important point we need to understand in communicating the truth is that trusting relationships are built in truth. Trust is as crucial in the doctor-patient relationship as it is in parent-child, husband-wife, brother-sister, friend-friend or any other close, personal relationship. It is doubtful whether the doctor and the dying individual's family could successfully "fool" the individual throughout the entire course of his illness. Likewise, the doctor and his patient have little chance of successfully concealing the seriousness of the individual's illness from other family members, particularly those who are closest to him.

When it becomes evident that people surrounding a dying individual are not being honest with him (or vice versa), the pain of betrayal accompanies the shock of the truth. This pain will then color the relationships of the individuals involved, introducing doubt into areas in which there had been honesty and openness. Being "shielded from the truth" will also contribute to feelings of aloneness and helplessness.

Although "honesty is the best policy," it doesn't negate the need for tact and wisdom. Revealing the whole truth may be inappropriate at times, and a person is not being dishonest if he gradually fills in the picture for another individual. However, both the content and the context of the communication between the doctor(s), patient, and family members should be honest. Such mediums as tone of voice, facial expressions, and posture can all be used to help communicate the truth tactfully.

Honesty allows doctors to frankly admit when they don't know what is going to happen. Labeling their guesses as guesses, especially if they are pessimistic, will allow the dying individual (or his family and friends) to maintain hope throughout the course of his illness. Doctors are not infallible, even if their instincts and experience make them predict a fatal outcome. God is the only One who knows *for sure* what will happen, and this fact can help everyone involved in the individual's illness to remain hopeful and comforting even under the most unfavorable circumstances.

GUIDELINES FOR COMMUNICATING THE DIAGNOSIS

Set Up a Chain of Communication

There is no set rule as to who tells whom the diagnosis. Obviously, the doctor has to tell someone first. If he tells the patient, then the patient may assume responsibility for sharing the information with members of the family and friends. But, for one reason or another, a patient may be unable to share the information with others. The responsibility then falls on other family members or friends who learn about the patient's condition from the doctor. Sometimes both the patient and those around him will share the diagnosis. A doctor may even choose not to tell the patient his diagnosis directly, but to pass the diagnosis along through a close friend, family member, or pastor. In some instances, the patient would prefer to be the one to break the news; on other occasions family members prefer to do it. Sometimes the doctor will not be willing or available to inform someone of the diagnosis at the patient's (family's) request.

If the request (or order) to withhold information from the patient (or family members or friends) comes from a member of the family, someone who is concerned about the situation should try to elicit support from the doctor, pastor, a social worker, or a nurse to include the entire family (and others) in the knowledge of the illness and its course. He should try to explain the benefits of facing the crisis together rather than trying to allow everyone to shield each other from the truth. It is also important for him to emphasize the necessity of truth in maintaining trust in a relationship and in the course of a terminal illness.

Be Tactful

Tact is very important. After you, as a concerned individual, have done and said all you can to reverse the decision to withhold information from the patient, family members, or friends and the decision-maker remains adamant, there is still one course of action you can take. Without actually defying the decision-maker's request (or order), you can allow the terminally ill individual to be open with you about his fears, anxieties, and hopes. You can do this by giving him the opportunity to express himself without censure, without interrupting him with such comments as "Oh, don't say that!" or "You shouldn't even think such things!"

You don't need to come out and say, "You have cancer!" or "You have had a serious heart attack!" to help the individual deal with his feelings. Instead, you can help him by making a comment such as, "Well, what if you *do* have cancer—what then?" and help him to express and face his fears and anxieties. Once you know what worries him, you may be able to help him without ever going into detail about the nature of his illness. This also holds true if the individual being "shielded" is a close family member or friend of the terminally ill person.

If the doctor requests (or insists) that the patient (or family member or friend) not be told the diagnosis, the first course of action is to ask the doctor for his reasons for keeping the individual(s) from knowing the truth. As a family member or close friend, you probably have more intimate knowledge of the individual and can mentally review the way he has faced crisis situations in the past. A discussion on the individual's ability (or inability) to face crises may be all that is needed to bring you and the doctor to an agreement on the matter. The doctor's reasons may convince you that his judgment is correct and that you should delay sharing the diagnosis, or vice versa.

If the doctor remains adamant that the patient (or family member or friend) should not be told the diagnosis and is unwilling to discuss the matter, you must make your own decision. This is also true if you and the doctor are able to discuss the matter but are unable to reach an agreement. You may decide that the uncertainty, anxiety, and fear produced in the individual by not sharing the diagnosis with him is unacceptable to you, then go ahead and talk to him.

If you decide to reveal the diagnosis, be sure you have the facts straight before explaining them to the individual. It is a good idea to write down what you are told and check it with the doctor to make sure you understand it correctly. Then use the following guidelines to break the news—gently, gradually, and at a rate determined by the individual himself—as he asks questions or refuses to discuss the topic.

(1) Careful, sensitive listening is the key. There is a right time to face a crisis; don't force the issue. When the individual asks you questions, your best answers will generally turn out to be truthful and limited. There is no need to "tell all." It takes time for the truth to sink in, and giving the individual information in installments as he asks for it gives him time to adjust.

(2) Go slowly. Start with a statement like, "You know, you're pretty sick," or, "I guess I'm pretty sick this time" (if you are the patient), and wait for a response.

(3) Listen to the reaction you get. If the individual drops the subject, he's not yet ready to hear more. If he says, in effect, "Don't be silly" or "Don't talk like that," you can repeat your statement a little more firmly: "Yes, I think we have to face the fact that the illness is serious."

(4) If the individual answers with a question, answer just the scope of the question asked. Be prepared in case he already knows the truth, is ready to face it, and just needs confirmation. For example:

Q: "How sick am I?"

A: "Well, the doctor said that you had a pretty bad heart attack."

Q: "I'm not going to die yet, am I?"

A: "The doctor was pretty worried about you. He said that you had a severe heart attack. I guess it was worse than expected."

(5) Be prepared to answer honestly if the patient asks a point-blank question. If, for example, the individual asks, "Do I have cancer?" it's usually best to answer point-blank, "Yes, you do."

ASKING QUESTIONS

Uncertainty, as we've seen, produces anxiety. The terminally ill individual (or his family or friends) naturally fears what he doesn't know. This is particularly true when the uncertainty is due to illness. However, once the individual knows what he's up against, he generally can find the necessary strength and resources that don't become apparent until he is in the midst of a crisis situation.

Which Questions Are Important?

Many important and legitimate questions deserve truthful answers, not just an "Oh, don't think about that" reaction. Once the terminally ill individual knows the name of his illness, he also needs to know what its consequences will be in his daily life. "What is its expected course of events?" he may ask, "and what kind of disability does it bring? Will it hurt, force me to curtail my activity, or make me feel tired? If the first type of treatment fails, is there an alternative? What will the treatment cost, in terms of my money, energy, well-being, and activity?"

Perhaps one of the most important but least asked questions is, "How do people who have what I have generally die?" This question regarding possible pain, coma, loss of control over mind and body, hospitalization, and medications says again, in effect, "What am I likely to face?" The individual's fear of dying can be much more acute than his fear of death itself, and it is important for him to know what others have faced. The question also has practical significance to the rest of the family and should be discussed. As the family watches the dying individual deal with his illness, they will think, *What will he have to endure? What will we be able to do for him as individuals and as a family? What danger signs do we have to watch for? How can we maintain control over our own lives and still do what we can for him? How will we know when he dies, and what will we do then?* Our lives touch the lives of others, so it is important for everyone involved in the terminal illness to communicate as much as possible the facts of the illness. The goal of communicating the diagnosis is to be prepared, as much as is possible, to face the situations as they come.

The Dying Individual's Questions

The information the dying individual needs varies somewhat from person to person and from illness to illness. Shirley Jones, for instance, has breast cancer. For her, the important questions include what will happen if the disease in her lungs spreads, what will happen if the cancer spreads to her bones, and how she will die if she dies from breast cancer. Since she is currently doing well and still has several avenues of alternative treatment available to her, I made sure that she knew this fact first. Then I went ahead and answered her questions to the best of my ability.

In this case, I gave Shirley a brief summary of what we know of the natural history of breast cancer. I was unable to be specific, since there were several equally likely courses her illness could take. It turned out that her major fears were of sudden disability or death and of pain. As we discussed her illness, I was able to reassure Shirley that sudden death was unlikely and that pain could generally be controlled satisfactorily.

Margaret Shaw has ovarian cancer. She did not respond to treatment and requested that I stop treating her. Her questions concerned the probable course of her disease, how long she would probably live, and how much weakness, pain, and general discomfort she should expect to face. While we were talking, we clearly emphasized the types of treatment she wanted and the types of treatment she desired to have withheld.

With Margaret, I was able to be much more specific about the course of her illness. I felt that her liver would fail and that she would die, and I was able to describe this to her. I assured her that she would be unlikely to have much pain, but I cautioned her about a continual decrease in energy and endurance. She then planned her schedule in order to use her energy for her most important activities and spared herself much frustration.

Do I Have the Right to Die?

In the current furor over the "right to die" issue, the individual's right to refuse "extreme" measures to prolong his life has been examined, and he now can request the right to die. This is particularly true if his chance of recovering from his illness is slim. Although the legal status of such a request from the individual and/or his family has not yet been fully clarified, the request carries a lot of weight with the medical profession.

If there are circumstances under which the terminally ill individual would not want to have any effort made to save his life, he should make this clear to his family and doctor. If, on the other hand, he wants medical personnel to make every effort to save or prolong his life under all circumstances, he should communicate this to his family and doctor too. These are not matters for silence.

The Family's Questions

As we've seen, communication should exist between the dying individual and his family and friends. But, as we've noted in earlier chapters, it may be difficult for all the facts to be understood and communicated.

The family should seek out experienced people. Sometimes nurses who have had experience with terminally ill individuals can give family members as much or more help than the family doctor. The nurses are frequently present at the deathbed. They also tend to become familiar with details of diet and activity that are useful in bringing the terminally ill individual the greatest possible comfort. Some ministers and church laymen also make a practice of visiting sick and dying individuals and have the experience and knowledge to answer some of the important questions about the final states of terminal illness.

When you, as a family member or friend, are asking for information, be specific. Let the doctor (or whoever you turn to for answers) know that you want a general idea of the usual events in the course of this particular illness. Then be sure that you receive the answers you need. "Will there be any pain?" you may ask. "And if he seems to be getting progressively weaker, is there anything I can do about it? At which point will it no longer be advisable to encourage him to do such activities as eat, get out of bed, or sit at the table? How will I know if he is dead? What should I do if I think he's dying or dead?" The basic guideline to follow is to list in your own mind the questions that are important to you and then be sure to get answers to them.

Mrs. McMillan, the wife of one of my patients, telephoned me a month or two ago. Hesitant and embarrassed, she obviously had something on her mind. I knew that George, her husband, was dying and that she was caring for him at home. Finally she blurted out, "I don't know what you'll think of me for asking, but this is something I need to know. George wants to be at home, and since I don't have any other responsibilities I can care for him here as long as I need to. But how will I know if he's dead? I know that sounds awful, but I honestly have never seen a dead person before, and I don't know if I'll be able to tell when he dies! Whom do I call when he dies? I've been worrying so about these things. I'm sorry to bother you with them, but I just have to have some answers!"

"I see no need to hospitalize George," I answered. I then explained the procedure to follow when he died. Mrs. McMillan was relieved, and George died peacefully at home a week or so later.

Not everyone has been as open and free with me as Mrs. McMillan in asking these kinds of questions. Yet, when I let people know that many people have questions about the final stages of terminal illness, these concerns are nearly universal. Almost without exception, patients and their families have wanted information that will enable them to cope with the illness at that point and help them to make future plans.

10

WHEN A CHILD BECOMES TERMINALLY ILL

ONE OF THE CRUCIAL factors in the care and well-being of a dying individual is the support and comfort he receives from his family. Except in the case of a severe emotional illness in one or more family members, such as severe depression or schizophrenia, lack of communication is the greatest barrier to realizing the full support and strength of the family during the strain of terminal illness.

THE IMPORTANCE OF COMMUNICATION

When the family circle is about to be torn apart by death, it is of utmost importance for those who will be left behind to strengthen their ties to each other while gradually loosening the ties to the one who is dying. It is easy to allow the break made by a death in the family to cause division in the family, which in turn causes each individual to go his own separate way and carry his own secret, unshared burdens. This tragedy can be avoided, however, if open communication is maintained in the family circle. In fact, open communication that is initiated or enlarged during the terminal illness of one member of the family can cement family ties in a way previously unknown to that family.

Twelve-year-old Jimmy Davis has two older brothers, Steve and George, a younger sister named June, and a baby brother named Allen. A year ago, Jimmy's mother noticed that he didn't seem to have any appetite and she asked her husband about it. "Dave, have you noticed how poorly Jimmy's eating? He just picks at his food. It's not like him at all. Do you think I should take him to the doctor?"

"Oh, I wouldn't worry about him, Ann," Dave said. "You know how boys are. He'll get his appetite back soon, and then you'll be complaining that he's always eating." Dave squeezed her hand for a minute and then continued reading the newspaper.

Although Ann was still worried about Jimmy's appetite, she didn't say anything more. Several days later she noticed that Jimmy's eyes looked yellow.

"Jimmy, do you feel all right?"

"Sure, Mom. I'm just a little tired."

"Dave, does Jimmy look all right to you?" she asked.

Dave nodded, said "Mm-mm," and went on eating, barely glancing at Jimmy. Ann was still concerned, but she didn't make a doctor's appointment for Jimmy.

A week later, the school nurse sent Jimmy home from school with a note saying that he had hepatitis and ought to see his doctor.

Ann took him to see Dr. Smith, who was very reassuring. "It's only a mild case, Mrs. Davis. Just keep him home until the yellow is gone from his eyes and his appetite is better, and you have nothing to worry about."

Jimmy returned to school two weeks later and soon was playing football and running on the track team. His appetite was good, and he seemed to have recovered completely.

Then, one afternoon, Ann noticed a large bruise on Jimmy's right leg. "How on earth did you do that, Jimmy?" she asked, pointing to his leg.

"Do what, Mom?" Jimmy answered, surprised.

"Get that bruise on your leg."

"What bruise?"

Ann looked closer and noticed several smaller bruises on his leg. "You must have walked into a wall, Jimmy!" she joked. "Doesn't it hurt?"

Puzzled, Jimmy looked at the bruises as if he were seeing them for the first time. "I don't know where they came from. I don't remember getting hit or bumping into anything."

Before those bruises cleared up, Jimmy had new ones all over both arms. "I don't know what to do with him," Ann told her husband. "I keep asking him to be more careful, but he's still black and blue all over. Would you talk to him?"

"Ann, he's a *boy*. A few bruises aren't going to kill him. Stop worrying about him." Dave didn't attempt to hide his irritation. "You're making a big fuss for no reason."

Ann still felt that something was wrong with Jimmy. His interest in sports dwindled. He avoided his older brothers and stopped playing with his friends. Soon Ann noticed that he had to stop to catch his breath every half block when he walked and that he didn't run anymore.

"Dave, I know you think I'm fretting, but I'm worried about Jimmy. There's something wrong, and I'm taking him to the doctor."

By this time, Dave also was worried. *What if Jimmy has something seriously wrong with him? Maybe I should have listened to Ann earlier,* he thought. *Maybe it will be too late to do anything now.*

Instead of supporting Ann, however, he exploded. "Goodness," he shouted, "leave the kid alone!" Ann began crying and ran out of the room. For a minute, Dave almost followed her to apologize. Then he thought, *Oh, it's probably nothing. Just a virus or the "flu." She's such a mother hen with the boys. They'd all be sissies if I left them to her.* He sat down heavily, turned to the evening newspaper, and avoided Ann the rest of the evening.

Ann determined to make an appointment for Jimmy with Dr. Smith first thing the next morning, but in the middle of the night Jimmy had a nosebleed. She and Dave tried everything they knew, but the nosebleed showed no signs of stopping. Terribly frightened, they rushed Jimmy to the hospital emergency room. The doctor on call, Dr. Anderson, took one look at Jimmy and knew that things were serious. Jimmy was covered with the purple of fresh bruises and the greenish-yellow of healing bruises. His skin was unnaturally pale. He was having trouble breathing, and his nosebleed wouldn't stop.

Dr. Anderson took a routine blood test, which showed that Jimmy was extremely anemic. "It looks as if Jimmy's bone marrow just isn't making normal blood," he told the Davises.

"Is it leukemia, Doctor?" Ann asked at the same time that Dave was asking, "It's serious, isn't it, Doctor?"

"I can't say why the bone marrow isn't making normal blood," Dr. Anderson stated. "It could be a leukemia or another type of blood disorder. We'll have to hospitalize Jimmy and do further tests to find out what it is. I'm afraid it's serious, but we won't know the cause for a couple of days. Why don't you two get Jimmy admitted and go home and get some sleep?"

All the way home, Ann prayed silently, *Dear God, please, not leukemia.* She hardly looked at Dave until they walked into the house at 2:00 in the morning. Then she saw that he, too, was exhausted and frightened. He held her, and they comforted each other. Unbelievably, they slept soundly until 8:00, getting up just in time to say "good-by" to their school-age children.

"Do you think you can manage without me, Hon?" Dave asked as he got dressed to go to work.

"I think so," Ann answered. "I'll take Allen over to Mother's and go to the hospital to be with Jimmy. I'll call as soon as they tell me anything."

Ann arrived at the hospital in plenty of time. The doctor hadn't even been in to see Jimmy yet. "How are you, Son?" she asked, fussing over Jimmy. She smoothed his pillow, adjusted the window shade, and tuned the television set.

"Aw, Mom, don't make such a big deal out of this," Jimmy said, grinning up at her from around the packing in his nose. "I'm okay."

For the first three days, Ann and Dave were in a daze, wondering what was wrong with Jimmy. Finally, Dr. Smith had a diagnosis for them. "It isn't a leukemia," he said. "Jimmy has aplastic anemia, which means that his body has completely shut down blood production. There's an effective treatment for it, but I can't promise anything until Jimmy starts taking the pills." Dr. Smith then reassured them, saying, "The nosebleed is causing him the most trouble, and as soon as it's stopped, he can go home."

The nights were the most difficult for Ann. She would fall asleep exhausted and sleep soundly for two or three hours. Then she would be wide awake, wondering, *What did we do wrong? Should I have taken him to the doctor sooner? Why did I listen to Dave? Why couldn't Dave have seen how sick Jimmy was? What if Jimmy doesn't get well? He's got to get well! Please, God, Jimmy has to get well. How can I stand it? How can I take care of Jimmy?* Scared and confused, Ann would fall asleep again, only to dream of Jimmy running in front of a truck, walking along the edge of a cliff, or calling out for help. It always seemed that she was just a little too late or a little too far away to help him. Dave never was around to help in her dreams.

Gradually the household adapted to the necessary routine. Jimmy had to have a blood count taken every Monday morning; Ann called for the results of the blood test every Tuesday. Jimmy continued to take his medicine and went to school as usual. After several weeks of tests, Dr. Smith telephoned. "Jimmy's count is low in all areas," he said. "His platelet count is low, which makes him bleed and bruise easily," he explained. "His white cell count is also low, which makes him a prime target for infections. His red cell count is low, too, which means that he is anemic. That makes him tired and short of breath. When his red cell count gets too low, he will have to go to the hospital for a transfusion."

Ann was concerned. "Dr. Smith, is it okay for Jimmy to go to school? Won't he catch colds and things from the other kids?"

"Jimmy will be all right going to school," Dr. Smith stated, "as long as he stays out of gym class."

Continuing to worry, Ann began to pester Dave when he would get home from work. "Do you think Jimmy's getting a cold?" she would ask, night after night. "Can't you make him stay inside and watch television instead of letting him play outdoors all the time?" she would beg. "Dave, don't you *care*? How can you let him play ball? He might get hit or fall down, and then he'd bruise!"

At first, Dave tried to reassure her. "Honey, he'll be okay. He's got to have some normal life, too." However, as Ann continued worrying, Dave felt more and more helpless. He did call Jimmy in early several evenings, only to have Ann fuss and fret over the boy until both he and

Jimmy were angry and frustrated. Finally, Dave stopped even hearing Ann's pleas and complaints.

Soon he began stopping off with some friends for a drink after work. He dreaded walking in the front door and facing Ann's continual demands. "Ann, can't you let the boy alone?" he would say. "After all, he's not a baby. He's got to be allowed some breathing space. Don't make a baby of him just because he's sick!" Whenever he would say that, Ann would close her lips tightly and look hurt. After awhile, she stopped talking to Dave about Jimmy at all. When she became worried about Jimmy, she telephoned her mother or Dr. Smith.

Whenever Dave tried to spend time with Jimmy, he felt uncomfortable. He didn't want Jimmy to be a sissy, but he was afraid of hurting him. They played touch football a couple of times, but once Jimmy fell and hurt his knee and the injury really scared Dave. He knew that any injury could be very serious. *I guess I'll just leave the responsibility for Jimmy up to Ann,* he thought. *After all, the mother is better at handling sickness.*

Dave began spending more time with the older boys, taking them fishing and camping during the summer. He wanted to take Jimmy, but Ann was determined not to let Jimmy go and Dave gave in. Gradually, Dave and the older boys drifted away from the family. By the time Ann noticed the distance that had developed between her and Dave, it was too late. Dave took the older boys and moved out; Ann kept Jimmy, June, and Allen.

Eventually Ann adjusted to Jimmy's illness. She is now able to let him go to school without worrying too much, lets him play with his friends, and manages to overlook the times he engages in medically forbidden contact sports. She has survived several critical periods in Jimmy's illness and now feels confident that Jimmy will be all right.

Although Dave checks up on Jimmy periodically, he feels shy and uncertain around him. He doesn't know how to relate to Jimmy, wondering if he should have had more say in Jimmy's care. It looks as if Jimmy won't turn out to be a sissy, and Dave is grateful for that. However, he knows that he has really lost his son and his ex-wife. Sometimes he wonders if things would have been that much worse if Jimmy had contracted leukemia and died.

As we see through this example, a gulf often is created between parents when their child contracts an illness that may prove fatal. Traditionally, the mother "knows" how to care for the sick child, while the father is "in the way." This attitude lessens the parents' abilities to cope with necessary changes in lifestyle while simultaneously causing tension to build up between them. *What did I do to cause this illness?* they inevitably ask themselves. *What could I have done to prevent it?*

Often, one parent places his or her guilt and self-accusation on the other parent. The father, for example, will blame the mother for pampering and "babying" the child, and the mother will claim that the father is insensitive to the child's needs. The parents' feelings of guilt and their accusations motivate them to "do something," and they may become overinvolved in the physical care of the terminally ill child. This response is costly in terms of time and emotional energy, for soon the husband and wife relationship in the family almost disappears, being replaced by the father and mother roles. In order for the parents to avoid this type of communication breakdown, they must recognize several points.

How to Avoid Marriage Breakdown

Recognize the Need for Reassurance and Love

First, both parents need love and reassurance during this time, as well as information that enables them to regain a sense of control in the situation. In a good marriage, the parents' love for one another is an important source of strength. Their reassurances that they are doing all they can and all that is expected of them is important.

Reassurances can come from other sources, too. I find that the praise of a doctor, nurse, or other health professional for the care given a child by his parents does much to counteract the guilt and hopelessness they feel. Friends can also comment in encouraging and helpful ways on how much the parents are doing for the child, how wisely they seem to be handling the illness, and how difficult it must be for them to determine what is right and then do it.

Recognize Anger and Blame

Second, parents can avoid the communication breakdown brought about by feelings of anger by recognizing their anger. It is easy for parents, when placed in a position where there is so little control, to develop feelings of helplessness and frustration which result in a general anger toward God, the universe, or whoever happens to be handy. When angry criticism or a retort to angry criticism comes to mind, each parent should pause for a minute and try to think of the feeling underlying the angry words and actions before responding. Each parent should also try to answer an angry, blaming statement in terms of the feeling expressed rather than in terms of its content. For example, the statement, "You never let that poor child do anything anymore," could be poorly, defensively answered with the statement, "You would let him kill himself just to prove that he's a normal kid." A more helpful answer might be, "It's so frustrating for both of us to see him sick and not be able to do anything. I get angry and upset about it, too."

It is important to remember that anger often results in depression and guilt. When one parent finds himself feeling worthless and depressed or interprets his spouse's manner to mean that he is worth-less, anger is usually at the root of the depression. When each parent recognizes his feelings of helplessness, vulnerability, and frustration and admits them to himself, his spouse, and to God, he opens the way for relief from the negative feelings and for a new closeness with God and his mate. Just admitting the feelings of helplessness and frustra-tion can open up a wave of compassion and reassurance from our spouse. It also helps us to see where our self-expectations are punitive and unrealistic. Sometimes, guilt and depression result from our not being able to control a situation that is hurting those we love. Once we recognize that we are demanding the impossible of ourselves, we are free to turn to God for His help and thus alleviate much of our guilt.

Recognize Areas of Self-blame

Third, each parent should try to identify areas in which he blames himself for the child's illness or for the direction his marriage is taking. These areas are extremely sensitive, and the parent will become angry whenever his spouse or someone else criticizes him for something he already feels guilty about. We all react defensively when we feel that our behavior is not defensible. But as the parent becomes aware of the areas of self-blame and asks for and obtains help from individuals whenever it is appropriate and from God, his feelings of guilt will de-crease. That, in turn, will make him less defensive and more under-standing when responding to his spouse.

COMMUNICATION DESPITE TREMENDOUS PHYSICAL WORK

Susan and John Hanssen had five children: Rebecca, twelve; Mark, ten; Judy, eight; Jennifer, six; and Matthew, three. Susan was used to childhood illnesses and the way they ran through her family. So when Jennifer came down with the "flu"—complete with a sore throat, cough, general achiness—she wasn't surprised when Mark developed a fever several days later. Mark's illness didn't improve, how-ever, and his fever climbed alarmingly, reaching 104 degrees two nights in a row. When he was still sick on the third day, she telephoned her doctor.

"Dr. White? This is Mrs. Hanssen calling. It may be a false alarm, but Mark has me worried. He has had a fever and sore throat for the last two days, and his temperature has been 104 degrees the past two nights."

Dr. White made an appointment to examine Mark that same after-noon at 3:30. Susan found a neighbor who was willing to take care of Matthew and left a note for Rebecca (who would hopefully be the first of the older children to get home), asking her to pick up Matthew from the neighbor's house and to give Jennifer and Judy an after-school snack. The note also said that she and Mark would be home in time for her to fix dinner.

Dr. White wasn't quite as busy as Susan had feared, yet it was almost 4:30 before she and Mark entered the examination room. Dr. White examined Mark thoroughly in almost complete silence. He noticed some bruises on Mark's arms and legs and asked Mark about them. When Dr. White was finished, he sat down. "Mark, I'm afraid that you're a pretty sick boy and that you'll have to spend a couple of days in the hospital." He then turned to Mrs. Hanssen. "I'm not sure what's wrong yet, but I think he belongs in the hospital. I would like to arrange for his admission tonight so that I can get the necessary tests done as soon as possible."

Susan nodded, only half hearing the rest of what Dr. White said. She caught the words "alarming," "may not be that bad," and "rest" as her mind raced ahead. *I'll go home and get dinner on the table. John said something about working late tonight, and I'll have to call him. I don't like to leave the kids alone at night. Should I call Karen? Maybe Carolyn could come over? What if I can't reach John?*

Dr. White left the room, and a nurse came into the room as Mark finished dressing. "Mark is expected at Lakeview Community Hospital as soon as you can get him there," she said. "He'll have to have a private room. You can stay with him as long as you like, to help him get settled."

By the time Susan got home, she had dinner planned and organized. Quickly she called the three girls together and told them that Mark had to go into the hospital. Then she divided up the work of preparing dinner among the four of them, giving Mark the job of amusing Matthew. Susan telephoned John's office, but it was already after 5:00 and the receptionist had gone home. She swore under her breath, recalling an earlier conversation with John concerning his habit of ignoring the telephone after hours.

"But what if I need you in an emergency?" she had asked him.

"Oh, nonsense!" he had replied. "I'm never that late. I can't be bothered with answering everyone else's calls when I'm staying late to get some work done."

It took four telephone calls to find a babysitter, and the one she got, Susan didn't know too well. *But at least,* she thought, *someone else will be there to help Rebecca.* "Now, I won't be long, children," Susan assured them as she left the house. "I'll get Mark settled and be back before bedtime."

At the hospital, she surrendered Mark to an orderly with a wheelchair and went to fill out the forms. They took longer than she had expected, and visiting hours were nearly over when she got upstairs to Mark's room. A technician was already there drawing blood. Mark had a thermometer in his mouth, but he managed to mumble that he had had a chest x-ray before he got to his room. After Susan saw that Mark was relaxed and enjoying the attention, she kissed him and hurried home.

John was already home. He had taken the babysitter home and was just putting Matthew in bed. As soon as Matthew was tucked in, John and Susan sat down for a talk and Susan explained what had happened. "It all took place so quickly. I'm still in a whirl. If Dr. White mentioned what he thinks it is, I didn't hear him. I sort of tuned out after he said that Mark had to go into the hospital. I still feel that I'm in a dream. I thought that Mark had the 'flu,' like Jenny." She wrung her hands. "Anyway," she continued, "Dr. White said that Mark wouldn't be in the hospital long, I'm sure of that. I can't really imagine what could be wrong with him!"

Susan telephoned the hospital the next morning, and Mark said that he felt fine. "There's a special doctor coming in this afternoon to see me. Dr. White says that the doctor needs to do a 'bone marrow' test and that you have to sign for permission. Can you come and be with me for the test? It's supposed to be at 2:30."

Susan still wasn't alarmed about Mark, although the news about a "special doctor" rang a warning bell in her mind. She couldn't imagine what a "bone marrow" test could be and only hoped that it wouldn't take too long. When she came to Mark's room, she found a big, orange sign on the door that read, "Warning: Protective Isolation." There was also a cart outside the door with masks and gowns on it. Shaking with fear and uncertainty, she went up to the nurses' station. "What does it mean?" she asked. "May I see Mark?" In her alarm, she wasn't even making sense. Later on, she couldn't remember whether or not she'd been crying.

"Mark is in 'reverse isolation,'" the nurse in charge explained, "to protect him from infections. His white cell count is quite low, and an infection could be very dangerous. Don't worry, Mrs. Hanssen. The specialist will be here soon, and he'll be happy to talk to you. You may go in. Just be sure to put on a gown and a mask and use gloves if you're planning to touch him."

When Susan entered the room, Mark was watching television. "Welcome to my cell, Mother!" he exclaimed, grinning. "How do you like this setup?" Although he was cheerful, his face was pale against the pillow and he had barely touched his lunch. A nurse came in first, explained what a "bone marrow" test was, and Susan signed the consent form.

By the time the specialist, Dr. Miller, arrived, Susan was composed. She sat with Mark during the bone marrow test and held his hand once when he winced. Then she followed Dr. Miller into the hallway. "There seems to be some kind of a blood disorder," he told her. Again, she only caught snatches of what he said, such as "abnormal cells," "danger of infection," "low platelets," "treatment," and "don't know yet."

"How soon will you know, Doctor, and how long will Mark be in the hospital?" Susan knew there was a word for what she feared. It was on the tip of her tongue. She groped for it and then, horrified, tried to push it away. She didn't want to know, not yet. *If I don't think of the word and no one else says it, maybe everything will be all right and Mark can come home tomorrow.*

Dr. Miller looked grave but only said, "Let me read the bone marrow test first, okay? Then I'd like to talk to you and your husband. How about the same time tomorrow afternoon?"

When Dr. Miller left, Susan looked at the clock. It was already 4:30. Matthew had been without her all afternoon. *Dinner isn't even started,* she thought, *and John will be home in less than an hour.* Concerned for Mark and thinking about her other children and dinner, Susan kissed Mark good-by and went home.

John took the next day off from work to go with Susan and talk to Dr. Miller. What he had to say was a real blow to them. "Mark has leukemia," Dr. Miller told them. "He will have to stay in the hospital six to eight weeks. For most of that time, he will have to be in a private room, in reverse isolation. The treatment for Mark is very promising. There is a good chance of arresting the disease and a slim hope for a complete cure. However, Mark will need to be treated for a long, long time. If everything goes well, the treatments can be given in my office later on."

Dazed, John and Susan then visited Mark. "What's wrong?" Mark asked.

Susan started crying, and John had to answer. "Dr. Miller says that you have leukemia, Son. He says there's a good chance you'll get better, but you'll have to take medicine for a long time. Later on, you can go to his office and get your medicine. Right now, you're going to have to stay in the hospital until things are under control."

Susan looked at John gratefully. He had said all the right things, and he seemed so calm! After fifteen or twenty minutes, she asked John to stay with Mark while she went home. John and Mark had a good visit. Although Mark was a bit frightened, he still was enjoying the novelty and distinction of the situation.

The next two months were a nightmare. Mark had a good response to treatment, but he developed pneumonia. For almost a week, he drifted in and out of a coma. Since the Hanssens didn't know whether he'd live through the illness, they tried to make arrangements to be with Mark all the time.

Rebecca was a big help at home. She was quiet and calm, and John and Susan thought that she had adjusted well to the news of Mark's illness. It was a real shock to them when Rebecca's next report card showed failing marks in three subjects, two of which had been her best subjects for the previous grading period. Matthew became tearful and clung to Susan every time she put on her coat to go out. He started misbehaving and refused to eat. Susan felt torn. She knew that her "baby" needed her and that Rebecca couldn't assume as much responsibility as she had previously. But how could she leave Mark in the hospital alone?

The laundry never seemed to get done. Either John or one of the girls would ask for an outfit, a shirt, or clean underwear, only to have Susan realize that the clothes were dirty. Meals became a succession of McDonald's, Kentucky Fried Chicken, pizza, and sandwiches, with an occasional casserole when Susan had time and energy enough to cook. Although friends invited them out, that was impractical on school nights, so meals continued to be a problem. Susan made half-hearted attempts at cleaning but didn't get very far with it. Finally John took over the vacuuming, trying to do it first thing every Saturday morning.

Visiting Mark was another problem. It took half an hour each way to go to the hospital and, since Mark was all alone, Ann and John felt they should try to spend several hours a day with him. John went to Mark's school to pick up his books and assignments, but Mark was lonely despite his homework. Finally John and Susan divided the hospital visitation, each of them going to see Mark every other night. This worked out for awhile, but then they realized they never had any time together.

Eventually, they made Sunday a family day. While the children were in Sunday school, John and Susan visited Mark; the rest of the family then attended church together and spent the remainder of the day away from the hospital. In addition, Susan left Matthew with a babysitter all afternoon on Mondays and spent the afternoon with Mark.

After Mark recovered from his pneumonia, he improved rapidly. Soon he was out of isolation and was able to go home. Now the Hanssens had to set up a new schedule. Mark had to go to Dr. Miller's office every Thursday afternoon for a blood test and an office appointment, which required most of the afternoon. Susan also had to get his prescriptions filled and never seemed to get to the pharmacy at the right time, usually having to wait up to three-quarters of an hour. Meanwhile, life at home made its usual demands. Meals had to be prepared and served; beds needed to be made; laundry had to be done; schoolwork had to be checked; and problems and victories had to be attended to and shared.

Although the time of Mark's remission was the easiest for the Hanssens, an underlying uneasiness remained. *Is this going to last?* they asked themselves. *What if he has a relapse? Is this only going to be a bad memory, or is this the only time we'll have with our son?*

Suddenly Mark relapsed, and the Hanssen's work tripled. Mark went back into isolation in the hospital with a severe infection. For two weeks, John and Susan took turns staying with him, twenty-four hours a day. John would leave work early and get to the hospital at 4:00. This allowed Susan to go home, have dinner, spend part of the evening with the other children, throw in a load of wash, and try to catch up on some of the household chores. John spent most nights at the hospital with Mark, leaving for work as soon as Susan got there in the morning. On weekends, John spent time with the other children while Susan stayed at the hospital.

Two months later, Mark went into remission again and got out of the hospital. The weekly doctor's appointments began once more. This time Mark had to go to the hospital outpatient department for a treatment once a month in addition to his weekly office visit.

The remission didn't last long. Soon Susan and John had to schedule additional trips to the hospital outpatient department for blood transfusions. Mark wasn't feeling well, either, and needed extra time and care at home.

Susan and John shared many of the added tasks relating to Mark's illness. John pitched in at home to help keep up with the essential housework. The girls were a big help—looking after Matthew, keeping their things in order, even doing some cooking. Still, it seemed as if there was never enough time. Three or four urgent, top-priority jobs came to mind every time John or Susan had a few minutes free. It seemed that there just wasn't any chance for them to sit quietly without any work and talk with each other or with the other children. Only Mark received that kind of time and attention, and sometimes John and Susan were just too tired to talk with him.

Finances had never been a major problem for the Hanssens, but eating out, paying babysitters, and commuting back and forth to the hospital and doctor's office were costly. Their insurance plan paid for most of Mark's hospital bills, including the private room, since it was medically necessary. Visits to the doctor's office were another story, however, and John found that he was required to pay for almost fifty percent of the doctor's bills.

In spite of these difficulties, John and Susan worked together through the course of Mark's illness to support each other and their children. Let's look at some of the ways in which parents are able to cope with the strain during this time.

Remember That the Marriage Will Go On

Some of the most important questions each parent must ask are: "After our child dies, will I still have a husband (or wife) to rely on? Will my marriage be stronger? Will it have just barely survived, or will I be bereft of both the child and my spouse because of the illness?"

By planning ahead, the parent can make sure that the experience of sharing the crisis of the child's illness or death will be instrumental in improving marital communication and in strengthening the marriage. This may not be possible, however, if one spouse has a severe emotional disability or if the marriage was shaky before the onset of the child's illness.

Recognize That Terminal Illness Is Exhausting

In many respects, a short, sudden, fatal illness is easier to deal with than a drawn out, terminal illness. Terminal illness, with its remissions and relapses, takes its toll in sheer physical energy. Doctor's appointments, treatments of various kinds, extra shopping or special diets, being awakened at night by a child's crying, cleaning up after nosebleeds, vomiting, or diarrhea, and getting prescriptions filled and laboratory tests done all take time and concentration. When the child is hospitalized, there is the additional work of making hospital visits without neglecting the care of other children in the family or disrupting the household routines too seriously. Meals, laundry, dishes, and cleaning need to be done regardless of death or illness. The normal processes of life must be dealt with.

Added to the physical energy demanded is the required emotional investment as hope flickers, grows stronger, nearly disappears, and then rekindles. With this in mind, it's not hard to understand that parental fatigue is a real, integral part of any child's serious illness.

"If only we weren't so tired," parents commonly say, "we would handle things differently." The parents must not make the mistake of minimizing or ignoring the fatigure incumbent in the care of a terminally ill child, for they will continue to be tired. If they plan ahead, making allowances for the fatigue and budgeting their energy to avoid complete exhaustion, they will find it easier to cope with the illness.

Set Aside Special Time for Each Other

The husband and wife are desperately in need of love, comfort, support, and reassurance during the course of a child's terminal illness. The bond of love between them and their mutual support of each other is of utmost importance during this time.

The illness of a child, no matter how serious and devastating, should not be allowed to usurp the priority of the husband-wife relationship. The family is based on the love and bond of the husband and wife. The weakening of that bond diminishes the entire family structure. Even with a critically ill child in the home, the husband and wife need to set aside time exclusively for themselves. It might be ten minutes at the breakfast table or half an hour at bedtime, but it is necessary to nurture and deepens the bond between the parents as husband and wife, not only as mother and father. Ideally, the major source of strength for each parent should be God first, then each other.

Maintain Sexual Intimacy

Sexual intimacy between parents is very important during the entire course of a terminal illness. The intimacy helps them to keep the close ties they might not be able to keep any other way. Since sex is unique to the husband and wife relationship within the family, some emphasis on sex helps to keep the husband/wife roles alive. Sex is a way of saying, "I still need you. You are still very important to me." Finding that they can still give and receive sexual fulfillment with each other can do much to restore the husband and wife's feelings of worth and meaning if they don't allow their enjoyment to be swallowed up by guilt for taking time away from the sick child and for enjoying themselves while he "suffers." If time and energy for sex don't seem to "happen" spontaneously (and they may not, in view of the emotional and physical fatigue the parents encounter), then the husband and wife should schedule such time.

Reciprocate Acts of Love

Parents of a terminally ill child should continue performing acts of love other than sex. Such things as a telephone call during the day to say "I love you"; a favorite dessert or dinner entree (even if the sick child can't stand it!); an evening out or spent at home listening to favorite records; reading favorite poetry; making popcorn; playing cards; or tucking a note that reads "You're still special" into a lunch box or under the telephone should be deliberately planned to help maintain the husband and wife relationship.

How Parents Can Relate to Their Children

I would like to share a few guidelines that have proved helpful to parents who are trying to maintain healthy family relationships with all their children during the course of a terminal illness.

Avoid Using the Illness to Gain Leverage

It is unwise for parents to use the illness of one child as a reason for asking the other children to do something. "Please play outside" should not be followed by the statement, "Can't you remember that Johnny is sick and that noise bothers him?" Mediation of sibling squabbles should also avoid mentioning that Johnny is sick. George shouldn't hit Johnny, take his toys, or do similar things even if Johnny weren't sick! Of course, some things will be related to Johnny's illness, and in those instances it is fair to mention them. For example, "We can't go to Grandma's for Thanksgiving because Johnny has to go into the hospital that week. We've already asked the doctor to make sure that Johnny isn't in the hospital at Christmastime, and we plan to go to Grandma's then."

Do Things as a Family Whenever Possible

Parents should remember that Johnny's death spells the end of family life only for Johnny. The rest of the family still has a number of years ahead as a family. During the illness, it is important to stay a family. The "well" children need their share of time and attention. Although such attention will be less than they would receive under normal circumstances, it should not be omitted altogether. Family outings, vacations, holidays, and traditions should be maintained as much as possible. Even with Johnny in the hospital, it is important for the rest of the family to go to George's basketball game, Janet's recital, the Sunday school picnic, out for pizza, or to a movie. If the family has planned to go somewhere and Johnny is too ill to go, consider the possibility of getting a sitter for him and the rest of the family going out.

Naturally, the sick child needs to be made to feel as much a part of the family as possible. Whenever possible, the parents should include him in family activities. Relaxation of discipline—probably one of the easiest things to do with a sick child—will make him feel that his parents don't really care what he does. He should obey the family rules and standards as much as possible, even though ill. His parents need to inform him about his class in school (if he's no longer able to attend) and the activities and plans of the rest of the family. Although he may not live long enough to see the plans carried out or the activities completed, it is better for him that he be included as naturally as possible rather than make him feel isolated and alone. His parents should encourage his friends and schoolmates to visit him or write cards or notes.

Keep the Other Children Informed

The other children in the family need to be informed as to what is going on, at a level they can understand. If they ask a question, it is important to give them a brief but truthful answer. When they want more information than they have been given, they'll ask for more. Remember, if the parents lie to their children now, they will remember that and it will color all the family's relationships. Parents cannot shield their children from the fact of death; sooner or later they will find out. It is much better for parents to prepare their children slowly, in stages they can grasp, than to have them say later on, "Our parents lied to us."

To gain insight into the thought processes and feelings of their children ages one and a half to five or six, parents should watch the children play "make believe" games with such things as dolls or toy animals and ask them to explain the pictures they draw. Parents should include children of this age group in their prayers for the sick child. They might, for example, pray "that Johnny won't be lonely in the hospital and won't miss us too much," "that Johnny's fever will go away," or "that Johnny's treatment won't make him real sick this time." Parents do not need to give elaborate explanations of the situation, but they should include the younger children in other family plans or concerns.

Parents usually need not volunteer information unless they feel that a child has unasked questions and that volunteering the information will open the way for the child to talk. If Susan asks, "Is Dave going to get well?" a parent can answer, "I don't know" or "I don't think so." To answer "No" is not really truthful, for no parent ever knows for sure until the child is actually dead. If Susan persists in asking such questions as, "Does the doctor think he'll get well?" or "Why aren't you sure?" the parent should answer as honestly as possible.

Maybe Judy is very attentive of her sick brother, Billy, and her father feels that she has questions about Billy's illness but is afraid to ask or doesn't know how to ask. Her father could open the conversation with a statement such as, "Having Billy sick is kind of hard on all of us" and wait for her response. He must not press the issue. If he lets her know that he's willing to talk about Billy's illness, she will ask questions when she is ready.

Be Aware of the Other Children's Reactions

There will be many explosive emotions in the family at this time. Parents should explore the most helpful ways of expressing these emotions with their family, making a distinction between the emotion and its expression. They must try not to scold a child (or censure an adult) because of the way he or she feels, but rather should help the child find appropriate wasy of expressing and dealing with the emotion.

(1) Guilt. When a child becomes terminally ill, the other children in the family tend to have a variety of reactions. They may, for example,

feel guilty because they think they are to blame for the illness and/or death. Very young children often do not know the difference between a wish and an act. If a young child wished that his brother or sister would become ill and/or die and the wish comes true, he may believe he caused the illness or death.

(2) Jealousy. Due to the necessary time, attention, and money spent on the care of the terminally ill child, the other children may become jealous. The jealousy may become evident in a number of ways. The children may compete in "naughty," attention-getting behavior or begin showing symptoms or having complaints of illness. They may have a tendency to wait on and care for the sick child, "making up" for feeling jealous and envious. They may, on the other hand, totally disregard the terminally ill child, denying his illness and sometimes even his very existence. The jealousy may, in turn, produce guilt, since the children are aware of the illness and feel that they ought to "understand" the time and attention the sick child is receiving.

(3) Anger. Although I believe that anger is an expected, natural, and normal reaction to the frustrating position of a family with a terminally ill child, I do not recommend uninhibited and uncontrolled expression of anger. For example, physical violence expressed angrily against an individual is not generally acceptable, while expressing that same anger in a vigorous workout with a punching bag is. A verbal outburst against the person who made us angry is usually more harmful and disruptive than the same outburst expressed to another individual. Writing down the angry thoughts and feelings is even better, for then no one can be hurt by them. Family members should attempt to express anger in the first person. "I am angry about your illness," a parent or older child may say, "because I can't seem to take care of you the way I want to and I feel as if I'm always behind on everything. I feel as if I'm always tired, worn-out, and in a hurry!" This is preferable to saying, "Why did you have to get sick and mess up my whole life? If it weren't for you and your illness, I'd be able to get out and do some of the things I'd enjoy doing."

As much as possible, family members should express their anger through prayer, looking to God for answers. Dwelling on anger can be dangerous; dwelling on the cause of anger can nurture destructive thoughts and actions. The expression of anger is good when it helps people regain their perspective and expel their angry feelings. Expression of anger should be a means of getting control, not a license to keep emotions seething. I repeat that the safest and sanest way to manage anger is to express it to God and turn it over to Him even if it's done in an "I dare you to do something about this, God!" attitude. With these points in mind, family members can find the safest and best means of expressing and dealing with their anger.

Allow Room for Friction

The gradual loosening of family ties will be a most difficult task, both for the sick child and the rest of the family. Friction will inevitably arise, and there will not always be harmony among family members. Billy will be ready to say "good-by" to Susan, while Susan isn't ready yet. Mother and Dad will let go of Billy at different rates, not necessarily in tune with Billy's own readiness. Everyone will make some mistakes!

The only safe guideline here is an honesty in facing the differing states of feeling among the family members, coupled with a willingness to try to let each member of the family proceed at his own pace. This may necessitate wirthdrawal by one or more members of the family from the family circle at some time. From the oldest to the youngest in the family, each individual will need some time by himself to sort out feelings and attitudes.

Don't Depend Too Heavily on the Children

Although the children can be of comfort and help, they should not be asked to assume the full burden of providing all or even most of the emotional support the parents need. Young children and adolescents should be informed, but they need to be shielded from the *full* impact of adult responsibilities, adult losses, and adult grief. As long as they still need to be taken care of, they should not be inappropriately leaned on by either parent.

Express Love

Open expressions of love in the family are important at all times, but particularly during crisis periods. Mother and Dad should hug and kiss in front of the children; children of all ages deserve hugs and kisses. Grandma and Grandpa, aunts and uncles, and other relatives all need overt expressions of love, too. I don't think that family members can say "I love you" too often or in too many different ways!

Present a True Picture of God

The parents' actions, words, prayers, and plans during this time will have much to do with their children's picture of God. Perhaps the best thing a parent can do for them in this situation is to exemplify a solid faith in God. It is futile for a parent to pretend to accept circumstances when he is rebelling inwardly, or to present the child with an explanation for the illness that the parent can't accept. The child will sense when his parents are putting on a front and will end up questioning his faith.

For example, to tell Susan that Billy had to die "because God loved him so much that He wanted Billy in heaven" is to present a distorted picture of God, His love, and death. It is much better to admit, "I don't know why God took Billy to heaven, but I know that God loves us and Billy very much and that He had a good reason for Billy's death. Someday we will be able to ask Him about it, and then we can understand, too."

All attempts to protect God and defend Him before questioning children conveys the impression that He is not capable of looking out for Himself. A child will then think, *How then can He take care of me?* God is the One who created little children. Surely He will be able to communicate Himself to them, even when their parents don't have the words to help!

If a parent is bewildered, upset, and angry about what is happening to his family, the fact that he can trust God enough to express his bewilderment and pain to Him can positively influence his children's faith. It is safe for parents to let children know that they don't understand what God is doing, for that means that God's understanding is "even greater than Mommy's and Daddy's!" A parent can let his children know that he is upset about the situation and at the same time let them know that he still is trusting God and expects Him to resolve the situation in the best way possible.

Be Willing to Say "I Don't Know"

As soon as a child is old enough to dislike "ouchies," colds, runny noses, or other ills, he is old enough to grasp the meaning of a new body "like Jesus'" that will never get sick and die. Heaven can become a meaningful and real place if Billy's going there, and this is a good time for parents to go over the Scripture verses describing heaven.

Again, when a parent talks about heaven, Christ's resurrection, God's will, and other important doctrinal truths relating to death and illness, he should never tell a child more than he knows. It is far better for the child and the parent-child relationship if the parent says, "I don't know. The Bible doesn't say anything about that, as far as I can find out. There's a lot in the Bible about heaven that I don't understand yet, and I can't tell you." Don't give the child an explanation just to keep him quiet. Particularly young children can be a help and a blessing in dealing with death, due to the refreshing grasp they have of Bible truths and their incessant questions that push their parents to find out just what the Bible says about specific matters. Once children have found a meaningful and comforting explanation, they will take it to heart and repeat it to their parents at a most unexpected (and sometimes needful) time.

For example, when our daughter had just turned four, we took her to the funeral of an old friend of my husband's, a man she had never known herself. We had spent time before this talking about the Resurrection and about dying (an unavoidable topic in our family) but were unsure about how much she had grasped of what we had taught her. She asked to go up to the casket and view the body and then sat quietly through the entire service. At the graveside, however, she began to ask questions about the grave, the vault, and what would happen next. Finally, seemingly satisfied with the answers to her questions, she turned to look at the casket again and said, "If Jesus comes back right now, they won't have to finish burying Dr. Harvey, will they? He'll get his new body first, and then we'll all get our new bodies." Don't underestimate the little ones. Sometimes it seems they have an advantage over us in learning and applying spiritual truths.

Work to Achieve Balance in All Areas

Finally, parents need to recognize that there is much room for common sense in dealing with terminal illness in the family. They shouldn't expose their children to the full magnitude of parental grief; some crying and questioning can rightfully be done behind closed doors. There is a balance between overinvolvement of the other children in the illness of one child and the overprotection that tries to shield them from the grim realities of life. Children should not be burdened with the full knowledge of the situation or given too much responsibility in helping make family decisions. Husband and wife should derive their strength primarily from God and from each other, and their children should feel secure under their protection and God's loving care.

The free expression of love among family members will provide the tie to keep the family together and will make anger, frustration, grief, and fatigue easier to bear. Family members should constantly look for ways to say "I love you" in an atmosphere of acceptance that allows other emotions to be expressed, explored, and dealt with. Most of all, the family should take situations one at a time, allowing God to provide His resources for each need as it arises.

11

WHEN THE FAMILY FACES
A PARENT'S TERMINAL ILLNESS

EVERY CHILD IN THE family handles the impending death of a parent differently. This is true even if the children do not form an integral part of the household, although the needs and reactions of children living at home have greater impact on the attitudes and feelings of both parents. The well parent particularly will feel a responsibility to these children to help them cope with the situation and to preserve a family circle that will survive the death of a parent.

Any of the various responses we have already discussed can be seen in the children at any time. However, the principle ways in which children cope with the impending death of a father or mother are withdrawal, expressing concerned involvement, or nonchalance. Withdrawal can be expressed quietly or through difficult, hostile absence. Concerned involvement will take the form of caring for the terminally ill individual (demonstrated in a variety of different degrees and done for a number of different motives). Nonchalance is an attitude of "business as usual" and can be evidence of either initial denial or a healthy, functional denial. In any case, the interactions of the various family members play an important part in determining the attitudes children will display during the course of the terminal illness.

ONE FAMILY'S REACTION

The Malone family's reaction is typical of a family facing terminal illness. When Marianne had a mastectomy at age forty, she and her husband, Joe, were alarmed and concerned. Dr. Harris, Marianne's doctor, assured them, however, that he had removed all the tumor and that Marianne had a good chance for a cure.

At that time, the family consisted of Marianne, Joe, and their three children. Darlene was sixteen and a junior in high school; Linda was fourteen and a freshman; Jimmy was a nine-year-old fourth grader. After a two-and-a-half month interruption of family routine while Marianne convalesced, things got "back to normal" and the Malones almost forgot about breast cancer.

Darlene graduated from high school a year and a half after her mother's mastectomy. She decided to go on to college, fulfilling her father's wishes, and chose a community college so she could live at home. In most respects, Darlene was an ideal daughter. She was dependable, courteous, and willing to help out at home. She applied herself to her schoolwork, made good grades, and seemed to know what she wanted out of life and how to go about getting it.

Linda was different. Although she knew that she wanted a good job when she left school, she never seemed to be able to settle down to her studies. College wasn't in her plans; it seemed to involve too much time and effort. Linda and her father clashed over this issue frequently. Joe would tell her, "I don't understand you! I've worked hard my whole life just to give you the chance I never had, and you don't want it! You won't get anywhere without a college degree."

Linda would either listen to him in mutinous silence and stomp out of the room the minute he was finished (slamming the door behind her), or she would lash out angrily. "You want to live my life for me!" she would exclaim. "You never let me make my own decisions. How do you know what's best for me? I've got to make my own life. You can't do it for me!"

Although Marianne talked to Linda once or twice, she usually tried not to interfere. Linda had been Joe's special "pal" as a baby and young girl, and Marianne felt that their relationship would iron itself out. She occasionally urged Joe to "let the girl live her own life," but basically she agreed that Linda needed an education to get what she wanted out of life.

Jimmy was the family peacemaker. When Linda and Joe got into a fight, Jimmy would distract everyone by playing the clown. Soon everyone would be laughing, and the fight would be forgotten. If Linda was in the "doghouse" with her parents, Jimmy would find her and cheer her up. Jimmy was also a special "pal" for Marianne. They would take walks and bike rides together, plan and plant the garden, read the same books, and sneak out together for a pizza or a late movie.

Two and a half years after her mastectomy, Marianne noticed some small lumps on her chest, around the incision. At the same time, she found a lump under her arm. She went back to her doctor, who sent her to see my husband and me for chemotherapy.

At first, Marianne responded well. Except for the new routine of weekly office appointments, life for the Malones was unchanged. Joe or Darlene usually brought Marianne to our office, but if it was impossible for them to do so, Linda would come along reluctantly. Jimmy seemed to have forgotten all about his mother's illness.

Nine months later, Marianne broke a tumorous rib while turning over in bed. X-ray studies showed that there was probably tumor in several others as well. Marianne's treatments changed slightly, altering the family routine. She had to be in the office once a week for blood counts. The new treatments were every three weeks, and they made Marianne sick. Linda's class schedule was light on Mondays, the day Marianne received her treatments, so she began bringing Marianne to the office. Darlene usually cooked on Monday nights and Tuesdays. If she was late getting home or had something else to do, Joe picked up something for dinner on his way home. Linda went out most evenings or shut herself in her room with the door closed. Whenever Joe or Darlene tried to talk to her, she would blow up at them. Marianne and Linda talked now and then, on their way to or from the office. Only Jimmy still got along with Linda in the same easy friendship they had always had.

As Linda's graduation approached, she and her father fought more and more. It seemed they were engaged in a continual battle over Linda's education. One night at dinner, they had a particularly violent argument. Joe ended up leaving the table to watch television, while Linda stomped out of the house in a fury.

When Linda returned home around midnight, she was surprised to see lights on. She slipped in quietly and found that her mother had begun vomiting just after dinner and couldn't stop. Darlene finally convinced her to call us for something to stop the vomiting, and Linda offered to pick it up since she was still dressed. She went to her father, wanting to apologize, but he just turned away.

As Linda drove to the pharmacy, one thought kept running through her mind. *I did it. It's all my fault. If I hadn't had that big fight with Dad, Mom would be okay. Why couldn't I have kept my mouth shut? Oh, God, please let Mom get well, please!* When she got home with the medicine, Linda told her mother how sorry she was. When Joe came into the room, Linda turned to him, said, "Dad, I'm sorry," and ran out before he had a chance to answer her.

No one except Jimmy got a good night's sleep. Joe was up with Marianne until she felt a little better; by then it was almost time for him to go to work. Darlene got up just before her father left, in order to keep an eye on her mother. Linda tossed back and forth in her bed, first feeling guilty, then furious. *It wasn't my fault. Dad makes me so mad. Why can't he leave me alone? If he wouldn't pick on me, I wouldn't yell. Oh, I hope we didn't make Mom sick! Please, God, don't let her die.* By morning, Linda was exhausted and finally fell asleep, only to hear Darlene knocking at her door.

"Linda, I hate to get you up, but I called Dr. Kopp and she said to bring Mom into the office today. Can you drive her? Dad's at work, and I have a class in half an hour. I'd cut it, but I've cut the last two sessions and I don't dare miss today."

Linda got up hurriedly, dressed, and went downstairs. Her mother really looked awful! She was pale and tired, with large circles under her eyes. Seeing her in the morning light, Linda again was overcome with remorse for the furious quarrel she'd had with her dad the night before. "Do you feel any better, Mom?" she asked. "I sure hope you got some sleep last night."

"Well, at least I'm not so sick to my stomach. But now I've got a pain in my back. It's been there a couple of weeks, but it got real bad last night when I was throwing up. I hope Dr. Kopp can do something about it."

Jimmy came in just then, ready for school. "Does your back hurt, Mom?" he asked, concerned. Then he brightened up a bit. "Too much heavy lifting. It's all those thick books you've been reading. You'll see, the Doc will tell you not to pick up anything heavier than a magazine." He kissed her shyly and ducked out the front door.

Marianne soon learned that a new tumor in her spine had caused her backache and probably had contributed to her upset stomach. Actually, the upset stomach turned out to be good, for without it Marianne might have waited longer before mentioning her back pain. That delay could have led to serious trouble. We put her in the hospital for a few days, started her on radiation therapy, and sent her back home. From then on, things started to get worse. She had good days as well as bad, but the bad days started coming more frequently. She was more tired, too, and seemed to be getting weaker.

As Marianne became worse, the family seemed to disintegrate. Joe had always been quiet, but with the extra work at home and his concern for his wife, he scarcely spoke at all. Linda spent more and more time away from home until, finally, she didn't come home at all one night. This resulted in a violent quarrel with her father, and she moved in with a friend. Darlene took over a large share of the housework and that made her bitterly angry with Linda and almost possessively defensive of her father. Even Jimmy became quieter. He began to spend more time at home, sitting quietly with Marianne or trying to make himself useful.

A few days after Linda moved out of the house, Marianne took a turn for the worse. She began to turn yellow, her feet became badly swollen, and she was always nauseated. Although she had been growing gradually weaker and more tired, now she would drift off, apparently asleep, several times a day. Soon Joe called me, and I had Marianne admitted to the hospital.

Before I even had a chance to see Marianne in the hospital, Linda called me. "Dad won't even talk to me anymore, but Jimmy telephoned last night and said that Mother was going into the hospital. Is it serious? What should I do? I would like to make up with Dad, but he's so angry with me that I don't know where to start!" I had to tell Linda that I seriously doubted that her mother would leave the hospital and, in fact, that I expected her to die within a week or two.

When I got to the hospital, Marianne and Jimmy were there alone. I "looked at" Marianne while Jimmy went out to get a drink of water. When he came back, he asked, "How is she?"

"Not very well, I'm afraid," I told him. Then I turned to Marianne and asked, "Have you or Joe said anything to Jimmy about how serious this is?"

Marianne shook her head, tears welling in her eyes. "No, I haven't said anything to him, and I know Joe wouldn't."

I turned to Jimmy. "Has Linda or Darlene said anything to you?"

"I don't want to know," Jimmy almost shouted, impatiently brushing away the tears in his eyes. "I don't want to know anything about it!"

"Jimmy, your mother's very sick. I don't think she has much time left. You knew that already, didn't you?"

Jimmy nodded. "We had so many good times last summer. We'd take Mom out into the yard, under the apple tree, and she and I would sit there. All the neighbors would come over to visit, and we would drink lemonade and talk."

Marianne took Jimmy's hand. "Jim and I are making plans for this summer, at least we're hoping for another summer."

After Jimmy left, I talked with Marianne. "I don't think you have much time left," I told her, "and I expect that you'll become more and more sleepy and maybe even confused. If you have things to do, you had better do them now, while you're well and alert enough."

"I know. Joe and I went out and bought a cemetery lot just before I came in this time. I'm ready. I don't feel well, and I'm tired of not feeling well. But I wish I could do something about Linda and Joe before I die. She was his favorite, you know. Until she started high school, they got along fine. Oh, they both have quick tempers, and they've always fought, but it's never been anything serious, not until just lately. This past year they haven't gotten along at all. Joe can't understand it. He's given her everything he always wanted, and she doesn't want it! He will do anything to give the kids a chance to go to college, and Linda laughs at him. I wish they would make up somehow."

Later, I talked to Joe, who repeated the same things Marianne had said. "I've spent my life working for the kids. I've tried to give them a good life. I've done all I could for them. They must know how much I love them."

"Have you told them specifically that you love them? Sometimes we're not as careful as we could be about saying things. Have you told Linda that you love her and want the best for her?"

"Well, I guess I'm not too good at saying those things. But she must know." Joe began to cry. "My own parents didn't care about me at all. We've barely spoken since I was in eighth grade. They made me get out and get a job as soon as I could get one, and they wouldn't even help me get through high school. I've always wanted my kids to be able to have the education I couldn't have, and Linda throws it away! Besides, here's Marianne, sick and getting worse, and Linda acts like it's too much for her to help out around the house."

I told Marianne to tell Joe how she felt about the way he and Linda were getting along.

Marianne told him what she had told me earlier. "Joe, I'm tired. I know I'm not going to get well, and I'm ready to have it over with. But it hurts me so to see you and Linda so far apart! I just can't die without knowing that you and Linda have made up. I would like to see you become friends again."

Linda began visiting Marianne in the hospital, and gradually she and Joe reached the point where they could talk to each other again. Linda and Jimmy grew even closer than they had been, and Darlene got over some of her resentment toward Linda and also began to get along with her.

Although Jimmy clearly knew the seriousness of his mother's illness, he continued to be the family clown—the one who could always bridge an awkward moment with a laugh or cheer the family up with his antics. His closeness to Linda gave him someone to lean on during and after the terminal stage of his mother's illness.

After Marianne died, Joe had a hard time adjusting. She had been his only source of strength and comfort, the only person in whom he had confided. For several months he withdrew from the family compeltely, going to work and drinking heavily. Darlene moved closer to her school but came home several times a week to visit Jimmy. Linda continued living with her friend, seeing Jimmy and Darlene occasionally and not seeing her father at all.

During the period of a year after Marianne's death, the members of the family worked through their own grief and were able to reestablish some loose family ties. Joe, Jimmy, and Darlene eventually became quite close, while Linda established a separate home for herself, even though she began visiting her family again.

MAINTAINING FAMILY STABILITY

When a family is faced with a parent's terminal illness, serious problems can result. The following considerations can make a world of difference in children's adjustment to the death of their parent.

Do Things as a Family

The children need to feel the security of knowing that the family will continue to function as a family, even after the death of one parent. New relationships within the family that will be necessary after Mom or Dad dies can be developed during this period of preparation. The family should maintain its identity as a family unit by continuing family activities, such as picnics, traditions, celebrations, and so on. These should sometimes include and sometimes exclude the sick parent.

If Mom is too sick to travel, the family should take the vacation without her but make it brief. On the other hand, a birthday party could be moved up to Dad's hospital room if he's feeling up to it so that he could be included in the fun. Keep in mind, however, that the ill individual should have the right to be absent from family activities if he feels he doesn't want to be included. The family should be free to continue their activities even if the ill parent does not or cannot participate.

Give the Children Time Alone

The healthy parent should give each child "breathing space"—his own time and privacy in which to work through his feelings and thoughts. The parent must not be surprised when children resent the additional work they are asked to do at home and the time involved in caring for the ill parent. He especially shouldn't respond to their expressions of resentment with the attitude, "After all Mother (Dad) has done for you, how can you feel like that?" or, "After all Mother (Dad) has done for you, this is the least you can do!" Again, he should answer the feeling behind the expressions, not the expressions themselves. Often the children's underlying feelings are a mixture of fear, guilt, and resentment. Although feelings should be "permitted," the unbridled expression of those feelings in destructive ways should not be allowed. Expressions of anger and resentment, particularly, should be found that help to relieve the children's emotion while also enabling them to relate constructively to the family. Such physical activities as walking, running, bicycling, and swimming are helpful, as are such expressions as writing a diary or writing a letter to God. Imaginative play, which includes playing with dolls and animals, is an excellent source of expression for young children.

Eliminate Future Uncertainty

Knowing that children will have to face the grief and bewilderment of bereavement, the healthy parent should try to eliminate as much of the children's uncertainty and insecurity concerning the future as he can. This holds true for elderly dependents as well. Even in a family where no specter of terminal illness exists, it is wise for the parent to choose a guardian for the children and to let them know about provisions he has made for them in the event of his sudden, unexpected death.

Maintain a Healthy Attitude

In order for the children to make a healthy adjustment to the changes ushered in by the death of their parent, the healthy parent must remember that his attitude will be the key to their attitude. He should involve them in the preparation for the changes and share his feelings with them, including those of sadness and reluctance to change. If his attitude is bitter and angry, he should not try to create a positive attitude in the children without first asking God to help him with his own attitude. By realizing the fact that God is looking after him now, as He has in the past, and knowing that God's care for the family will not change, the parent can better deal with his negative attitudes.

Again, in this type of situation, the parent may be surprised at the support and encouragement his children will provide, even the youngest one. Their faith and trusting dependence on God can be refreshing and heartening. If the healthy parent has no past examples of God's provision for his family, he can use scriptural examples to show how God has provided for others in the past and take advantage of the opportunity to prove Him faithful in his own family at that moment.

Involve the Children in Preparations

Involving the entire family—particularly the children—in preparations for the death of the parent to some extent eases the strain felt in loosening the close family bonds. The farewells said during this time will be painful and sad. However, using the family's time to prepare for the future will help ease the pain. Children of all ages should be included in the preparations to the extent that they are able to understand what is going on. Again, the healthy parent must not force information on a child who isn't ready for it.

Recognize and Redirect Anger

Longstanding and unresolved family conflicts will tend to surface violently during this time for two reasons. First, emotional fatigue caused by strain makes it harder for family members to act "reasonably." The members should try to see the other person's viewpoint and in general try to keep the peace. Secondly, the family members' anger and resentment caused by the situation of terminal illness over which they have no control can easily be directed into "safer," more familiar quarrels. Anger toward the terminally ill individual, the doctor(s), God, and/or the universe in general is more difficult to handle than anger against another family member, especially in the context of a longstanding and familiar quarrel.

Because anger has the potential to destroy family ties, it is important to learn to cope with it. First, an angry individual has to recognize that he is angry and then ask himself, *Why am I angry?* He should check to see if fatigue, frustration, or hopelessness are causes of his anger. Adequate rest—even if it means fifteen-minute naps from time to time—is an important peacemaker! Frustration, helplessness, and futility can be shouted out at God and worked out through physical exercise that will cause physical fatigue.

To summarize, I would like to say that the same basic guidelines offered in the previous chapter apply in this situation, but several are especially important.

(1) Be eager and constant in expressing love in any and every way.

(2) Use common sense in coping with fatigue, upset schedules, and all the changes in life style necessitated by terminal illness.

(3) Allow each family member to set his own pace and sort out his own feelings. Give emotions their legitimate recognition while setting up rules about expressing the more negative emotions in harmless ways.

(4) Take it easy! No situation needs to be faced fully until it comes, and God's grace doesn't anticipate your need but rather coincides with it. You can cope if you take things as they come and rely on God.

12

TILL DEATH DO US PART

WHEN A HUSBAND or wife is dying, feelings of helplessness, frustration, and guilt may create a gulf between him and his mate. "What did I do wrong?" each may ask. "What could I have done differently? Is the illness my fault?"

A woman with breast cancer, for example, may feel guilty for not noticing a certain lump sooner or for not getting to the doctor sooner. Her husband may feel equally guilty for not noticing that something was wrong or for not insisting that she see a doctor. Their guilt feelings may then lead to self-blame, depression, and/or avoidance of the one who is causing the feelings of guilt.

Due to the fact that communication among family members will vary according to the family's basic structure, we need to separate into different categories the situations a family facing terminal illness can encounter. In this chapter we will look at families in which one of the spouses has terminal illness and see how that situation can affect marriage. In some cases, the children will be living at home; in others, the children will be grown and have homes of their own. Many of the principles and guidelines we examine will also apply to two people living together (friends, brother and sister, and so on). We will also consider the experiences of two, two-parent families in which children are still living at home and the dying individual is one of the children. The case material has a base of factual information but is largely fictionalized.

Tina Jacobs, a high school senior, had been dating Chuck steadily for two years. They planned to get married as soon as they both graduated and Chuck found a job. When Tina learned that she had Hodgkin's disease, it took a week before she had enough courage to talk to Chuck about it. Finally she telephoned him. "I think I want to break our engagement," she told him. "I just found out that I have a form of cancer."

Chuck listened to her arguments but refused to call off the wedding. "Let's make an appointment with the doctor first," he stated, "and see what he has to say."

A week later, they walked into Dr. Williams' office and sat down. "I don't want to marry Chuck and then have him tied down to an invalid," Tina said. "I don't think it's fair. Maybe I won't be able to take care of the house, or cook, or do anything else. I think we should just forget about getting married."

Dr. Williams shook his head. "Tina, you have a very early form of Hodgkin's disease, which is easily treated and can sometimes be cured. In any case, you don't have to jump to the conclusion that having this disease will make you unfit to be a wife and mother. It won't automatically cripple you." After further reassurances from Dr. Williams, Tina and Chuck decided to get married.

Following graduation, Chuck and Tina found good jobs, in spite of Tina's diagnosis. Having begun chemotherapy treatment several months before the wedding, Tina was accustomed to the treatment and its side effects by the time they were married. She was delighted to find out that she felt well most of the time and could continue working while on treatment. As soon as she completed her course of maintenance therapy, Tina became pregnant, and Karen was born shortly after Tina and Chuck's third wedding anniversary.

At the end of her second year of treatment, Tina relapsed. Although both she and Chuck were worried, they tried not to let it show. However, they became tense, and tempers flared for several weeks. Soon Dr. Williams placed Tina on a new form of treatment, and she had an excellent response. Both she and Chuck breathed a sigh of relief and settled back into the routine of doctor's appointments, blood counts, and periodic chemotherapy. Tina's doctor's appointments soon were as normal and natural as Karen's regular checkups and immunizations.

A week before Karen's third birthday, Tina found a small lump under her right arm while taking a shower. Almost as a reflex, she checked herself for other lumps. She found a large, tender lump on the left side of her neck and a small, painless swelling in her left groin. *Oh, no!* Tina thought. *It's the cancer again, I know it is.* She went back to bed to think about things and began crying.

Karen's calling, "Mommy, Mommy, where are you?" brought her back to herself. Tina dried her eyes and went to check her calendar to find out when she was due to see the doctor. Since her appointment was only two weeks away, she decided to try to forget about the lumps and wait for her scheduled office visit. *After all, it doesn't necessarily have to be the Hodgkin's disease,* she told herself. *It might go away by itself, and then I'd be worrying for nothing.*

Tina succeeded in forgetting about the new lumps for a few days—most of the time, anyhow. Every now and then her hand would stray to her neck, just to see if the lump was still there and if it had become smaller. Then, one day, Chuck noticed her feeling the lump.

"What's the matter, Honey? Have a sore throat?" he asked.

"Oh, I don't suppose it's anything," Tina replied. "I thought I could feel a swelling in my neck a couple of days ago, but it's smaller now. I don't think it's anything serious, but since I have to go to Dr. Williams next week, I'll ask him about it." Not wanting to alarm Chuck, Tina didn't tell him she had found several other lumps. He had been working extra hard lately, and she knew he was tired. All the same, she was let down and disappointed when he just nodded, said, "That's a good idea," and dismissed the lump from his mind.

That evening, before they went to bed, Chuck started to tell her about some problems that had come up at work. Tina, still hurt by his response to her worry about the lumps, listened with only a fraction of her attention. Chuck then felt she didn't care about his problems. By bedtime, they had become cool and silent.

For the next couple of days, the family atmosphere improved. Tina managed to put aside her worry about her health and really paid attention to Chuck; Chuck forgot about her coolness and was again open and loving with her.

Then the day of Tina's doctor's appointment arrived. Tina was both looking forward to it and dreading it. As she sat in the waiting room listening for her name, her heart began to pound and her hands felt clammy. Finally she was called to the examining room, and Dr. Williams' sure fingers found the lumps she had worried about. His face was grave, but he didn't say anything until he had finished his examination. Then he asked, "How long have you had these new nodes?"

"I noticed the one under my arm two weeks ago. When I found that one, I checked to see if there were any others and found one in my neck and one in my groin. Does this mean another relapse?"

Dr. Williams nodded and said gently, "I'm afraid so. I would like to put you into the hospital for some additional tests and have a specialist take over your treatment."

Tina went home and told Chuck that she had to go into the hospital for tests. She wanted to cry and have him hold her, but she put on a brave face and told him the news in a matter-of-fact way. She knew he was having problems at work, and she didn't want her health to upset him. *After all,* she thought, *maybe the specialist will have another "miracle" drug and things will get back to normal again.*

Chuck was alarmed at the thought of Tina going into the hospital. *Now I'll have to find someone to look after Karen and make time to go back and forth to visit Tina most days.* In the back of his mind, he worried that this would be the end, that they would finally face the specter of the cancer they had lived with.

Chuck was also annoyed. Facing a crisis in his job, he wanted to tell Tina about it and receive her comfort and sympathy. Now he didn't dare mention it. In spite of the fact that she was being brave and breezy, he knew Tina was really scared and sick. They spent the evening in silence, Tina brooding about her illness and Chuck anxious about his job. Each of them felt responsible to help the other, so they both felt guilty.

The next day Tina was admitted to the hospital. During her brief hospitalization, my husband and I were asked to examine her and take over her care. We did have another "miracle" drug, but it was a very short-term miracle. In a matter of months, it became obvious that Tina was facing another relapse. From that point on, Tina's health gradually went downhill, interrupted with good times. She began to feel ill, tired, and depressed more frequently. We decided not to hospitalize her again but to treat her on an out-patient basis.

At home, Tina found that eating required an enormous effort and cooking nauseated her. She had to force herself to fix meals for Chuck and Karen. Once she had cooked a meal, she couldn't bring herself to eat it and began to lose weight. Chuck could hardly bear to look at her. *Is this thin, pale, listless skeleton of a woman really the pert, vivacious girl I married?* he kept thinking. Once Tina had been an attractively dressed woman, showing off her excellent figure in well-chosen skirts and slacks; now her well-cut clothes hung shapelessly on her thin frame.

Chuck and Tina had once been good companions as well as husband and wife. Tina had a knack for listening to Chuck's problems—putting her finger on the sore spot, making a useful suggestion for coping with it—without being cold or unsympathetic. Chuck was at a point where he could use her suggestions. Several nights he had come home late, ready to share his problems with her, only to be met with her tears and complaints. "Why couldn't you have called and told me you'd be late?" Tina would complain. "I've been waiting and waiting for you to get home. You knew I wasn't feeling well!" After such a greeting, Chuck didn't feel he could burden Tina with his problems. Although he tried to be sympathetic to her complaints, he soon began to "tune her out" when she told him about her illness.

One afternoon, Chuck stopped off for a drink after work. He was surprised to find how much easier it was to be sympathetic with Tina that evening, and soon his drink after work became a habit. Then he met Tina's friend, Nancy, and took her out with him. Nancy was easy to talk to. Chuck could tell her how confused and guilty he felt about Tina. "You know, I feel like a heel when I get mad at her," he confessed. "She's really sick, and I shouldn't get angry, but I do. I want to talk with her the way we used to talk, but she's so sick. I'm afraid to worry her about my work. Still, I have to have someone to talk to!"

Chuck found that Nancy was a good listener, and he began to spend a lot of time with her. The guilt involved in seeing her wasn't as bad as the guilt of being around Tina. He felt guilty because Tina was sick and he wasn't, because he wished she would pay more attention to him, because he criticized her housekeeping, and because she made him feel angry and depressed. Nancy, on the other hand, made him feel good. She made him feel like a man, worth looking up to and admiring.

Tina didn't know what was wrong, but she knew something was happening. Chuck was coming home later and later. When she asked him about work, he answered briefly and absent-mindedly. When he asked her about what the doctor had said, she knew that he wasn't listening to her answers. Once or twice, she had persisted and tried to get him to talk with her the way they used to talk, but he had become furious and accused her of wanting to run his life. After that, she just left him alone. She tried to cook and clean, but it seemed that Chuck didn't even notice. Soon she made only half-hearted attempts at the housework.

Since her relationship with Chuck had deteriorated, Tina began to concentrate on Karen. She spent most of her energy playing with Karen and reading to her. She fixed Karen's meals regularly and on schedule, laundered Karen's clothes, and cleaned up Karen's room. Whenever she could drive the car, Tina also took Karen to her grandparents, since she wanted Karen to feel completely at home with them.

One afternoon Tina told me that her concentration on Karen was carried on with ambivalent feelings. "I love her so, and I don't want her to suffer because I'm sick, Dr. Ruth. I can't bear to have her see me when I'm really bad. Sometimes I get so frustrated, and the next thing I know I'm yelling at her, as if my illness were all her fault! How can I take it out on her when I love her so much?

"There are other times when I can hardly stand to have her around. I want to tell her, 'Save your love. I'm not worth it. I'll be gone soon.' She comes to hug me or bring me flowers, and I want to push her away and tell her to leave me alone. Then I feel awful! I can't believe that I would feel like that about my own baby!"

Since Chuck spent more and more time away from home, Tina's parents were around more. Soon Tina moved back to her parents' home, and they began caring for her and Karen. When Tina went into the hospital for the last time, she said "Good-by" to Karen and didn't want to see her again. By then, Karen was used to being with her grandparents and was able to let her mother go. At the end of her life, Tina was almost like a little girl again, having surrendered her adult privileges and responsibilities. After Tina's death, Chuck married Nancy, took Karen, and avoided Tina's parents completely.

REASONS WHY TINA AND CHUCK'S RELATIONSHIP BROKE DOWN

What caused the total deterioration of Tina and Chuck's relationship? We can look at two problem areas that can easily crop up in *any* husband-wife relationship.

Difficulty in Communications

Tina needed desperately to discuss her illness with Chuck and to experience his comfort and support, but she didn't know how to express her need and her blaming accusations drove him away. She also was unable to ask him for his support and love in a way that made him feel useful instead of guilty. At the same time, she couldn't find a way to offer him the tenderness and support she still had to give.

Chuck, in turn, needed Tina to be a wife to him. Feeling that he couldn't ask anything of her because she was sick, he turned to Nancy for encouragement and support. Neither he nor Tina were able to break through their misconceptions and reach out. When Tina wanted to discuss her illness with Chuck, she decided to keep it inside because he was "having a hard time at work." Chuck, on the other hand, decided not to talk about his job with Tina because "she doesn't need to hear about that when she's worried about being sick." As they faced the necessary separation of death, they experienced premature alienation from each other, brought about by the overwhelming needs they could not express and the rejection each felt from the other.

Failure to Recognize Cultural Standards

Paradoxically, Chuck's need for his wife to be his wife caused him to turn to another woman. His action may well reflect our cultural standards for men. Generally speaking, men are supposed to be strong, assured, and supportive, whereas women are allowed to be weak and to lean on others. Add to a man's self-expectations for strength and endurance the unthinkable nature of asking for help and comfort from his dying wife and it's easy to understand why a man may feel compelled to turn to someone other than his wife for emotional support and love.

It is much less common, at least in my experience, for the wife of a terminally ill man to turn to another man for comfort and encouragement. It seems much easier for a woman to "lean" on a dying husband. Perhaps this is because the kind of protectiveness a wife feels for her husband is different from that which a husband feels for his wife. Perhaps it is because we have been told so often that a man needs to be built up and admired by his woman. At any rate, the women I have known have been able to derive support and comfort from their terminally ill husbands more easily than men in the same situation have been able to accept help and comfort from their wives.

It is important for me to point out, however, that it is not common for either spouse to turn to someone other than his or her dying mate for love and support. The feelings and reasons underlying infidelity in the case of a terminally ill spouse are nearly universal, however, and should be understood and handled in a way that will enrich both partners rather than leave them both feeling isolated and rejected.

Even a healthy, secure marriage can hardly survive if one spouse suddenly becomes totally responsible for all the physical, emotional, and spiritual needs of the other, while the other spouse becomes exempt from all responsibilities to his partner and cannot be "burdened" with his partner's needs and problems. Of course, if there are other stresses in the marriage, it is easy to see why the marriage bond might not survive the added strain of a terminal illness.

GUIDELINES FOR BOTH HUSBAND AND WIFE TO FOLLOW

There are some practical guidelines that apply to a marriage in which one of the partners is terminally ill. Through an awareness of the following guidelines, the husband and wife can become closer rather than farther apart.

Recognize Emotional Stress

Although most of us would look to our husbands or wives for emotional support during a time of stress, we often feel it is unfair to ask a terminally ill spouse for that support. We are afraid to add the burden of caring for us to the burden of the spouse's illness. So we bravely try to bear our burden alone—and become alienated from the one we love most, and feel depressed and extremely lonely.

On the other hand, the terminally ill individual often has resources available to help his spouse. However, he may sense his mate's need to "spare" him a share of his troubles and may not intrude. So, at a time when sharing and closeness would mean so much to both partners, they both experience alienation, which occurs abruptly and seemingly without reason or warning. As a result, both feel alone, rejected, and depressed.

If the "well" spouse can communicate his frustration, loneliness, and anxiety to the terminally ill mate, he will usually find great comfort in the love and understanding of his mate. The "ill" individual, on the other hand, will have the satisfaction of both being needed and having an important place in his mate's life. The problems and emotional stresses that each individual faces during the course of a terminal illness tend to be different, and sharing the burdens lightens the load of each rather than increasing it.

Understand the Mother/Father Role

The view that each parent has toward his (or her) role in the family structure is important to the marriage's strength or weakness. Tina, for example, was able to direct her tenderness and love toward Karen and receive comfort in return. Generally speaking, a woman is "supposed" to be closer to her children and to depend on them more than her husband. It is legitimate for a mother to go to her children for companionship, support, and approval. It is, again, inconceivable that a father would seek emotional support and aid from his children in a crisis situation. He is supposed to "provide" and protect, not derive emotional support.

Again, let me emphasize the fact that we do not injure our children by letting them see our needs and weaknesses. If they never see anything but our strengths, they will be much less able to accept their own weaknesses. If, on the other hand, we can let them see our needs and the ways in which they are met through other people and our faith in God, our children will learn valuable lessons in handling life's crises for themselves.

Recognize Physical Stress

During a period of remission, the terminally ill individual may be able to continue many of his duties, get to appointments at the doctor's laboratory and hospital on his own, and require little extra care. However, during the terminal phase of his illness or anytime he is bedridden in the hospital or at home, the individual is unable to share in his own care. He is also unable to continue performing his normal household duties.

Often, this increase in responsibility results in feelings of insecurity. The parent who must do the work his spouse used to do may feel insecure in assuming tasks he is not accustomed to doing. When he temporarily assumed responsibility from his spouse, he normally looked to her to let him know whether or not he was doing a good job. In terminal illness, however, the spouse who is well tends to eliminate this source of reassurance and comfort, believing that it is "unfair" to ask anything of the terminally ill person. Add feelings of aloneness, fatigue, and depression to feelings of insecurity, and it is easy to understand why marital communication can break down.

So what can a terminally ill wife do for others? She can approve of the way her husband cares for her, can commend him for the efficiency and neatness of his housekeeping, or can comfort him in his suffering because of *her* illness. Although her strength and resources may be limited, the fact that she can give him encouragement, approval, appreciation, and comfort—and that they are important to him—can add to her own sense of personal worth and help do away with the fearful aloneness she faces.

If there are children at home, she can also take time to help them (if they are old enough) to understand the jobs that must be done and help them assume responsibility for those jobs. She may, for example, help her children assign themselves different jobs in keeping the house clean. She can help them work out a practical schedule. She can pass on her tips about shopping and alert them to things they might be likely to run out of and how to avoid it. She can help them in menu planning and, if she has enough time and strength and her children are the appropriate ages, she can even help them become fairly good cooks!

What can a terminally ill husband do for others? He can do the same things for his wife. He can appreciate her care for him, show approval of the way she manages tasks that were traditionally his, help her evaluate her own worth, and emphasize her importance. Being able to make this contribution to her life, even though he is dying, will give him fulfillment and help realize that he does, indeed, "have a place in the world."

If the husband has handled the family finances, it is imperative that he explain the financial aspects of the family to appropriate family members. His wife or an older child, or both, need to know where to find such important documents as his will, life insurance papers, property and/or house titles, car insurance papers, and bank books. If there is time, he should explain the family budget and the means of paying bills, outline monthly expenses, and alert family members to bills that come annually or semi-annually—such as taxes and insurance premiums—so they can be prepared for them. He should also go through health and hospitalization insurance with them, so they will know how to take care of the hospital and doctor bills after the funeral.

In addition, he could explain to them how often and where he has had the car(s) serviced; what type of house paint to buy; how to change the filters in the furnace; how to turn off the water, electricity, and gas in the house in the event of an emergency; and other details that might come to mind.

In providing his wife and/or family with the information he has accumulated over the years, the terminally ill husband is able to give his wife and/or family a head start in functioning effectively after his death. He will also gain positive reinforcement and love in the process. The transfer of roles and responsibilities can be easier if the dying individual can help his family assume his former responsibilities.

Write Details Down

It is a good idea for both spouses to keep a notebook handy to jot down important matters when they come to mind. The notebook should include: names and addresses of people to contact (doctor, lawyer, funeral director, minister, friends) at the time of death; location and identification of legal documents (will, insurance policies, deeds, titles, et al.); pertinent information concerning the smooth running of the household; and any other details that are important to the family.

Encourage Open Expression

As the husband and wife work together to get the physical work done and prepare for the eventual separation due to death, communication continues to be critical. If either spouse feels that what he is doing is going unnoticed and unappreciated, it is better for him to express his feelings than to brood over them. The simple statement, "I feel that I'm doing everything I can and that no one cares," or "I'm working as hard as I can to keep the family going, and I still feel that nothing I'm doing counts for much," can open the way for a partner to express his appreciation. Remember, too, that the things that "go without saying" sometimes need to be expressed loudly!

Confront Feelings of Guilt and Blame

During the course of a terminal illness, we have seen that feelings of guilt and blame can widen the gulf between husband and wife. Either one can blame the other. The "well" spouse can resent and blame the other one for becoming ill; the terminally ill individual can resent and blame the one who is well for having good health.

The feeling of anger against a spouse often triggers guilt. *I'm not supposed to become angry with someone I love,* one individual may think, *especially when he is sick (or is taking care of me when I'm sick).* Such guilt generates depression and encourages the individual to avoid the one who is making him feel guilty, angry, and depressed. In a husband-wife relationship, it is easy to recognize the fact that the avoidance will, in turn, produce more guilt, loneliness, resentment, frustration, and depression.

Several methods of avoidance are common. Drinking is one way of "coping" with the problems of guilt and blame, but it tends to induce more guilt and perpetuates a vicious cycle. A more "acceptable" means of avoidance in American society is to bury oneself in work, either in one's career or profession or in volunteer or church work. This method produces fewer feelings of guilt but still results in the same feelings for both parties in the relationship.

When dealing with guilt and self-blame, both partners should realize that anger, flare-ups, and times of distance will occur during the course of a terminal illness. Since the feelings between a husband and wife are much more intense than those between parent and child, and since a husband and wife depend more extensively on one another for support than a parent depends on a child, there will be more "touchy" areas and more tendency for self-blame and guilt. Rather than tormenting each other with regrets for letting them occur, the husband and wife should use them as occasions for reconciliation and forgiveness.

When feelings of guilt and blame surface, both individuals can handle angry, blaming accusations by answering the feelings behind the accusations rather than the words themselves. Let's say, for example, that the wife says, "Why did you promise the children fish for dinner tonight? You know that I have my chemotherapy today and that fish makes me sick even at the best of times."

The husband could respond, "I wish for once you would stop feeling sorry for yourself and think of the rest of us." However, he could handle the situation much more effectively by saying, "I'm sorry that you're feeling sick. I've often wished that you could be on some kind of treatment that didn't make you so nauseated."

As both marriage partners work to improve their communication and become honest in their expressions, they will be drawn closer together. Accompanying this closeness will be a multitude of regrets covering the past nature of the relationship, such as "I wish I had only . . ." or "Why did I ever . . . ?" Many of these regrets are unavoidable, but the individuals involved don't have to indulge or wallow in them! If regrets are causing a marriage partner to feel angry, guilty, and depressed, he should take them to God in prayer, confess what he did (or didn't do) and accept God's forgiveness.

God can deal with negative emotions far more effectively than can family members. Each spouse should find time to be alone with God and reserve some of his doubts and discouragements for His ears alone. Whether the guilt is real or imagined, it can be dispelled by forgiveness. When the individual has received the strength and comfort God has promised, he will be doubly able to strengthen and encourage his spouse and his family.

Sometimes an individual will also find it necessary to confess a sin to his spouse and receive forgiveness. However, let me caution someone in this situation to think before he confesses the burdensome knowledge of some "secret sin" (I'm referring to attitudes of heart and mind that hurt as well as to physical infidelity) to his spouse. In many instances, the spouse will not need to know about it, and it can be settled between the individual and God.

Budget Time and Energy

Time and energy are both precious resources during the terminal phase of an illness. Both the healthy and the sick individuals should budget time and energy carefully, making sure that there is enough to invest in their relationship with each other. A wife who is terminally ill can learn to budget her energy (by trial and error) so that she has the emotional reserve to meet her husband's needs. Being relieved of some of the household chores and the responsibility of planning and running the family's activities will allow her to apply her energy to encouraging and supporting her husband and family. A terminally ill husband who has been relieved of the pressures and responsibilities of his job can turn his attention and energy to encouraging his wife and family and giving his wife the approval and support she needs.

Both individuals should plan and schedule many of the "spontaneous" acts of caring and tenderness in their marriage during this time. They must set aside times for physical closeness, times to talk, times for special meals for two, times to listen to a concert or special records, times to watch a favorite television program, times to read poetry or the Sunday comic section together, or times for similar activities. If "together" times aren't planned and carried out, both individuals may miss out on the love and sharing they would like and need.

Recognize the Need for Physical Closeness

I don't think it's possible to overemphasize the value of physical closeness. At times, we must be absent from those we love, no matter how much we wish we could be with them. However, many of us avoid a sick individual because we "don't know what to say or do." In general, we feel useless and superfluous. Yet, it is often enough just to be there. To sit quietly beside a hospital bed may seem insignificant, but often it means more to the sick individual than we can imagine.

Jane Jones was a pretty, scared, and lonely young lady. A tumor had been removed from her spinal cord shortly before we were called to examine her, and her outlook wasn't good. Although we tried various means of treatment, her tumor soon recurred. She suffered excruciating back pain, severe headaches, progressive weakness of her legs, and complete paralysis from the waist down. She also lost control of her bowels and bladder and required constant care.

There was never a clearcut diagnosis of Jane's case, since each of the doctors who was caring for her had a slightly different opinion about her illness. Although no doctor openly contradicted any of the others, Jane was aware of the uncertainty. "I wish I could be more sure that I'm getting the right treatment for my tumor," she told me one day. "It's so confusing. You tell me one thing; Dr. Ellis tells me something slightly different; Dr. Warren's opinion is still something different. Do you think I'll ever be well again?"

Up to that point, I hadn't met John, her husband. Jane told me that he was "busy" and that he telephoned her every night. However, I sensed her loneliness and her longing to see him. One day, Mrs. Jones,

Jane's mother-in-law, came to me in tears. "Do something about Johnny!" she said. "He hasn't been to the hospital to visit once since Jane was admitted two weeks ago, and Jane is getting desperate."

I telephoned John several times during the next two days and finally reached him when he wasn't out on a service call. He seemed nice enough on the telephone but was a bit shy. "Could you come to the hospital to visit Jane?" I asked, after telling him who I was.

"Well, I get off work at 6:00," he answered, "and I would barely get there before visiting hours are over."

"It's certainly not that long a drive, is it? I think you easily could get here by 6:30 and have dinner with Jane."

"Oh, but I couldn't come straight from work! I work as a mechanic, and that's dirty work! I would have to go home and get cleaned up first."

I reassured John that no one would mind if he came to the hospital directly from the garage. "Jane really needs you. If it's necessary, we can even give you special visiting privileges after hours."

John came to the hospital three times that week, and Jane was almost a different person. She was much more relaxed and peaceful, and her pain was easily controlled with moderate doses of narcotics.

I telephoned John again to thank him for visiting Jane. "She's having a lot less pain now," I told him, "and she's sleeping a lot better, too."

John was embarrassed and ill at ease. "I don't really do anything," he said quietly. "I don't know what to talk to her about, and mostly I just sit there. Do you really think it makes a difference if I come?"

I told John again that Jane was needing less pain medicine and was sleeping better now that he was visiting her. "You don't really have to say anything," I continued. "All she wants is for you to be there, to know that you care."

The message must have gotten through. After that, whenever I was in the hospital late in the evening, I'd see John sitting by Jane's bedside. Sometimes he held her hand. Sometimes he read his copy of *Popular Mechanics*. Sometimes he just sat there, half asleep. But he continued visiting his wife.

The nurses kept in touch with him. When Jane had a bad night, they told him, and he would try to stop by before he went to work. When she became concerned about their children and what would happen to them after her death, John took several days off work and got her will in order. He still didn't say much, but he managed to visit at least three times a week. That was enough for Jane, and he was able to be with her just before she died.

More than a year after Jane's death, John telephoned our office. "I just wanted you to know that the kids and I are doing okay," he said quietly. "Thank you for all you did for Jane."

In cases in which a husband has been holding his wife when she died, or vice versa, that moment has been something the survivor has remembered with comfort and gratitude. Also, I've noticed that patients who tend to be restless, or in pain, or have trouble sleeping, do much better when someone they love is in the room with them. This is particularly true if the husband or wife is present. These patients actually need less medication during the times their spouses are with them.

Realize the Importance of Touch

It is important for the husband and wife facing terminal illness to touch, hold, and caress each other, and especially to use words that express tenderness and love. When a spouse is terminally ill, both partners tend to feel isolated and very much alone, and they each carry a great burden of responsibility. The assurance that the other partner cares for him, loves him, needs him, and in some sense shares and understands his burdens can make the way much easier. There are times when a touch conveys much more than can be said in words.

From time to time, couples ask me about intercourse, and, to my surprise, I have learned that they have avoided it unnecessarily. Although physical intercourse may not always be possible—due to side effects of medication, surgery, radiation, the disease itself—it may be possible. The well individual may also be concerned about the comfort and sexual enjoyment of the sick partner. Usually, in my experience, the well individual would like to have intercourse but is afraid it will hurt or harm his partner. On the other hand, the sick individual may want to have intercourse and be quite bewildered by his partner's lack of interest! Obviously, there is a need for better communication here.

If one partner doesn't feel free to express his desires and needs to his spouse, I suggest that he discuss the issue with his (or his partner's) doctor, nurse, pastor, or someone else who could counsel or advise him. Of course, if there is any question about the advisability of intercourse, he should consult the doctor most familiar with the situation.

GUIDELINES FOR THE HEALTHY SPOUSE

There are several important guidelines concerning the effects of terminal illness on marriage that specifically apply to the healthy spouse.

Prepare to Become Single

As the husband-wife bond loosens, the surviving spouse must deal with the deep loss he will feel, not only of a partner but also of a large part of himself. The deeper the marriage bond, the more "self" the survivor will lose. Shared jokes, memories, habits, rituals, and all the "together" aspects of married life will be lost when the partner dies. The survivor must be willing to accept this loss, discover his new self, and begin making a new life for himself.

This principle is particularly important when the terminally ill individual is an invalid or semi-invalid or when he is hospitalized. The well individual needs to schedule time off from visiting his spouse. He should make arrangements for a friend, another family member (not one of the children), or even a hired sitter to take over for several hours a week so that he can have time for himself and for the rest of the family.

Remember That He Is Not Alone

There is no requirement that the healthy spouse handle all his problems and crises alone. His own extended family, church, friends, and specific community resources are all designed to be of help to him in his need. A time of crisis is a particularly good time to experience the warmth and concern of the family and the love that exists within the body of Christ. He mustn't rob himself of this love and comfort by refusing to ask for help.

Do Not Become Overinvolved With the Children

As the surviving partner makes plans to resume life as a "single" individual, there is a danger (particularly on the part of mothers) of overinvolvement with the children. The temptation for the healthy parent to submerge himself in his children will be supported by a feeling of obligation toward them, since he soon will be the only parent they have left. He must remember, however, that the goal of successful parenting is to produce mature, independent adults who can leave their parent to lead their own lives. Relaxation of discipline, overindulgence, and overprotectiveness cost too much in terms of the insecurity they give the children and the time and energy they rob from the healthy parent. The remaining parent must set aside time for himself and his own interests apart from the parental role as much as it is feasible, both before and after the death of his spouse.

When there are no children at home, there is no need to preserve the family circle for them. Although close ties with grown children are sometimes possible, often the children will be scattered across the country and involved with families, jobs, and other pursuits that make it impossible for a parent to tighten the parent-child bonds even if he wants to.

WHEN THE CHILDREN OF A DYING INDIVIDUAL ARE GROWN

The first thing I noticed about the Smiths was that they seemed to be a devoted couple. Joe always came into the office with Mary, and they always carried on an animated discussion during the whole time they were there. In fact, they never seemed to run out of things to say to one another. I also noticed the way they enjoyed each other's company.

Mary had widespread cancer of the colon. A year and a half after surgery she had a recurrence, followed by evidence of tumor in the lungs three months after that. My husband and I began treating her at that time with a considerable amount of success.

Joe, a retired businessman, thoroughly enjoyed his retirement. He loved to work around the house and lavished hours of loving care on his garden. He also enjoyed the free time he had to go fishing or hunting with his friends.

The first winter Mary was on treatment she got the "flu" and became severaly ill. For four days, she was unable to keep anything down, and we hospitalized her. Joe was frightened. At first, he was there twenty-four hours a day, sitting by her bedside. When one of the nursing staff came in to care for her, he offered to help. Soon he was watching her intravenous feedings, taking care of her bedpans, serving and clearing her meal trays, and helping in countless other ways. During her third day in the hospital, Mary was able to eat, with help. By the fifth day, she was out of bed and sitting in a chair. After a week, she and Joe were taking short walks up and down the hall. Two weeks after her admission, she was home, looking well-rested and much better.

The next eight months passed quickly. Mary came into the office periodically for treatment, and Joe was always with her. She felt well and was able to continue keeping house. Joe kept up the garden and kept ahead of the odd jobs around the house.

The inevitable relapse finally came when Mary developed new tumor in the liver. Although we used another form of treatment, Mary became weaker and weaker. She was able to do less and less around the house and also ate less.

One day, Joe came in. "Dr. Ruth," he said, pacing back and forth, "Mary just isn't eating! I can't seem to fix anything she likes (and, you know, I'm a pretty fair cook). I don't know what to feed her. What should I try to feed her to get her strength up?"

"Well, you know that she might not get much better," I answered. "Still, a high protein diet would be worth a try." Joe and I discussed the various way he could add extra protein to his wife's diet. I was impressed with the quick understanding he had of the diet I suggested and the remarkably sound suggestions he had to offer. Soon he had Mary eating and even enjoying her meals again! When she ate, she became stronger.

Again, things remained stable for six or eight weeks. Then, during one office visit, Joe came to me. "I'm really worried this time, Dr. Ruth.

Mary's so sleepy and confused all the time, and she seems to be getting yellow. What do I do now?"

I examined Mary. It was true, she was quite jaundiced and slightly confused. Her liver was about the same size, however, and I didn't think her condition was quite as bad as she looked. "Joe, I think it's time to cut down on the protein in her diet. Her liver has gotten worse, and it just can't handle that much protein anymore."

Joe telephoned two days later. "Dr. Ruth," he exclaimed, "you can't believe the change in Mary! I did what you said, and now she's completely alert. Her color's even better."

Finally, however, Joe could no longer take care of Mary at home. She was experiencing some pain and was too weak to get up by herself. Joe was all alone at home, and he wasn't quite strong enough to lift her up and down by himself.

The Smiths' single daughter, Jenny, was a schoolteacher downstate. She took a leave of absence and came home. She and Joe took turns staying with Mary in the hospital. One of them would stay there all day, and the other one would spend the night. Joe was still very attentive. When Mary needed oxygen, he got it for her. When she needed a bedpan, he got it. When she was restless and discouraged, he sat by her bed, holding her or stroking her hand or her forehead.

Mary lingered. I began to notice that Joe was taking a "break" now and then. First one afternoon a week, then a couple of times a week, Joe would leave. He asked me if it was all right and explained, "I don't want to do anything that wouldn't be good for Mary. But as long as Jenny is here, I like to go out now and then to go to a movie, putter in the garden, or fix the garage door. You don't think it will hurt her, do you?" I assured Joe that this would be fine and was, in fact, good for him. It seemed to me that he had a healthy balance between his concern for Mary and his beginning a new life for himself.

Mary died one night, quietly. Joe was sitting by her side, and she began to choke. Quickly he took her into his arms and gave her oxygen. "She breathed easily a time or two and then looked at me as if to say 'good-by,'" he told me later. "Then she was gone."

Joe had many things to attend to immediately after Mary's death. It wasn't an easy time for him. However, he had already begun the adjustment. Mary hadn't lived in their home for several weeks; he had begun going out and doing some things for himself before she died. He had made plans for the future and was able to begin carrying them out.

DISSOLVING THE MARRIAGE

The balance between maintaining the husband-wife relationship and gradually severing the marriage bond will vary from family to family. It is not likely to be a completely smooth transition and is more likely to be a "backwards and forwards" movement than a steadily progressive dissolution of the marriage bond. There seems to be a tendency during the course of terminal illness, from what I have observed, for the husband-wife type of bond to be replaced by a parent-child type of bond in which the well individual assumes a maternal role and the sick individual assumes a child's role. The well partner "mothers" the sick one—cooking for him, caring for him, dressing and undressing him, sometimes bathing him—assuming the duties that a mother undertakes for a small child. The relationship also tends to become less verbal, with more communication by touch and holding than by an exchange of words and ideas. Conversations are simpler, shorter, and less frequent. Perhaps this change from husband-wife to mother-child relationship is a major step in loosening the tie between the two individuals, making the final separation easier. Of course, the substitution is rarely complete, and there is often a large part of the husband-wife role left even at the end.

In many cases, the actual date of death on the death certificate is weeks or even months after the death of the marriage. Particularly in cases where there is mental deterioration or personality change due to illness, the "husband" or "wife" known to the spouse is already gone, even if the individual is still alive.

An effective period of preparatory grief can sometimes fulfill the task of loosening the marriage bond and can accomplish almost all of the mourning. Since this period varies widely from individual to individual, some people who "get over it" too soon have actually had a head start on their mourning and have finished with it sooner than those around them expected. So, while the terminally ill individual withdraws slowly from the world, the one who is to be left will begin the work of rebuilding his life. This seems to be particularly true in cases where the remaining spouse has done all he could to care for the ill one and is able to see himself as adequate without having regrets or feeling overwhelming guilt. Remarriage does not necessarily demonstrate a lack of love or consideration for the one who died. Sometimes it evidences the completeness of the work of mourning and the success in breaking ties with the past.

As an individual involved in the course of a terminal illness admits his own needs and accepts the help his partner (well or ill) can provide, he becomes better able to help the partner. In this way, he finds fulfillment of his needs and gains a position of usefulness. Honest communication of feelings and needs is the tool by which individuals maintain love, support, and respect throughout the shifting roles and difficult work of a terminal illness.

SECTION FOUR

RESPONSES TO TERMINAL ILLNESS

13

THE CHRISTIAN'S RESPONSE TO TERMINAL ILLNESS

WHEN THE TRUE nature of their terminal illness sinks in, many Christians are overwhelmed with their absolute helplessness before a cruel and unjust fate. They feel vulnerable and powerless, and these feelings lead to frustration and anger. They look to God for help and may find that He is silent. No one hears their prayers, answers their pleadings, or helps them in their hour of need. They've done everything they can, and now their very lives are in someone else's hands. They are dependent on doctors, drugs, and treatments that are usually foreign to them. They are helpless even to judge the competence of those who are now making major decisions about their treatment that affect the length and quality of their lives. Is it any wonder they cry out in helplessness, desperation, and anger, "My God, my God! Where are You? Why have You left me alone like this? Why have You forsaken me?" Christians facing terminal illness are subject to the same emotions, fears, and psychological reactions as those who are not Christians.

As children of God, Christians have the sobering responsibility to live the type of lives God the Father wants them to live. Using what might be termed "parental discipline," God seeks to perfect the image of Jesus Christ in Christians. In addition, their spiritual nature grows and develops as their fellowship with God and other Christians deepens. This fellowship opens up the vast resource of Scripture to Christians, who can use it as a guide and can help them face crisis situations. They can be assured that Jesus Christ understands them, is interested in their problems, and is willing and able to come to their aid.

THE CONCEPT OF CHRISTIAN "REWARD"

Accompanying the concept of the parent-child relationship between God and His people is the concept that He punishes "bad behavior" and rewards those who are "good." Christians have the idea that God's favor automatically brings safety, security, a good reputation, good health, material prosperity, and long life. When physical health fails and death seems imminent, Christians automatically ask, What did I do wrong? What is my sin? Why am I being punished?

Christian friends, who have similar assumptions about the outward signs and manifestations of God's favor, may further compound the terminally ill individual's feelings of dismay and confusion. "Confess your sins and have faith," they may say when illness and disaster strike. They may even suggest that the individual should "get back into fellowship with God." If the one who is ill or in trouble holds to slightly different beliefs or practices, some of his Christian associates and friends may automatically jump to the conclusion that "Harry never was a Christian" and spend their time and energy trying to convert him. In order to see whether or not this system of "Christian reward and punishment" is a correct interpretation of scriptural principles, let's examine some people who "found favor with God."

Mary

Mary, the mother of Jesus, had God's approval. The angel Gabriel, in Luke 1:28, declared to Mary, "Greetings, you who are highly favored! The Lord is with you." Gabriel went on to describe to Mary the specific way in which God's favor would become evident in her life. "You will be with child and give birth to a son, and you are to give him the name Jesus. He will be great and will be called the Son of the Most High."

Startled, Mary asked, "How will this be, since I am a virgin?"

Gabriel replied, "The Holy Spirit will come upon you, and the power of the Most High will overshadow you. So the holy one to be born will be called the Son of God."

Mary, remember, lived in a strict society where the penalty for adultery was death by stoning. Joseph, already betrothed to Mary, knew that he was not the father of her child. He had every legal and moral right to deliver her to the Jewish court of law and have her stoned for infidelity. Even if he went ahead and married her, her firstborn son would always bear the stigma of illegitimacy. Indeed, the Scribes and Pharisees taunted Jesus during His public ministry. "We are not illegitimate children," they said. "The only Father we have is God himself" (John 8:41). Yet Mary was "highly favored."

Job

In Job 1:8, we learn that God also favored Job. "There is no one on earth like him," God said. "He is blameless and upright, a man who fears God and shuns evil." Yet, we know how Job was "rewarded" for his faithfulness. His crops were destroyed, his livestock was decimated, his children were killed, and he was afflicted with open, draining, stinking, painful boils.

As Job sat on his ruined estate—enduring the deaths of his children, aching, heartsore, wishing he had never been born—his three friends immediately jumped to the conclusion that his condition was

God's punishment for some terrible sin. They "comforted" him by assuring him that God was just and would not allow these terrible things to happen unless he deserved them! Even his wife deserted him in his hour of need. "Are you still holding on to your integrity?" she asked him. "Curse God and die!" (2:9) In effect, she was saying, "What's the use of your faith? Why don't you just give up and get this over with?" Yet, Job had done nothing wrong in God's eyes.

Christ

In talking with His Father, Jesus said, "I have brought you glory on earth by completing the work you gave me to do" (John 17:4). In Matthew 17:5, we read that God was well-pleased with Jesus. Even though Jesus always did those things that pleased His Father, He was "rewarded" with His humiliating death on the cross. He endured physical pain and anguish alone, and His closest earthly friends, as well as His Father, turned their backs on Him during the hour of His greatest need. Only after the agony of Good Friday did Jesus achieve the triumph of Easter Sunday.

How Does God Deal With His Children?

Based on these examples from Scripture, we can draw several conclusions about how rewards and punishment relate to illness and death. First, we must acknowledge that we see only part of the picture. In many instances, that which is yet to come may completely change the entire picture. God has clearly told us that His ways are not our ways and that His thoughts are above ours (Isa. 55:8, 9).

Second, we must recognize the difference between punishment and discipline. Webster's Dictionary defines discipline as: "1. INSTRUCTION, 3. training or experience that corrects, molds or perfects the mental faculties or moral character."* The definition for punishment is: "1. to impose a restraint or penalty (as of shame, suffering, strict restraint, or loss) upon for some fault, offense, or violation."** While discipline can and usually does involve punishment, there is more to discipline than its punitive aspect.

This principle holds true in God's dealings with us as His children, as evidenced in Hebrews 2:5–18. There, the writer of Hebrews discusses Jesus and His superiority over the angels and establishes the difference in the way God dealt with His Son and with the angels. Part of the difference lies in the fact that God allowed Jesus to suffer. "In bringing many sons to glory, it was fitting that God, for whom and through whom everything exists, should make the author of their salvation perfect through suffering" (2:10). Since we know that Jesus was

---

*Webster's Third New International Dictionary, p. 644
**Ibid., p. 1843

sinless, His suffering was not a punishment brought about by a violation of God's laws. Rather, Jesus learned obedience "from what he suffered" (5:8), for the suffering molded and perfected His character.

In short, God may permit us to endure illness, suffering, and death as part of His program to perfect in us the attributes He wants us to have. In Hebrews 12:5–7, the writer emphasizes the necessity of discipline. "My son, do not make light of the Lord's discipline, and do not lose heart when he rebukes you, because the Lord disciplines those he loves, and he punishes everyone he accepts as a son. Endure hardship as discipline; God is treating you as sons. For what son is not disciplined by his father?"

The Comfort of Christ's Example

Jesus Himself faced the cross in the spirit of, "Oh, no, not this!" In the Garden of Gethsemane, He pleaded with the Father to let "this cup" pass from Him, untasted (Matt. 26:39). He asked to be spared. His revulsion at the thought of the undignified, cruel death on the cross can be compared to the horror many of us have of the debilitating, disfiguring, and incapacitating features of terminal cancer, heart or kidney disease, or other diseases. Christ's victory was demonstrated in the words, "Yet not my will, but yours be done" (Luke 22:42).

I am convinced that Jesus' submission to His Father's will was made in trust and love, not out of a sense of defeated resignation. Throughout His life, Christ evidenced a remarkable ability to take things as they came, living life a moment at a time. From the Garden of Gethsemane to the cross, the cross to the tomb, and out of the tomb to the glory of the Resurrection, Jesus took things one at a time. His confidence in His Father was not misplaced. Easter Sunday dawned bright and triumphant after the gloomy darkness of Good Friday. Christ was not spared the agony of crucifixion; the glorious victory of the Resurrection was His reward for His faithfulness to death.

As Christians, we can look to Christ for our hope and encouragement. His example in suffering, His confident submission to the Father's will, and His ultimate, triumphant vindication through the Resurrection are examples of His faithfulness. Whatever suffering and agony we must endure, we are assured of His presence. Our resurrection, when we will be clothed with an incorruptible, pain-free, and immortal body like His, is our future hope.

Meanwhile, our business is to trust God and submit to that which He gives us to bear. In obedience, we follow Jesus, who Himself was perfected by the things He suffered (Heb. 2:10). Knowing that God is working to perfect us in the image of His Son, we can more easily submit, obey, and endure the moments and hours of approaching death.

THE CHRISTIAN'S CONCEPT OF PRAYER AND HEALING

There are many Scripture references concerning prayer that Christians can cling to in a desperate situation. In John 14:14, for example, Jesus says, "You may ask me for anything in my name, and I will do it." We read in James 5:14, 15, "Is any one of you sick? He should call the elders of the church to pray over him and anoint him with oil in the name of the Lord. And the prayer offered in faith will make the sick person well; the Lord will raise him up. If he has sinned, he will be forgiven."

It is easy for us as Christians to feel guilty of hidden sin or to berate ourselves for our lack of faith if we pray for healing and are not healed. We remember the words of the psalmist in Psalm 66:18: "If I had cherished sin in my heart, the Lord would not have listened." We remember Jesus' statement in Matthew 21:21, 22: "I tell you the truth, if you have faith and do not doubt, not only can you do what was done to the fig tree, but also you can say to this mountain, 'Go, throw yourself into the sea,' and it will be done. If you believe, you will receive whatever you ask for in prayer." We may "confess our healing" in the face of evidence to the contrary, as we saw in the chapter on healing, trying to have faith and to believe so that we may be healed. If by chance we manage to overlook these Scriptures, we can be sure that friends and family members will point them out to us!

Christians throughout the ages have had to face the fact that God does not heal everyone who prays for healing. Hebrews 11 answers my questions concerning lack of faith and sin in the lives of those who suffer death and torture. In verses 38–40, we read, "The world was not worthy of them. They wandered in deserts and mountains, and in caves and holes in the ground. These were all commended for their faith, yet none of them received what had been promised. God had planned something better for us so that only together with us would they be made perfect."

These verses were written after the author listed many people who obtained great things of God and endured hard things through faith. Some were tortured; some were bound and imprisoned; some were stoned to death, sawed in two, or put to death. Obviously, their faith did not guarantee them deliverance. Since they had all received a "good report," I find it hard to believe that their lack of deliverance was a result of sin in their lives or that their trials were punishments for sin. On the contrary, their trials occurred because of their faith. With this point in mind, I find it easier to understand why the Lord doesn't give me or someone else physical health.

In James 4:3, we read, "When you ask, you do not receive, because you ask with wrong motives, that you may spend what you get on your pleasures." Before we consider our lack of healing as an evidence of "guilt," we should look at it in conjunction with the above discussion on God's discipline. Our requests for deliverance from our physical, emotional, and/or spiritual trials may be misguided in terms of the training and character development God plans for us. Perhaps our desire to escape a particular situation conflicts with His design to mold and form in us the image of Christ. If Jesus learned obedience by the things He suffered, then we—as His followers—should not necessarily expect our lessons to be any easier.

Why Me?

As we've seen, when a person learns he has a fatal illness, he is numbed by disbelief. Then the awful truth breaks through the denial. He stops saying "I can't believe this is really happening!" and the questions come pouring out as he realizes the facts of his physical state. "Why me? What have I done to deserve this? Why?"

The psalmist David, in Psalm 22:1, 2, 6, expresses that feeling well when he writes, "My God, my God, why have you forsaken me? Why are you so far from saving me, so far from the words of my groaning? O my God, I cry out by day, but you do not answer, by night, and am not silent. But I am a worm and not a man, scorned by men and despised by the people" (see Matt. 27:46; Mark 15:34).

As Christians, we seem to have a host of answers to the question, "Why me?" As we begin to search our past and present, we come across all the things we have done that we shouldn't have done and all the things we ought to have done that we left undone. Soon our answer to the question, "Why me?" becomes "Why not me?" We begin to feel that we are only receiving what we deserve and should not have expected anything better, realizing that we are guilty and deserve to suffer for our sins.

In this frame of mind, it is easy for us to focus on God as the just Judge, totally forgetting about His love and mercy. The doctrine of original sin then takes precedence over the doctrine of the Atonement. Instead of finding comfort and succor in our faith, we discover that it has become a tool to torment us, to remind us of our unworthiness. At this point, our faith seems to slam the door on our hope, for we begin to believe that we are totally unworthy to ask God for help. *Why should He listen to someone like me?* we reason.

In order to better understand the complex feelings and beliefs that a Christian placed in this position experiences, let's examine what happened to Joanne Young, an attractive woman in her mid-fifties. She led an orderly, well-organized life and had raised two sons and two daughters who were a credit to her. Although her life hadn't been easy, her faith in God had sustained her through difficult times. Fifteen years earlier, for example, her husband, Bill, had been involved in a terrible auto accident that severely injured his spinal cord and left him helpless, unable to care for himself. For five years, Joanne had nursed him while caring for her four teenagers. During the sixth winter after the accident, Bill died.

Joanne continued living without complaining. Not only did she continue to run her house and care for her children, she also began caring for an elderly aunt in her home. Aunt Ellen had suffered a stroke and was moderately disabled. She could get around in a wheelchair and care for herself, but she couldn't help with the housework. Furthermore, she had "bad days" when she was almost impossible to get along with!

Joanne kept going. One daughter, Peg, married and moved away from home. Lisa, the other daughter, was nearly through school, engaged to be married, and planned to remain in her home town. David, the eldest son, finished college and went to work as an electronics engineer, while Rick, the youngest, was in his final year of college and planned to become a teacher. Everything appeared to be going well until Joanne discovered a lump in her breast a week before Lisa's wedding. In an almost absent-minded way, she made a doctor's appointment and continued with the wedding plans. Even though her doctor wanted to operate sooner, she pleaded with him to schedule the biopsy for the day after the wedding. "Another couple of days won't make that much difference," she told him. "Lisa's getting married only once."

The biopsy was just the beginning for Joanne. Since the small lump was malignant, surgery was extended and she had a mastectomy. "There's almost a 100 percent chance for a cure," her doctor told her. "The cancer was so small that I'm sure we got it all, even without the extensive surgery. There certainly is no need for any further treatment at this point! Just be sure that you come in for a checkup every six months, and you should be okay."

When Joanne got home from the hospital, she couldn't believe that she had had breast cancer. Only the sight of her lopsided chest while changing clothes served to remind her.

Spring passsed into summer and summer into fall. Joanne found out that Lisa was expecting and began to make preparations for the new baby—her first grandchild. One day while helping Aunt Ellen move into the wheelchair from the bed, Joanne got a sharp, excruciating pain in the small of her back. "I thought at the time that I had strained a muscle," she explained later, "and I knew that it would go away so I didn't do anything about it." She lay down with a heating pad on her back for several hours and was careful for the next three days whenever she lifted anything.

Her back didn't improve, however, and Aunt Ellen noticed that

Joanne was limping and seemed to be in pain. "Jo, you'd better go see a doctor about that," she scolded. "I think you're getting worse instead of better."

The next day, Lisa dropped by for a visit. "Mom, what's wrong with your back? Have you seen a doctor?" When Joanne admitted that she hadn't, Lisa also scolded her. So Joanne telephoned Dr. Cummings, and he asked her to have x-rays of her back and a bone scan taken before he saw her. "That way," he said, "I'll have all the information at hand and you won't need to come in a second time."

When Joanne entered Dr. Cummings' office, she still wasn't worried. It never occurred to her that her pain had anything to do with her breast cancer. She later told me, "By then, incredible as it seems, I'd almost forgotten about my mastectomy. Everything was going to be all right, and I had stopped thinking about it. I felt so well," she continued, "and how could I feel so well all the while the cancer was growing? Wouldn't you think that I'd have had some warning, some premonition?"

Gentle and sympathetic, Dr. Cummings looked grave and concerned when he came in to see her and had nothing but bad news. "Joanne, it looks like we didn't get that lump out in time. There's a spot in your spine that is a tumor, and several other spots are also suspicious."

Joanne almost didn't hear what he said. "You mean, it's cancer?" she asked. "My backache is caused by cancer? But why? Why me? How did this happen?" She was thinking, *I'm hearing wrong. In a minute, he'll explain things and I won't have to worry about cancer any more.*

Instead, Dr. Cummings scheduled her for several additional tests and then made an appointment for her with me. "For an opinion and probably for chemotherapy," he told Joanne, "I think it best that you go to Dr. Kopp."

Joanne had the additional tests done, and was still walking around in a daze. At home, she functioned mechanically. When someone asked her something, she would take several minutes to answer and often the question had to be repeated three times before she could understand it. "I was lost in a fog. All I could think about," she told me, "was that there was cancer in my bones that shouldn't be there. And I kept telling myself, 'It's not true. There's a mistake. They got the wrong x-rays. Any minute now I'm going to wake up.'"

When I finally saw Joanne several weeks later, she was still dazed and I had more bad news for her. "There is tumor in your liver as well as in the bones," I said quietly, "and it's time to start treatment." I explained the drugs that we use to treat breast cancer.

"Why me?" she burst out, her fists clenched. "It was so small when they took it out! How could it spread?"

I waited for her to calm down and talked with her awhile. Then I repeated my recommendations. "Mrs. Young, you don't have to decide now, but I would like to know your decision when you come back a week from today. I would like to see you get started on treatment without further delay." When Joanne left my office, I felt that she at last understood the diagnosis, although she was not ready to decide what to do next.

Joanne's next move wasn't surprising. Three days after she left my office, she telephoned to ask me to send her records to a university-affiliated medical center in Chicago. "I need another opinion," she stated, "and a little more time to think."

I didn't hear from Joanne for three months. The medical center suggested an operation as an alternative to chemotherapy, and she agreed to undergo surgery. After surgery, complications began. Her blood pressure dropped every time she sat up or stood up, making her dizzy and weak. After this was controlled, she developed a high fever that lasted nearly a week. Then she experienced severe nausea, vomiting, and diarrhea.

Meanwhile, her back pain was getting worse instead of better. When she complained to her doctors, they put her off. Finally, she angrily insisted on a repeat bone scan, x-rays, and a liver scan. The test results were worse than she had expected. The operation had been a complete failure, and she would have to start chemotherapy immediately with the added disadvantages of dizziness and her recent operation to complicate things. "I'm going back to Dr. Kopp," she told her doctors. "At least that way I can be treated near home." The doctors made arrangements to move her to another hospital near home, and I examined her a few days later.

For the first few days, everything went smoothly. Then something changed. Although none of us on the hospital staff could put a finger on anything specific, we found that Joanne was an upsetting patient. "I don't like to complain, Dr. Kopp," she would tell me as I made my rounds, "but that Dalmane isn't a good sleeping pill for me. I found in Chicago that I had to have Nembutal by injection before I could sleep, and if I can't sleep there's no way I can feel any better."

The next day it would be something else. "Dr. Ruth, do I have to ask for pain pills? In Chicago, they gave them to me every four hours and that seemed to work better. Here, if I need one and ask for it, I may have to wait almost forty-five minutes for it and by then the pain really gets severe."

The nurses, too, experienced constant problems in caring for her. "Can you send this tray back and get me a hot dinner? I don't feel like eating anyhow, and cold food is impossible to get down." Or she would say, "I can't get up in my chair now. Can't we do that later?"

Although Joanne was responding well to chemotherapy, she wasn't getting any better, in her opinion. She "never had a good night's sleep," her appetite "was always poor," and she seldom reported feeling well at all. As her x-rays and laboratory tests improved, we made plans to send her home and met with steady, defiant resistance. "Aunt Ellen can't take care of me," she would say, "and I'm certainly in no shape to care for her." Or, she would state, "Lisa's just had a baby, and you can't expect her to be able to help me!"

On and on went the objections. In her mind, she could not possibly go home! By this time, I had noticed that her family didn't visit very often. The nurses avoided the room whenever possible. I, too, had a tendency to miss seeing Joanne on rounds if I could justify it. Finally, my husband and I had had enough of the situation. There was no reason why we shouldn't be able to work out a way by which Joanne could receive care at home, and there was no reason why everyone around her should have to put up with her thinly veiled hostility any longer.

One morning we both went into her room and sat down. "Mrs. Young," Jim said, "I don't know if you realize it, but you arouse a lot of hostility in the people who are caring for you."

"Dr. Kopp, I don't know what you mean! I try not to be a bother. But when I'm nauseated all the time and can't sleep at night, I don't see how I can be getting any better."

"How do you feel about being here in bed, with cancer, and feeling that it would be impossible for you to go home?" he asked her.

"I feel awful. I'm nauseated most of the time. You know, I haven't been getting my Compazine before meals the way I was before. I really think that that would help."

"Mrs. Young," I interrupted, "you didn't answer the question. How do you feel about being sick, bedridden, and alone? If I were in your position, I think I'd be upset and lonely, maybe even angry."

Again Joanne changed the subject. "I have so much trouble sleeping at night. When Lisa went home at 8:00 last night, I asked for my Nembutal. You know when I got it? It was almost ten o'clock! By then I was wide awake, and I couldn't settle down for hours."

"Mrs. Young, how did that make you feel? Don't you ever feel that this is unfair? Don't you ever feel hurt and angry and upset? I would."

Joanne's eyes filled with tears. Barely whispering, she said, "I can't understand it! I've tried to be a good Christian. I took good care of my husband. I've taken the best care I could of Aunt Ellen. Why this? Why now?"

I nodded. "It doesn't seem fair, does it?"

Joanne went on, crying and talking loudly and angrily. "The kids had just grown up. I was ready to have time for myself. I've spent all my life taking care of other people, and when I finally have a chance for myself I get cancer. Why?"

Jim moved closer and took her hand. "I know it's hard to understand, but if you ask God, maybe He will help you understand things a bit better. We are promised a better understanding in the future, however, when we will be with Him and see Him face to face."

We talked some more about Joanne's children and how she hoped they would help care for her, about Aunt Ellen and what to do with her, and about practical matters—a visiting nurse to help care for her at home, house calls instead of office visits until she became stronger, arrangements for meals and housekeeping services.

Three days later, Joanne went home! She was excited about the prospect of being home again and anxious to be on her own as soon as possible. Gradually she recovered her strength and energy. Lisa began bringing Chuck, the new grandson, over nearly every day and helped look after her mother and the house. Joanne learned to walk again, taking her first steps the same time Chuck was taking his.

THE CHRISTIAN'S FEAR OF DEATH

We must remember that the Bible calls death an enemy, and the Christian who faces death with reluctance or fear is not necessarily weak in his faith. One does not run to the door and fling it open to allow an enemy to enter!

The apostle Paul himself confessed to being torn between the desire to die and be with Christ and the need to continue his work in the churches. He wrote, in Philippians 1:22–24, "If I am to go on living in the body, this will mean fruitful labor for me. Yet what shall I choose? I do not know! I am torn between the two: I desire to depart and be with Christ, which is better by far; but it is more necessary for you that I remain in the body." Paul was unmarried, single-mindedly devoted to the work of the Lord. His ties to earth were the churches that needed him and his spiritual children. If we add the concerns for a spouse and family that most terminally ill individuals have, we can understand how the conflict of desire is even stronger.

It is, of course, necessary for the Christian to find courage and strength in facing death through his faith because of the nature of the enemy he faces. Although the Christian stands to gain much after death, there are still tremendous losses as well. If he denies his human needs to fall in line with a concept of "spirituality," he is robbed of his humanness and his Christian faith is deprived of its vigorous, robust human character. Only as he faces death realistically, in all its horror, can he see the true magnitude of Christ's triumph in the Resurrection, the true glory of God's promises, and the true grandeur of the God who has so amply supplied *all* his needs.

Strength of God's Sovereignty

There is one final area in which the Christian faith speaks to us, as Christians, who are trying to cope with terminal illness. When everything is out of control and we seem to be drifting along without a sense of direction in a nightmare, the doctrine of the sovereignty of God becomes meaningful. We are helpless to do anything on our own behalf; we are at the mercy of strangers for our treatment and the outcome of our illness. Our ability to plan for the future has been wiped out completely. What a comfort in the midst of all this to turn to a God who is in control! Psalm 104 speaks of God's control over the natural world—His might in the heavens. His power over clouds and wind, His founding of the earth and establishing boundaries for the seas, His provision for the beasts and birds with their need for food, water, and shelter, His control over the crops and growing plants, and His ordering of the heavenly bodies. The theme of the second psalm, which speaks of God's power over the rulers of the world and His control over the affairs of men, is reiterated throughout the psalms and the prophetic books. Our situation, then, is not out of control. God still knows, still cares, and still orders our daily lives.

Personally, I have found that my belief in God's control over all circumstances gives me the ability to keep going. It means that there is no purposeless suffering, no meaningless trouble. It is an enormous relief to be able to give the burden of each individual into His capable hands, believing that He cares, and knowing that His knowledge of the situation far surpasses my own. Knowing that I am responsible to Him as my Master, and need to do only that which He assigns me with the assurance that He sees and attends to the details that are not in my assignment, allows me to do my work with a lighter heart and to be encompassed in His peace.

An acceptance of God's sovereignty, coupled with the fact that He allows many things to happen that are puzzling to us, is born of a solid trust in His love and wisdom. We who are Christians need to avoid the mistake of assuming too much responsibility for what does or does not happen in our lives. God is still in control—in spite of our humanness, our denial, our battles. He will still accomplish His purposes. Furthermore, He understands our weaknesses and forgives us for our procrastination. Rather than berating ourselves for being human and vulnerable, we would do well to look to God for acceptance and forgiveness. Then we can draw on His strength to endure whatever is before us.

14

THE ROLE OF ANGER
IN TERMINAL ILLNESS

ANGER PLAYS A real role in the course of terminal illness. Despite opinions to the contrary, anger is not automatically or necessarily a sin. It just happens. Sometimes anger is appropriate and appropriately expressed. For example, anger can result in great personal benefit when we express it openly to God and allow Him to respond to it. In this situation, we may find ourselves face to face with Him in a new and wonderful way.

It is important for us to recognize anger—in ourselves, in our loved ones—if we wish to deal with death in an intelligent fashion rather than acting and reacting in a disorganized way. Individuals who show no evidence of anger whatsoever tend to worry me. I have learned that the absence of anger often indicates either a lack of true acceptance of the fatal diagnosis on an intimately personal level or a block within the individual between his mind and feelings.

ANGER CAN BE POSITIVE OR NEGATIVE

Occasionally the anger and energy of the terminally ill individual will be turned outward. To some degree, the outward expression of anger motivates many terminally ill individuals to work in special areas. For example, cancer society volunteers have had cancer themselves or have had family members with cancer, heart society workers have had a personal experience with heart disease, and concern with birth defects often comes from the families of children who have birth disorders. This can be a healthy means of expressing hostility and can reap an enormous benefit for the community at large as well as for the individual who directs his energy into these channels. Anger can also spark important research, career choices, and organizational action.

Anger can, of course, also have serious and detrimental effects. When anger is not recognized and dealt with, it can result in severe depression, physical symptoms or bizarre behavior. The anger of family members or friends surrounding the angry individual can produce further hostility and resentment, leading to alienation and deep divisions in the family circle. The angry individual (or family members or friends) may find that what he has feared has happened; no one understands him, no one seems to care about him, and he has been abandoned in his helpless condition.

How Should We Deal With Anger?

There is no simple answer to anger, just as understanding and acceptance of difficult circumstances do not come easily to most of us. The first step in dealing with anger effectively, however, is recognition. We must learn to recognize our own anger and that of others when we see it.

Perhaps the best indication that we are dealing with an angry response toward someone close to us is our own hostility, resentment, or desire to avoid the person. By using our own discomfort, defensiveness, and hostility as a barometer, we can usually uncover anger even when it is buried beneath a facade of depression and guilt.

When we feel helpless and vulnerable, it is easy to lash out, blaming others for our situation. Those who are nearest (and often dearest) usually bear the brunt of both anger and blame. So the husband or wife, close friends, family members, and the nursing staff (particularly if the terminally ill individual is hospitalized) must face a fair share of the anger.

In Joanne's case, which we studied in chapter 13, her feelings of despair contributed significantly to the hostile attitude others perceived in her. She blamed her slow recovery (and possibly the fact that she had cancer in the first place) on the facts that: (1) she couldn't sleep because the hospital staff wouldn't give her the "right" medication; (2) her food was cold or hot and she couldn't eat it; (3) she was in pain and couldn't get the nurses to bring her any medication for it; (4) the doctors in Chicago had handled her case wrong; (5) she blamed herself for going to the doctors in Chicago in the first place. Time after time, she asked, "Would I have had a better response if I had started on chemotherapy when you recommended it? I should have listened to you in the first place."

For the most part, such questions are unanswerable and I rarely attempt to answer them. I did, however, try to explain to Joanne that most of the decisions and recommendations in her case had been made in good faith and that my husband and I couldn't have predicted the outcome any more than we could have told her how she would have done if she had started chemotherapy earlier. "Joanne," I would say, "that's all over now. We can't go back and undo it. I don't know why, and you don't know why. All we can do is start where we are and do the best we can with each day. Somehow, it fits into God's will, and if we ask Him for explanations, He may or may not give them. On the other hand, if we ask Him for strength, guidance, and direction each day, He will not fail us."

MANIFESTATIONS OF UNRESOLVED ANGER

Depression: Unresolved Anger Turned Inward

Sometimes, when our anger is hidden, those around us can only see our feelings of utter helplessness, guilt, and extreme depression. There are several important reasons why we don't allow our anger to show. When we encounter situations in which our frustrations and vulnerability might provoke us to anger, our culture cautions us that something is wrong with expressing anger. For the Christian, anger is doubly taboo, for it is frowned on by society and totally forbidden by the church. "Good Christians," we hear people say, "do not feel, express, or deal with anger."

As a result, we learn instinctively to repress our angry thoughts and feelings and focus on our worthlessness, hopelessness, and helplessness. Weighted down by the enormity of the diagnosis, we start to believe that all is lost and totally lose hope. The resulting depression may be mild or profound, and its symptoms will vary in degree. However, they will probably include some or all of the following: sadness and the tendency to weep; loss of appetite that may be accompanied by actual inability to swallow or the feeling that there's "a lump in my throat"; decreasing mental and physical activity, as if everything was an unbearable effort; the tendency to sleep long hours during the day, sometimes accompanied by the tendency to wake up early in the morning and not be able to get back to sleep. In its extreme forms, depression may require medical or psychiatric intervention to prevent suicide through either active or passive means, such as inadequate intake of food and liquids.

Passive Suicide

Madeline Barnes was only forty-five when she developed lung cancer. Although she had never smoked, she had been exposed to high concentrations of chemical fertilizers and insecticides in the farming area where she grew up. Her lung cancer was highly treatable, however, and since it had not spread there was a fairly good chance for a complete response, possibly even for several years.

Madeline responded quite well throughout her course of radiation therapy. She tolerated the treatments better than many people, seldom having nausea and suffering no skin discomfort. A month after her last radiation treatment, we began to treat Madeline with chemotherapy.

Her husband, Fred, would do anything he could for her, and they were very close. They had never had any children, and in some ways Madeline was Fred's child as well as his wife. For both of their sakes, I was delighted to find Madeline responding so well to chemotherapy.

On Madeline's third office visit, I noticed she had lost some weight. This symptom usually alarms me, and I wanted to find out why it was occurring. "Are you eating well, Mrs. Barnes?" I asked.

"Oh, I'm doing pretty well, Doctor," she answered. "I just can't seem to get the food down, though. And then, if I eat the wrong kinds of things, I vomit them."

Fred shook his head. "I don't know what to do with her, Dr. Kopp. I'm glad you asked about her eating. I've been wanting to talk to you about it. She won't eat anything solid at all. She says that she can't swallow it and claims she has no appetite. I can't get her to eat any meat or anything." Soon I found out that any kind of meat except hamburger "stuck in her throat." She couldn't eat most vegetables, milk made her sick to her stomach, and she was living on baby food, soups, and an occasional soft drink or cookie.

First, I suggested she drink half a glass of wine before dinner to relax her and spark her appetite. This worked moderately well for a few weeks and then Madeline went back to her original state of being unable to eat most foods. So I got "tough." I scolded Madeline and insisted that she eat one thing a day she didn't want. I also insisted that she begin to eat other types of meat besides hamburger and to drink some milk. Madeline gained five pounds in two weeks. Then the meat began to stick in her throat again, and she spent nearly a whole week vomiting constantly.

"Mrs. Barnes, why do you suppose the food sticks in your throat?" I asked. "Do you have any pain there? Have you ever had an ulcer?"

"No, I haven't," she replied.

"Do you have any idea what's wrong?"

Madeline showed me several pinkish, raised spots on her chest. "This is tumor, isn't it? It's grown through the lung and now it's in the skin. That's why I can't swallow. A tumor in my throat makes the food stick." By the time she had said this, she was nearly hysterical. Her face was flushed, and her voice had risen. She practically gasped out the last words and looked anxiously at me.

We took x-rays of her chest and esophagus that same day. As I had expected, they were completely normal. I went over them with Madeline and pointed out in detail the areas where she thought there was tumor, explaining how normal it all looked. "Madeline," I said, "you can't swallow because you're scared! When we get frightened, we tighten up our muscles. The esophagus—or throat—is a muscle, too, and when you are scared it tightens and you can't swallow. Now, the only problem is, how can you relax?"

"Dr. Ruth, I have cancer and I'm dying, aren't I? It's spreading here inside, and I can feel it. I'm so scared, I don't know what to do!"

I asked Madeline about her faith. "I believe in God," she recited, a look of panic on her face. "I believe that I'm saved through Jesus' death and that He will take care of me."

"But, Madeline," I pointed out gently, "you're still scared and anxious. Do you know why?"

Madeline shook her head, and tears came to her eyes. "I try to believe, Dr. Ruth, but I can't! I guess my faith just isn't good enough. I try to praise God, but all I can do is pray that He'll help me get well. You know," she continued, "I haven't been very good about going to church or about reading my Bible and praying at home. I guess it's just too late for me to learn how to believe, now. Dr. Ruth, I'm so scared," she whispered, holding my hand tightly.

Madeline kept telling me how much she feared and hated the hospital. Yet, as she lost more and more weight and became weaker and weaker, it became impossible for Fred to care for her at home. "I don't know what to do with her, Dr. Kopp," he told me. "She has me up two to four times a night. I would let her get up by herself, but last week she fell in the bathroom and couldn't get up. She won't feed herself at all; I have to feed her all her meals. She won't even pour herself a cup of tea from the thermos I leave in her room! I can't keep this up much longer; I'm almost worn out!"

Eventually, it became necessary to hospitalize Madeline. In the hospital, she did very well at first. The nurses encouraged her and sat with her, and she began to eat by herself again and even sat up in a chair once day. After she had been in the hospital for several days, I stopped in her room and saw that she was being fed again. "What's the matter, Madeline?" I asked.

"Oh, Dr. Ruth, I'm so weak! I just can't eat by myself. And I had to vomit three times yesterday and once already today. I just know I'm getting worse!"

I had the previous studies repeated, with the same results. Madeline didn't have an ulcer, there was no narrowing or tumor of the esophagus, her lungs looked normal on x-ray, and there was no evidence of cancer anywhere. Since Madeline was becoming weaker and weaker in the hospital, I finally discharged her to a nursing home. She lived another three months, scared, anxious, and growing continually weaker.

Madeline had an excellent mental knowledge of the Bible and what it said. However, she had always depended on herself and her husband to solve their problems and had never really learned to trust the Lord. In addition, I believe that Madeline never worked through her anger caused by her illness. I would ask her, "Don't you ever feel that this is all unfair? Doesn't it ever make you angry to be here, sick, when you could be well?"

Her only answers were, "Oh, I wish I could get up and walk!" or "I'd like to be able to have a good appetite again!" or "It isn't any use, anyhow." If I asked her how a living God could let her become so sick, she always stated, "God knows what He's doing, and He's doing what's best for me." I never saw any expression of anger in Madeline, only depression and hopelessness.

This extreme form of anger-related suicide is not very common. A sort of reverse denial accompanies it, a selective hearing of "bad news" to the exclusion of good news. After the word "cancer," I don't think Madeline ever heard a word I said. When I told her that effective treatment was available, she heard me say, "A few people don't respond." When I described the side effects of treatment, she heard everything but my final statement, which was, "Of course, very few people have all these side effects. Most people feel a little bit sick on the day of treatment but don't have any problems after that." When I told her that her swallowing problem was not due to tumor in the throat, she didn't hear me.

In many respects, Madeline behaved like a sulky child. She temperamentally refused to eat certain foods or went ahead and ate things that she knew would make her sick. She pleaded with God to help her, then turned her back on Him and refused to wait for His answer. Although people would read Scripture to her, her mind was so full of her illness and her depressed resentment that there wasn't room for God's Word. Like a child who stops playing a game when it looks as if he's losing, Madeline seemed to say, "If that's the way I have to live—if I have to learn to get along with cancer and its treatment—I just won't live anymore!" In short, Madeline's death was a passive form of suicide, due to her unresolved anger and resulting depression.

Feelings of Helplessness

When we learn that we have a terminal illness, we must deal with feelings of helplessness, another by-product of anger. Perhaps the worst aspect of our helplessness is our complete inability to make future plans. No one can give us a definite answer to the question, "How long do I have?" No one can say for sure what effect the treatments will have on us, what course the disease will take in us, or list the side effects of treatment or consequences of illness we may have to live with. Not only are we unable to know how long we will live, but there is also the possible loss of mental and physical capabilities due to illness or treatment that might shorten our useful lives even more.

The more we feel the pressure of limited time and the more pressed we are to make plans to occupy our time, the more aware we become of the large number of unknowns in our future and the difficulty we have in making any plans at all. No one in our immediate surroundings can really understand our position. We can do almost nothing to affect the course of our illness. Exercises, diet, and positive thinking are all pitifully inadequate and are unlikely to alter the outlook significantly. We are thrown into an unfamiliar medical world, with few guidelines to help us find our way around. When we are faced with conflicting medical opinions or when newspaper and magazine articles seem to disagree with our doctors, we can only hope we are in competent hands.

We look to our doctors, ministers, and family, hoping they will have answers to our questions. Sometimes we are bewildered by the apparent or even real contradictions among different members of the medical team treating us. Disagreements among members of the nursing staff or minor errors in their care frighten us, for we can envision serious errors arising from the confusion around us.

When we return home again, we wonder who we should turn to when trouble shows up. By now, we may have a family doctor, a surgeon, a radiation therapist, a cardiologist, or even more doctors. Who is *really* our doctor?

Our family and friends offer help by suggesting different doctors we could see for another opinion or other research centers we could visit. They bring us newspaper and magazine clippings, health foods, diets, exercise programs, and anecdotes, each person being sure that what he suggests is the best for us. In the midst of this bewilderment, we must make decisions, trying not to hurt or alienate our family and friends.

We turn in desperation to our minister, and he may tell us that, since we have trusted in Christ and heaven is our true home, we have nothing to worry about. "Just leave the matter in the Lord's hands," he may say, "and He will take care of you." Wanting to hear more—much more—from our minister, we are again confused. *Maybe he is right after all,* we think, *and our own attitudes and feelings are wrong!* We can echo Job's words with feeling, wishing in part that we had never been born.

> May the day of my birth perish, and the night it was said, "A boy is born!" That day—may it turn to darkness; may God above not care about it; may no light shine upon it. May darkness and deep shadow claim it once more; may a cloud settle over it; may blackness overwhelm its light. That night—may thick darkness seize it; may it not be included among the days of the year nor be entered in any of the months. May that night be barren; may no shout of joy be heard in it. May those who curse days curse that day, those who are ready to rouse Leviathan. May its morning stars become dark; may it wait for daylight in vain and not see the first rays of dawn, for it did not shut the doors of the womb on me to hide trouble from my eyes. Why did I not perish at birth, and die as I came from the womb? Why were there

knees to receive me and breasts that I might be nursed? For now I would be lying down in peace; I would be asleep and at rest with kings and counselors of the earth, who built for themselves places now lying in ruins, with rulers who had gold, who filled their houses with silver. Or why was I not hidden in the ground like a stillborn child, like an infant who never saw the light of day? . . . Why is light given to those in misery, and life to the bitter of soul, to those who long for death that does not come, who search for it more than for hidden treasure, who are filled with gladness and rejoice when they reach the grave? Why is life given to a man whose way is hidden, whom God has hedged in? For sighing comes to me instead of food; my groans pour out like water. What I feared has come upon me; I have no peace, no quietness; I have no rest, but only turmoil (3:3–16, 20–26).

When Jack Miles noticed a swelling in his groin, he went immediately to his family doctor. Dr. Norton knew Jack well, and he knew that if Jack thought something was wrong, there probably was. Although it was a busy week for him, he made sure Jack could see him right away. He finished examining Jack, and things didn't seem quite right, although he couldn't put a finger on just what it was that worried him. Swollen lymph nodes in the groin weren't an uncommon finding and might mean nothing at all. *Jack has lost five or six pounds in the last two months,* he thought, *but I've been after him to lose weight for a year now. His color isn't just right, but his blood tests are normal.* Dr. Norton ordered a chest x-ray and told Jack to come back in ten days.

After ten days, the nodes in Jack's groin were slightly smaller. However, because there was one suspicious spot on the chest x-ray, Dr. Norton told Jack, "The nodes will have to be biopsied, and you should go to Dr. Sommers for the biopsy. I don't really expect that it's anything serious, but it never hurts to be sure."

When the biopsy came back, it showed nonspecific changes in the lymph nodes. There was no hint of cancer, and Dr. Norton gave Jack the "all clear." However, Jack still didn't feel well. His appetite was getting worse, and he continued to lose weight. The swelling in the groin became larger from time to time and began to give Jack some discomfort.

In the course of his business, Jack took frequent trips to New York and San Francisco. Since he had a number of New York trips planned during the next several months, he went to see Dr. Anderson at a research hospital in New York.

Dr. Anderson repeated the same tests, and they showed an abnormal shadow on the chest x-ray and a slight abnormality in the liver tests. Because the lymph nodes were still swollen, he did another biopsy. "Jack," Dr. Anderson said, "the biopsy was malignant, containing cancer cells that appear to originate in the colon. It looks like cancer. I guess your doctor at home got the wrong lymph node," he added, laughing and conveying the impression that the "doctor at home" wasn't quite up to par. "Anyhow, it looks like you need further surgery and a course of radiation therapy. We've got your surgery scheduled for first thing tomorrow. I'll see you this evening to get a permit signed."

As Dr. Anderson left the room, Jack thought, *I don't even know what kind of cancer I have or what kind of surgery I'm scheduled for. And the radiation therapy! How long will that take? How should I plan? How many extra days will I need in New York?* Jack took out his appointment book and began to look it over, a tight, hard knot forming in his stomach. After awhile, he rang for the nurse. "Sorry to bother you, but Dr. Anderson didn't tell me what kind of surgery I'm having or how much longer I'll be here. Do you have any idea? I need to make arrangements for my business."

"I'm sure I couldn't say," the nurse answered. "I wouldn't worry about it if I were you. Just look at it as an unexpected vacation and enjoy your free time." She patted his pillow, smiled at him, and left the room.

Jack could feel his stomach churning. *I guess I had better relax or my ulcer will start acting up,* he told himself. *But how can I call my wife and tell her I'm going to surgery tomorrow when I don't even know what kind of operation it's going to be? I really have to call Betty at the office, at least to get her to reschedule my appointments for this week. When should I tell her I'll be back home?*

When Dr. Anderson came back that evening with the permit, Jack was ready for him. "Explain in detail the surgery that will have to be done and how long it will take," Jack said. "Why will I still need radiation therapy? How many treatments will that be, and how long will it take?"

"We're entering you in a study for treatment of colon cancer," Dr. Anderson explained. "One-third of our patients get radiation after surgery, one-third get chemotherapy, and the rest get a combination of radiation and chemotherapy. This treatment is for people whose cancer hasn't spread, of course."

Jack was confused. "What about the spot on my lung? Isn't there a question about the liver? And anyhow, didn't the cancer in the lymph node in my groin spread?"

Dr. Anderson stopped short, looked hard at Jack, and went to get his chart. He came back to the bedside briefly, leafing through the chart. "Sorry, I got you mixed up with someone else," he said, and left the room!

Now Jack was really in turmoil. *If Dr. Anderson has me confused with someone else, how much of what he told me is still true? Am I really going to surgery in the morning? And if I do, will it be for an operation that I really need?*

Late that night, another doctor stopped by. "Mr. Miles, I'm terribly sorry. Dr. Anderson tends to rush around a bit too much, I'm afraid. I'm Dr. Olson, and I'm going to do your surgery. You do have cancer in the colon and, although it has spread, we feel that it's advisable to take out the tumor in the colon. Otherwise, it will give you serious trouble. After surgery, we want you to have a course of radiation, and then we will start you on a program of chemotherapy. I'll come and explain it to you when you're ready to start."

"Dr. Olson, can you give me any idea of when I can plan on getting home?" Jack asked. "I need to call my secretary and have her rearrange things, and it would help a lot if I knew about when I could plan on being back."

"I can't promise," Dr. Olson explained, "but if you make satisfactory post-operative recovery, you can probably be home in two weeks." Jack felt the knot in his stomach start to unwind, and his headache improved. *Two weeks isn't too bad. Betty is good at rescheduling and especially good at placating angry clients. She should be able to handle this situation just fine. I have some idea of what's going on, and Dr. Olson promised to explain things to me again later.*

For some reason, however, Dr. Olson didn't get back to explain the chemotherapy to Jack. Instead, Jack saw yet another doctor, who went over the treatment program with him and got his signed consent. Jack extended his business trip and stayed in New York to undergo more extensive surgery and a full course of radiation therapy treatments. Then he was advised to find a doctor at home who could start him on chemotherapy. He was given a six-month return appointment, a copy of his records, and his first dose of chemotherapy.

On the plane on the way home, Jack was tense and jumpy. Having to take two and a half weeks off had put him in a position of having to catch up. *I'm sure Betty has things well-organized,* he thought, *but I've lost the feel of the work and will have to spend two or three days getting back into the routine.* He kept thinking about the chemotherapy and how he would have to start all over again with another doctor.

When Jack returned, he went in to see Dr. Norton immediately. Dr. Norton reviewed the records from New York and told Jack that he was happy he had been cared for there. However, Dr. Norton was totally unfamiliar with the chemotherapy they had used and referred him to my husband and me for treatment.

We looked over Jack's records and reviewed the treatment plan as well as the treatment he had already received. Then we went over everything with Jack, explaining that he would be treated on the first, eight, and fifteenth day of every six-week period and that he would need weekly blood counts. Jack wrote down the schedule in his appointment book and jotted down on his calendar the days he would need his next appointments.

Jack left the office feeling relieved. *Everything will work out all right after all!* he thought. *I now know when I need to visit the doctor and can plan my out-of-town trips around my office appointments.* The feeling of helplessness and frustration that had been with him ever since he had been in the hospital in New York began to ease.

For the first several months we were treating Jack, things went well. His blood counts remained in a safe range, and so we were able to treat him on schedule. He was able to organize his trips and his appointments to his own satisfaction. He even began eating better and gaining some weight. Then we had to delay starting a scheduled treatment course because of a low white count. This meant that a business trip had to be rescheduled and it threw everything off by a week. Jack found this upsetting, and he realized that it could happen at any time. "Dr. Kopp," he asked, "is there anything I can take, or anything in my diet, that will keep the counts up? I wish there were some way I could be sure they would stay up there!"

"Jack, the treatments themselves drop the blood counts. We just have to wait for them to recover. They will, you know, but not always as quickly as we expect. I don't know of anything that we or you can do about it."

When the time came for Jack to go back to New York, we repeated the studies and found that the chest x-ray was completely clear. The liver tests were normal as well, which made us very happy. We gave Jack a complete set of his records and told him to telephone when he got back in town.

Much to our surprise, Jack telephoned a week after he had left. "I'm going to have surgery," he explained. "I guess Dr. Olson wants to see if there is any tumor in the abdomen. He said something about radiation. I'll keep in touch with you."

Again, Jack found himself scheduled for surgery before he even knew what the surgery was for. Doctors gave him several explanations that only served to confuse him. Finally Dr. Olson told Jack that the surgery would allow him to look inside and see if there was any obvious tumor. "You've done so well otherwise that I feel it's a good idea to see how things look inside. Then, if there is some tumor still left, we can use radiation in hopes of giving you a better long-term outlook."

Jack went to surgery and waited to hear the results. Dr. Anderson stopped one day to visit, but he was on a different rotation now and wasn't involved in Jack's care. Jack asked about Dr. Olson, only to find out that he had gone on vacation. Suddenly, one afternoon, Jack was placed on a cart and wheeled to radiation therapy. *Well, that's one way to find out, I guess,* he told himself, convinced that more cancer had been found at surgery.

Jack tolerated his radiation treatments well and soon was back home to continue his chemotherapy. But we began to run into serious trouble. Not only were Jack's white cell counts low, but his ulcer began bleeding again. Several times he tried to telephone Dr. Olson for advice and reassurance; we, too, tried to contact Dr. Olson for records and a copy of the treatment plan that would tell us what the alternative treatment(s) was.

One day Jack came in to talk. "I don't think I'd better take any more treatments until you or I talk to Dr. Olson," he said. "I have to be in New York next week anyhow, so I'll try to see him then. I'll call you as soon as I find something out."

We again tried to contact Dr. Olson—without success. Several weeks went by, then two months, and we didn't see or hear from Jack. Then one Friday morning, our secretary came in with a clipping from the obituary column. Jack had cleared off his desk, left his affairs in order, gone out into his garage, and hanged himself.

Few people are placed in such a helpless position, and many who are do not have Jack's overwhelming need to be in control of their daily lives. In Jack's case, the only way he could bring order out of the chaos of his illness and regain some measure of control over his life was to determine the time and circumstances of his death.

Overt suicide is an extremely rare occurrence in terminally ill individuals, and it generally arises out of the helplessness and vulnerability felt in the stage of anger. Often it is the well-organized, efficient, and orderly individual who commits overt suicide, which may be a desperate attempt to gain some kind of control over what he believes to be a hopeless situation. Instead of waiting meekly for treatment programs and their results under the uncertainty and pressure of limited time—waiting for the natural course of his illness and any unforeseen accidents—the individual who commits suicide is able to set the time of his death and leave his affairs in an orderly fashion.

One who is used to ordering, organizing, and arranging his own life is particularly vulnerable to the unexpected, unpredictable nature of a terminal or serious illness and will be greatly threatened by it. Perhaps such an individual could better handle his frustrations by voluntarily handing over control of his schedule to one doctor, one person, or—perhaps the best alternative—to God. Friends, family members, and medical personnel caring for such an individual would do well to see to it that he is allowed as much involvement and information concerning decisions as is possible.

Anger Toward God

Throughout Scripture, we read that God is all-powerful (see Gen. 18:14; Jer. 32:17, 18), compassionate (see Ps. 86:15; Rom. 3:25), loving (see Jer. 31:3; 1 John 4:7, 8), all-knowing (see Isa. 46:9, 10), in charge of all things (see Isa. 45:7), and the source of all knowledge (see Prov. 2:1–6). These and other passages indicate that He is personally concerned about each of us.

Yet, it often seems that God hasn't done anything to prevent our illness (or the illness of another) or intervened on our behalf as we had expected. We agree that doctors are human and can make mistakes. The same thing might also be said of our friends and family, who might be unaware of our condition, preoccupied with their own concerns, or incapable of understanding and responding to our needs. *But God claims to make no mistakes,* we think, *and yet He didn't prevent this calamity.* So God easily becomes the object of our anger. The feeling that God has turned His back on us and doesn't even care about us is more devastating than being left at the mercy of doctors, tests, and treatments. Often when we turn to God for reassurance in times of confusion, He is not there. We pray, and there is only emptiness and silence. It seems that no one is listening, that our prayers are bouncing off the ceiling. When this happens, we feel like crying out to God using the words of the psalmist: "My God, my God, why have you forsaken me?" (Ps. 22:1).

C. S. Lewis, the well-known English scholar and writer, experienced this type of situation after the death of his beloved wife. In *A Grief Observed,* he notes that "instead of 'ask, and it shall be given unto you' (see Matt. 7:7) the rule seems to be, 'Them as asks don't get.'"* Why does this happen?

Have you ever tried to embrace an angry child? The love you try to express meets the barrier of the child's anger—stiff shoulders, head turned aside, muscles struggling and writhing to get away! Perhaps we are like that with God. While calling desperately for Him to hear, do we react receptively when He reaches down to comfort us or are we like the stiff, struggling, angry child?

One reason our questions go unanswered is because we refuse to ask God our "why" questions and don't give Him the opportunity to answer them. As Christians, we quickly realize that being angry with the world about terminal illness or other devastating situations is ultimately being angry with God, resenting the situations He has allowed to happen. Since God can do no wrong, we decide that our anger against Him is unmerited and quickly suppress it. Yet, we become overwhelmed with guilt and are unable to accept our circumstances.

---

*A Grief Observed (New York: Bantam, 1976), p. 11.

While affirming intellectually that God knows what He's doing, we are seething inside with rage, frustration, and resentment over what seems to be His will for our lives. Many of us stop at this point—seething inside, condemning ourselves for our inability to "thank God in all things," overwhelmed with guilt, self-reproach, and hopelessness. Ultimately, if we have any sense of God being an omnipotent, omniscient Being, we must reach the point where we hold Him responsible for our plight.

Guilt

Our anger toward God almost inevitably leads to guilt. How dare we question what God has done? Who are we to tell Him what He should and shouldn't do? Even worse, who are we to expect His favor, ask His mercy, and anticipate His care? Our guilt can lead us to minute self-examination, and few of us could not find sins and faults in ourselves that would invite God's wrath rather than His mercy.

It is interesting to note that, in the Bible, we have evidence that others before us have blamed God for situations they felt were unfair and hopeless. In John 11, we read the account of the death of Lazarus and his resurrection by Jesus. Notice in verses 21 and 32 that both of Lazarus' sisters, Mary and Martha, blamed Jesus for their brother's death. Both said to Him, in effect, "If You had been here, our brother would be alive now. Where were You when we needed You?" Then both of them went on to state their belief in Jesus' power and to ask Him to do something, if He could.

Jesus did not rebuke them. He didn't explain His delay, nor did He deny that His delay had been a factor in Lazarus' death. After they asked Him, "Where were You when we needed You?" they saw their brother restored to life! When Jesus' disciples later questioned Him about His delay in going to Lazarus, He told them that they didn't understand God's purpose in the situation (see John 11:5–16, 37, 40).

I do not believe that God expects us to accept our difficult situations automatically and without question. When we ask our questions, He will respond, although He may not always give us direct answers. In some cases, He will make part or all of His purpose behind the situation clear. In others, He will reveal the purpose to us when we ask Him. The rest of the time we must be content to know that He has a purpose. We must trust Him in light of what we already know and in light of the new knowledge of Him that we acquire while in the midst of our trouble. Although God may not satisfy our desire to understand, I am confident that He will always satisfy our need for His presence and His love. When we need Him, cry out to Him, and wait for Him, we will find Him!

CONFRONTING GOD FACE TO FACE

Once we as Christians are forced to confront our terminal illness, we face a severe test of our faith. If our faith is built on a solid belief in God's past faithfulness to others and to us, it will remain strong and solid. The more we learn about God's character through our own experiences with Him, the more secure our faith will be. The bigger our concept of God, the greater our faith can become.

Yet, we will have a time when we earnestly seek answers to our questions and relief from doubts and confusion in order to testify to God's ability to meet and satisfy our needs. By allowing our doubts and questions to be expressed to God, we learn that He is big enough to handle issues of life and death and to give us meaningful, satisfying answers. We must not be afraid to confront God face to face.

We read in Scripture about individuals who found themselves in desperate situations. Some of them dared to go to God and tell Him, in effect, "You got me into this! Now what are *You* going to do about it?"

In Numbers 11, Moses complained to God that the burden of responsibility for the Israelites was becoming too heavy. "What have I done to displease you that you put the burden of all these people on me? Did I conceive all these people? Did I give them birth? . . . Where can I get meat for all these people? They keep wailing to me, 'Give us meat to eat!' I cannot carry all these people by myself; the burden is too heavy for me. If this is how you are going to treat me, put me to death right now" (vv. 11–15).

God answered Moses' angry remarks by providing a practical solution to his problem. Rather than being the only individual providing leadership for the people, Moses was to choose seventy of Israel's elders. "I will take of the Spirit that is on you," God said, "and put the Spirit on them. They will help you carry the burden of the people so that you will not have to carry it alone" (v. 17).

God then dealt with the Israelites' demand for meat. Moses said, in verses 21, 22, "Here I am among six hundred thousand men on foot, and you say, 'I will give them meat to eat for a whole month!' Would they have enough if flocks and herds were slaughtered for them? Would they have enough if all the fish in the sea were caught for them?"

In response, God stated, "Is the LORD's arm too short? *You will now see* [ital. added] whether or not what I say will come true for you" (vv. 21–23).

Throughout Scripture, and in the lives of believers today, God responds in this way. When Moses asked, in effect, "How are You going to do this impossible thing, Lord?" God stated emphatically, "Wait and see!" In essence, God emphasized the fact that He was God and promised that Moses would see what that meant. Moses did wait, and he did see God's supernatural intervention in that difficult situation.

During the Midianite occupation, a man named Gideon was secretly threshing wheat in a winepress to keep it from the Midianites. The angel of God suddenly appeared to him and said, "The LORD is with you, mighty warrior" (Judg. 6:12).

Gideon then faced God with an accusation, much the same way Moses had done. "But sir," Gideon replied, "if the LORD is with us, why has all this happened to us? Where are all his wonders that our fathers told us about when they said 'Did not the LORD bring us up out of Egypt?' But now the LORD has abandoned us and put us into the hand of Midian" (v. 13).

"Go in the strength you have," God answered, "and save Israel out of Midian's hand." In case His orders weren't perfectly clear, God added, "Am I not sending you?" God then gave Gideon specific instructions to tear down his father's idol to Baal, replace it with an altar to God, and offer a sacrifice.

Gideon wasn't convinced. "If now I have found favor in your eyes," he said, "give me a sign that it is really you talking to me" (v. 17). God gave him a sign, and Gideon followed His orders and tore down the altar to Baal. Then the entire town became angry with him. God understood Gideon's plight, however, and the people decided to let Baal defend himself and didn't kill Gideon.

After the Midianites, Amalekites, and other eastern peoples joined forces and crossed over the Jordan River, Gideon summoned the Israelites to war. But he still wasn't convinced that God would do as He had promised. "If you will save Israel by my hand, as you have promised," he told God, "look, I will place a wool fleece on the threshing floor. If there is dew only on the fleece and all the ground is dry, then I will know that you will save Israel by my hand, as you said" (vv. 36, 37). God answered by fulfilling both this request and a second one.

Satisfied that he was doing God's will, Gideon went ahead with plans to fight Israel's enemies, and God went with him. Using God's own strategy, Gideon and his band achieved a rousing victory and freed Israel from bondage. All of this happened, however, because Gideon took his anger and confusion over Israel's desperate situation to God and God answered him.

Many of us are familiar with the prophet Elijah's plight after his showdown with the priests of Baal in 1 Kings 18. Afraid of what Queen Jezebel would do to him, and both angry and depressed, Elijah "ran for his life" (see 1 Kings 19:3). He sat down under a broom tree and prayed that he might die. "'I have had enough, LORD," he said. "'Take my life; I am no better than my ancestors'" (19:4).

Again, God met Elijah's need. On a practical level, He sent an angel to feed Elijah and to make sure he got some rest. Then God gave Elijah some tasks to do and told him that he could see only part of the picture.

Even though Elijah thought he was the only person left who was following God and that the situation was hopeless, God still had 7,000 followers "whose knees have not bowed down to Baal" (v. 18). God granted Elijah's request, and it wasn't long before Elijah was taken to heaven.

The Book of Job contains the most remarkable answer we have from God to accusations made against Him. Even though Job had always been a just and righteous individual, he was stripped of his possessions, his family, and his health. Job's three friends added to his miseries by insisting that he was being punished for his sins. If you will only admit, confess, and forsake your sins, they insisted, God will forgive and heal you. After all, we know God, and He would never repay good with evil! (see Job 4:7, 8:3, 11:4–6; 5:21–30).

God didn't defend His actions toward Job. He merely gave Job a long dissertation about who He is. Job's friends were punished for lying about God (presumably in their confident assertions of what God would and would not do), and God asked Job, in essence, "Who are you, Job, to question Me?" The wonderful part of it, however, is Job's final statement to God before God restored his fortune and family. Nothing positive had entered Job's circumstances. Yet he was able to say, "My ears had heard of you but now my eyes have seen you" (42:5). This, then, was God's answer. Whereas at first Job knew God only through hearsay, at the end he had seen God for himself.

These selected illustrations from Scripture serve to support my feeling that God is capable of handling our anger and answering our accusations. So it seems to me that when we, as Christians, become angry, we should remember that God is able to speak for Himself. Others have been angry with Him, and He has understood. We must tell Him about our anger, our feeling about the injustice of the situation, our confusion and doubt. We then must wait for Him to answer us. Although He may not always answer every question we ask, He will give us the satisfaction of knowing Him. He alone can satisfy us and help us resolve our anger.

RESPONSES TO ANGER

As I began writing this chapter, I could feel my shoulder and neck muscles tightening, for when I recalled the angry patients I've known, I could feel myself responding emotionally. From time to time, I could even relive the hostility and resentment I have felt toward some of those individuals. In order to learn how to deal with anger, we must understand the various responses people have to anger.

Responding to Anger With Hurt, Hostility, and Avoidance

The easiest response to anger is to become hurt and hostile. Because these feelings tend to make us feel uncomfortable and/or guilty, we stay away from the person who produces them in us. Even though the person provoking irritation and resentment may be a close friend or relative, we leave him alone. Inevitably, our avoidance creates more guilt. We will examine the cases of two individuals who made people respond in completely opposite ways.

Louise Durham was in the hospital for treatment of advanced breast cancer. She was extremely weak, had trouble sleeping, suffered from severe nausea, and was quite depressed. The first day I visited her on my rounds, I asked, "How are you feeling?"

"Oh, terrible," she snapped. "I never slept a wink last night. That sleeping pill—it was Seconal, wasn't it?—didn't do any good. I always need Nembutal by injection in order to sleep."

"Mrs. Durham," I answered, "your platelet count is a bit low, and injections aren't a good idea. However, I'd be happy to change you from Seconal to Nembutal capsules."

The next day, Mrs. Durham again confronted me. "Those Nembutal capsules were useless," she stated. "It has to be a hypo or nothing. I know I won't start feeling well until I get some rest. How can you expect me to get well without any sleep, Doctor?"

Later that same morning, after her breakfast tray had been delivered, Mrs. Durham called the nurse back. "I have such a headache; I can't possibly sit up. Can you roll the bed up and move my tray over here?"

At lunchtime, she called the nurse back again. "My soup is cold," she said. "You know, I don't like to complain, but I have so little appetite anyhow. Cold food just makes me nauseated at the best of times."

"We'll see what we can do for you," the nurse answered, removing the soup from the lunch tray.

At 4:00, the nurse was called back again. "Isn't it time for my hormone pill?" Mrs. Durham asked. "I always take it at 8:00 A.M. and 4:00 P.M. at home."

Soon the nurses were dreading her call. Although she was always polite and "never wished to complain," her attitude was angry and hostile. My husband and I noticed it too, and we would occasionally skip her on rounds, rationalizing that there was "nothing to do for her today, anyhow."

Perhaps symbolic of Mrs. Durham's situation was the fact that the door to her room was always closed. She rarely had visitors, and nursing personnel never stopped to visit with her. Although she never failed to say "Thank you," she didn't have a grateful attitude. Needing people desperately, she succeeded in driving everyone away.

In the room next to Mrs. Durham's the situation was different. Betty David, another patient of ours in the terminal stage of her illness, was in that room. Her door was always open, and a steady stream of visitors came and went—friends, family, nurses both on and off duty. When nurses looked in on Betty, they would linger to talk with her and her husband. Even though Betty needed a lot of attention, perhaps more than that demanded by Louise, the nurses and her family were quick to care for her and attend to her needs because she had a gracious attitude of thanks.

When Louise's son, John, flew home from college in Miami after his mother was hospitalized, everyone knew he was there! He had come to his mother's side and now planned to see to it that she was properly cared for.

First, he made an appointment with me to discuss his mother's "situation." The morning I was to see him, he telephoned several times to be sure that I was running on schedule and would see him at the appointed time. When he came into my office, he began firing questions at me. "Who made the diagnosis on Mother?" he asked. "Why was a liver scan done? What did it show?" He then continued, "Why did you repeat the chest x-ray, and what did it show you? Why didn't Mother get her chemotherapy last week? How often do you do blood counts? Are they really necessary? What do they tell you?"

I answered John's questions as best I could, and he left. However, I soon learned that his attitude toward others in the hospital was the same. If his mother requested a bedpan and didn't receive an immediate answer, John would show up at the nursing station, demanding attention. If the nurse was five minutes late with his mother's medicine, John would go on the warpath. He took detailed notes of the care his mother received and gave a report to the nurse in charge every two or three days, letting her know where the problems were and what she should do about them!

Of course, John's lack of sincere communication and understanding alienated the nursing staff even further. Still, he visited with his mother every evening from 5:00 to 8:00, and the two of them got along. Since they shared their anger and directed it at the same people, it didn't disrupt their relationship. John was able to provide much comfort for his mother, and became her close companion.

Responding to Anger by Becoming Depressed

Agnes Welch was a petite, older woman with cancer of the colon. Her slight figure, blue-gray hair, and clear complexion made her look like a china figurine. Everything about her was porcelain and neat, except for her anxious-looking, blue eyes! "Please, please help me, Dr. Ruth," she begged when I first saw her. "I'm so scared! I don't know what to do!"

I tried to reassure her. "We'll try the treatments we have and hope for a good response. You'll notice that once you've started on treatment you'll be less nervous. Everyone gets a bit apprehensive to start out with, but it usually gets better as time passes."

The next week when I came to give Agnes a treatment, she was still anxious. "Dr. Ruth, I just can't eat!" she exclaimed. "I can't seem to swallow the food. There's a big lump in my throat, and the food just won't go down. I think it's a tumor."

Again I reassured her. "No, there isn't a tumor in your throat," I said. Thinking that most of her problem was her nervousness, I prescribed a soft diet and a tranquilizer. During the following month, Agnes steadily lost weight and strength. Sally, the niece she lived with, was trying hard, but she couldn't get Agnes to eat.

"Agnes," I said again, "you know that you won't get stronger if you don't eat! I think it's time for you to make an effort. I want you to eat three meals and two snacks a day—not a lot at a time—but often. You can swallow, you know, if you try." I renewed her prescription for tranquilizers and tried to encourage her again.

Several weeks later, Sally stopped to talk with me. "I'm at my wits' end. Auntie will barely swallow a spoonful of broth or tea. She's so weak I have to feed her. And she's waking up two or three times a night. Of course, I have to get up with her, since she's so weak. I'm so afraid she'll fall. But I'm wearing out, too, and she can't go on like this."

The next time I saw Agnes, I became quite stern with her and actually told her that she had to make up her mind whether to remain living or die. "You know, I don't think it's all over for you yet," I emphasized. "If you make up your mind to live, I'll help you all I can. But if you decide to die, there's nothing I can do to stop you. I can't make the decision for you. I still think it's too soon for you to give up, though."

Although Agnes seemed appreciative of the concern Sally and I were showing, she made no effort to care for herself. Ten days later, I hospitalized her. By then she was extremely weak, emaciated, and severely depressed. During her first days in the hospital, the nursing staff went all out for her. They sat by her bed. They coaxed her to eat. They cajoled her into taking short walks and sitting in a chair. Agnes remained weak and pathetic. It seemed that the more attention she received, the less she tried.

Finally a night nurse exploded in anger. "We've done all we can! She's well enough to eat by herself. She's strong enough to sit up. I'm fed up with babying her. If she doesn't want to get well, there are plenty of people here who do! I'm going to concentrate on them." Sally finally made arrangements to have Agnes transferred to a nursing home and, in a sense, we all washed our hands of her.

Although the helpless aspect of depression can be very appealing and can arouse instincts to care and serve in those around the terminally ill individual, the accompanying hopelessness is usually overwhelming. Where others might tend to respond to the individual's helplessness with an eagerness to serve, the hopelessness eventually gets them down, and they begin to agree that there is, in fact, nothing that can be done to help.

Like open hostility, depressive anger usually results in avoidance and alienation. In a case like Agnes's, there seems to be no alternative but to avoid the angry person. It is better, perhaps, for us to recognize this early and put a psychological distance between ourselves and the angry person in order to maintain some sort of relationship. Otherwise, our own anger and hostility toward the angry person can become so overwhelming we cannot maintain or reestablish a relationship. This leads to total alienation and generally leaves us feeling guilty and angry.

My own reaction to Agnes was a marked tendency to avoid her. There have been times when I have forced myself to remember her illness and her need to talk with someone. Since I disengaged my emotions rather early in her case, I was able to spend time with her and talk with her. I can also recall occasions when I felt angry with her for the irrational way in which she was behaving toward me and for refusing to try to get well.

GENERAL GUIDELINES IN DEALING WITH ANGER

Since anger can destroy much needed relationships, let's examine a few guidelines in dealing with anger:

(1) Try to remember the cause of the anger—the angry individual's frustration, hopelessness, and helplessness. Even if you become the target of the person's anger, don't take it personally. Answer the feeling expressed by the angry individual, not his specific accusation. For example, you might say, "I can see that you're feeling upset" or "You are very angry."

(2) It is probably best not to respond by saying, "I understand." Substitute a statement such as, "I can see how that would make you upset"; "If it were me I'd . . ."; or "You are in a very difficult situation and I sympathize with you."

(3) Try to avoid judgmental statements such as, "How can you say that to me, after all I've done for you?" or "How can you treat the doctor (nurse, minister, social worker) that way? He/She is only trying to help you." Remember that the angry individual probably knows he is acting abominably. He has probably tried to "be good" without much success. Berating him about his behavior will tend to make him feel more guilty and depressed. There is a difference between scolding and compassionately pointing out the way an individual is acting and asking for an explanation.

(4) Make it easy for the individual to talk about his anger and

frustration. Unexpressed anger doesn't go away; it shows up in a new form (often guilt or depression). If you are able, convey by your attitude that it is okay for the terminally ill individual to be angry and that you are willing to listen to his expressions of frustration and rage.

(5) Don't expect too much of yourself. Remember that you have feelings of your own to deal with and at times you will find it impossible to be around the angry individual. Under these circumstances, an explanation for your leaving would be in order (if you can handle it). Assume responsibility for your own feelings. Rather than saying, "You make me mad" or "Your attitude about this illness upsets me," tell him "I get upset by your illness" or "Right now I feel that I can't cope with the fact of your illness." A statement such as this may open the way for the individual to talk with you about his anger and can relieve you of guilt feelings. If you must leave, plan to go back in the future to find out if the situation has improved and become easier for you to handle.

(6) Remember the helplessness and the feeling of uselessness that are present in anger. Look for ways to say, "You are still an important individual." For example, ask him when he would prefer you to visit instead of dropping in on him at your own convenience. Suggest that he call the office from time to time and keep in touch with his work. Depending on his role at home, it might be possible for him to assume responsibility in teaching other members of the family how to assume responsibilities he previously carried.

For example, suppose Dad has always cared for the garden and the yard, and now he is sick in the hospital. Consult him about the garden, and ask such questions as, "What should be done this week? Is it too early to plant (or harvest) this? What do you use to spray the roses? How often should they be sprayed? What special plans do you have for the garden, and what can the family do to help you get it ready?"

Let's suppose, on the other hand, that Mom is in the hospital. She has always been responsible for the house, the meals, and the schedule of activities. Consult her about menus. Ask such things as, "Do you clean the house in a special order? (Maybe there's method to her habits.) Are there things I need to remember, such as putting salt in the water softener or getting the garbage out for the garbageman?"

In implementing this suggestion, I have one further caution. Don't overdo! Ask for advice and help in one area at first and see what kind of response you get. A terminally ill individual can be overwhelmed by being asked to assume a lot of responsibility at once. Take it easy. On the other hand, don't ask if you don't intend to follow the advice. If you are merely "humoring" him, he will realize this right away and resent it.

As I pointed out earlier, I believe that God is ultimately the rightful object of our anger and frustration. After all, if He is God, then He could have prevented our (or another's) impossible situation! Not only that, even now He can intervene and change things. The fact that He does not change things and prevent them from occurring makes Him responsible for the situation in which we find ourselves. If it makes us angry, then He should share the force of that anger.

Don't try to protect God, either from your own anger or from the anger of someone near you. He is perfectly capable of defending Himself. More surprising than the fact that God *can* take care of Himself (His honor, the glory of His name, His reputation, et al.), is the astounding evidence we have that He will, in fact, answer accusations against Him!

Once we have worked out our anger toward God, the way is open for a new understanding and acceptance of our situation. Admitting that we are angry with God allows us to go to Him and ask Him to help us forgive Him for permitting the situation that is so intolerable for us. In this attitude, we can learn acceptance of our circumstances, which brings us new peace and often opens up a way for God to work in our situation.

15

LET'S MAKE A DEAL

RUBY CARTER WALKED into my office for her regular chemotherapy treatment and said, "I don't care what happens to me after Sheila's wedding. I just want to be able to go." I nodded, knowing that this attractive, vivacious, sixty-year-old woman hadn't complained or had a real problem with her treatment for breast cancer since she started planning for the wedding. Truly on "good behavior," Ruby was living for the wedding, which was three months away. Her oldest daughter, a successful lawyer in San Francisco, would be married to a "wonderful man" and the wedding was going to be a great occasion in the Carter family. Like many other patients I have treated, she was bargaining to gain a little more time in order to do something she really wanted to do.

Bargaining is a emotional buffer similar to denial. People who bargain are aware of the real nature of their illness. However, they are not quite ready to fully accept the truth and try to "make a deal." "I will face facts," they say, "if you can guarantee that I will live to participate in the wedding (or graduation, Christmas, birth of a grandchild, or another type of special event)." They then set a definite date. At that time, they tell themselves, I will no longer try to avoid the seriousness of my situation or the fact that my death seems to be inevitable.

The bargain consists of several parts. First, there is a specific time limit usually related to a special event. Second, the person bargaining implicitly promises not to ask for anything else if that one request is granted. Third, the individual offers a spoken or unspoken promise of good behavior in exchange for the time he has asked for.

The bargaining individual says, "I'll be satisfied if only I can have this last request." That request may be the "last thing" the individual intends to ask for; if it is granted, he agrees that he won't want anything more. Of course, once he has been given one "stay of execution," he is generally ready to try another bargain. Few people are content with getting only "one last thing."

The third aspect of bargaining, the promise of good behavior, may be a spoken agreement between the patient and the doctor or nursing team. "If you let me go to the wedding, I'll be good," she may say. Or, "If you have me well enough to go on this special vacation, I won't ever complain to you again." A doctor, when placed in this situation, will generally do everything in his power to see to it that the patient can participate in the event that is so important to him, but he can't guarantee anything. Beyond that point, the matter is in God's hands.

To further understand the bargaining process, let us examine some examples of bargaining found in Scripture.

SCRIPTURAL BARGAINS

Hezekiah's Bargain

One of the best-known examples of bargaining found in Scripture is in Isaiah 38:1–22 and 2 Kings 20:1–11. Hezekiah was dying of an illness, and Isaiah the prophet went to him and said, "Put your house in order, because you will die; you will not recover" (2 Kings 20:1).

Not wanting to die, Hezekiah prayed and wept before the Lord, reminding Him of all the good things he had done and of the way he had followed Him. "Remember, O Lord, how I have walked before you faithfully and with wholehearted devotion and have done what is good in your eyes" (Isa. 38:3).

After hearing Hezekiah's prayers and seeing his tears, God agreed to extend his life and said to Isaiah, "Go and tell Hezekiah, 'This is what the Lord, the God of your father David, says: I have heard your prayer and seen your tears; I will add fifteen years to your life. And I will deliver you and this city from the hand of the king of Assyria'" (Isa. 38:4–6). As a sign, God moved the sun's shadow back ten steps on the stairs of Ahaz. It is interesting to note that God then gave Isaiah a prescription for Hezekiah—a lump of figs to lay on his boil so that it would heal (see 2 Kings 20:7).

Hannah's Bargain

Hannah also bargained with God, although her bargain was not a matter of life or death. Her story is recorded in 1 Samuel 1:1–20. Elkanah, her husband, loved her dearly and showed a preference for her above his other wife, Peninnah. But Hannah was barren, and Peninnah mocked Hannah's childlessness. "Because the Lord had closed her womb," we read in verses 6 and 7, "her rival kept provoking her in order to irritate her. This went on year after year." Finally, in great anguish, Hannah bargained with God for a son. She told God that if He would give her a son, she would dedicate him to temple service. "O Lord Almighty, if you will only look upon your servant's misery and remember me, and not forget your servant but give her a son, then I will give him to the L ORD for all the days of his life, and no razor will ever be used on his head." The Lord agreed to Hannah's bargain and gave her Samuel. Hannah, in turn, kept her promise to return Samuel to the Lord. God blessed Hannah further, making Samuel a leader of his people and one of the foremost prophets. To complete the picture, He gave Hannah three more sons and two daughters.

David's Bargains

David frequently included reasons in the psalms why it would be to God's advantage to grant him his requests. Many of the psalms include bargaining transactions with God. In Psalm 88, David describes his plight in the first nine verses. Then, in verses 10–12, he gives the reason why God should save him. "Do you show your wonders to the dead?" David writes. "Do those who are dead rise up and praise you? Is your love declared in the grave, your faithfulness in Destruction? Are your wonders known in the place of darkness, or your righteous deeds in the land of oblivion?" In other words, David is saying, "Look, God, I'm no good to You if I'm dead. I won't be able to praise You or tell others about You in the grave. Let me live so that I can go on praising You."

In Psalm 13, the writer asks God to come to his rescue so that his enemies will not be able to glory in his defeat and so bring dishonor to God's name. In Psalm 6, David again emphasizes the fact that it is to God's advantage to save him, since he will abundantly praise, honor, and give glory to God if he is rescued, and he could not praise Him in the grave.

In the scriptural examples we just examined, all three individuals bargained with God. This is usually the case when the individual who bargains is a Christian. The individual asks God to give him an additional number of weeks, months, or years of life. The basis for such a request is either: the past service the individual has given God; the praise, thanks, and glory that God will receive for honoring the request; and/or the future service that the individual will give God in his "extra time."

E XAMPLES OF B ARGAINING FOR L IFE

Due to extensive tumor in most of her bones, Ellen Bailey had several fractures and suffered severe pain. She couldn't go for more than three hours without an injection for pain—which sometimes wasn't even enough—and the pain made her nauseous, miserable, and irritable.

Yet, Ellen wanted to attend her son's wedding, and things changed the week before the wedding. Ellen became much more agreeable, and in the excitement of planning she was better able to tolerate her pain and discomfort. Although some of us had grave doubts about her ability to be away from the hospital for the entire day, she insisted that she wanted to go to the wedding and reception and spend the night at home. Her doctor wrote a medical pass, and everyone joined in to help Ellen get ready for the wedding.

On the day of the wedding, someone fixed her hair and made up her face. We helped her get dressed, gave her an extra-strength injection for pain and some pills to take along, and sent her off. The following day (and for more than a week) when Ellen returned to the hospital, she was walking on air! Nothing seemed to bother her, and her pain was markedly improved.

Hospitalized in a near-terminal phase of breast cancer, Sheila Cooper wanted desperately to attend her only daughter's wedding. All the nurses on her floor—even the cleaning ladies and orderlies—knew that her goal was to attend the wedding. Everyone tried to cheer her up and keep her morale up. The nurses worked hard to help her overcome her problems with nausea and pain. Family, friends, and medical personnel worked together to get Sheila home for the wedding. Implicit in their minds was the thought, *Let her have this one last request before she dies.*

In spite of everything, Sheila didn't make it. She got to the point of leaving the hospital to go to the wedding and then was too weak to even get up from her bed. A friend who attended the wedding told me later that the wedding was "almost like a funeral" because everyone was so conscious of Sheila's absence and the reason for it. Shortly afterward, Sheila died.

BARGAINING IS NOT DENIAL

There is a small but important difference between bargaining with God for extra time in a terminal illness and the denial-motivated belief in divine healing. Denial is an attitude that still claims, "This is all a bad dream, and I'm going to wake up any minute now and find out it's not so." Bargaining, on the other hand, says, "Yes, I'm living in a nightmare. I will have to cope with it, but not yet. Let me do this one thing first."

After beginning a new type of chemotherapy treatment, Ellen Matthews described her reaction to the fact that her breast lump was malignant:

> I just knew that the surgery would cure me. After all, God wouldn't let me die of cancer. Hadn't I worked hard for Him all my life? I was important to the overall Sunday school program in my church; I had a good witness before my neighbors and a vital role in the Christian growth of my family. I didn't seriously believe that there was any possibility of my dying from cancer.

Contrast Ellen's viewpoint with that of Rena Owens:

> When I found out that I had a breast lump, I was a widow with five children under the age of six. After the surgery, I forgot all about the cancer. I remarried and began a normal, happy life, and the doctors told me that there was tumor in the bones. I prayed and told the Lord that it wasn't fair to Bob to leave him alone with my children. I asked Him to give me enough time to raise my children so that they could look after themselves. Then I would be ready to die.

Ellen didn't seriously believe that she *could* die of breast cancer; Rena realized that she could die and asked God to let her raise her children first. Ellen was saying, "Oh, no, not me!" Rena, on the other hand, had the attitude, "Yes, it's me all right, but not yet!"

The Importance of Bargaining

Helps the Individual Face Death

Although there is a difference between denial and bargaining, they have a similar function. The bargaining individual is one step closer to facing his own mortality. In fact, he is ready and willing to face death at a definite point in the future if only he can be granted a "good conduct prize," a guarantee of extra time. Bargaining also serves to keep the final impact of a person's serious illness from overwhelming him, in a way similar to initial denial.

It is important for us to notice that the bargains often succeed. The bargaining individual is frequently, but not always, granted his wish, and this helps him to better face his death. God does answer prayer in this area many times. Yet, no one involved in the course of a terminal illness should discount the psychological value of positive thinking in the healing process.

The person with a "bargain" or positive attitude tends to be more at peace and more relaxed. He sleeps better at night and expends less energy in nervous tension. His muscles are more loose, so that the pain he may experience is lessened. He does not have the stimulus of anxiety to produce extra acid in his stomach or more active bowels, thereby minimizing nausea, vomiting, and diarrhea he might otherwise have. Relief from anxiety, therefore, decreases pain and nausea, promotes good nutrition and adequate rest, makes chemotherapy and radiation treatments more tolerable, and decreases the amount of medication needed to control symptoms associated with illness or therapy. In addition, individuals who are at peace with themselves seem to heal faster than those who are under stress.

It Gives Family and Friends the Opportunity to Help

Those who care for an individual who has made a bargain, as well as his family and close friends, probably know about the bargain, and most of them will do whatever they can to make the bargain succeed.

It Provides Hope

Because bargaining gives the dying individual a goal to look forward to, it helps him to gain control of his life again, which in turn brings him peace, purpose, and interest in life. It is important to realize that a bargain is not a cheap, trite way to try to live longer. It is a psychologically sound, natural response to death's approach and can offer a person additional hope that comes from within—the most valuable kind of hope available.

How Should We Respond to a Bargaining Situation?

As we have seen, a bargain generally involves the terminally ill individual and those people around him and/or God. Occasionally a parent or spouse will enter into a bargain with God on behalf of his sick child or mate. Usually, though, the individual will make a bargain with God, "fate," "the universe," or "the powers that be." As outsiders, our position in responding to an individual's bargain simplifies our responses. Either we agree wholeheartedly, adopt a "wait and see" attitude, or become frankly skeptical.

Wholehearted Agreement

When I first began treating Chuck Parsons for widespread cancer of the colon, he was incredulous. "Dr. Harris told me he got it all when he operated last January," he told me. "I just can't believe it! I never smoked. I never drank. I always got my exercise. I've been careful of my diet. What went wrong? How did I get cancer?" I carefully explained to Chuck the available treatment and warned him that it was effective in only one-third of the people who used it. That was enough for him, however. He was sure he would be the one out of three to have a successful cure!

As the months went by, I began seeing signs that Chuck's disease was spreading. Little by little, he was losing ground. Finally he, too, noticed that he wasn't feeling as well as he had been before. "Is this it?" he asked me.

"I think we've reached the end of medical treatment," I explained, "although I think you will still feel relatively good for another couple of months."

The next time I saw Chuck, he was almost bursting with excitement. I had barely entered the examining room when he began to tell me what had happened. "Dr. Ruth, last time I was here you told me that things were out of your hands now. You said that there was nothing more you could do medically. Well, when I went home, I started thinking. You know, I've lived a good life, but I've been kind of selfish. I never was very religious. Oh, I believed in God, and I would pray, but I never was much good at church or that sort of thing.

"Well, I decided that things would have to change. The next day, I telephoned our pastor, I told him that I wanted to join the church and asked if I could become an usher. The last three Sundays, my wife and I have been to Sunday school and church, both. I start ushering this next week. Dr. Ruth," he continued, "I know God's going to give me more time! I want a chance to do good, to do the things I ought to do. I know that God will let me live!"

Then Chuck's wife broke in. "Oh, yes, Doctor! Chuck is really a changed man. I believe God's going to heal him and make a wonderful testimony of him."

Both Chuck and his wife believed in his bargain. They "knew" that he would be "rewarded" with an extended life for turning to God and that he would be given an opportunity to serve Him. Although the bargain was Chuck's, his wife agreed completely.

The "Wait and See" Attitude

After Chuck and his wife stopped talking, I looked at Chuck and smiled. "Mr. Parson, I'm glad to see you looking so well. You certainly have managed to stop worrying, haven't you? I'm glad you have decided to join the church and go regularly. I'm sure that will help you be at peace and less anxious." I then proceeded to examine and treat him, and neither of us mentioned his bargain again. I didn't agree or disagree with his statement that he would be healed. Instead, I agreed that his promise of good behavior was a good thing. I also commented on the obvious fact that he was now much less anxious and concerned than he had been earlier.

Responding With Skepticism

About eight weeks later, Chuck brought up the subject of his bargain and his healing again. "Dr. Ruth, do you know that it's been almost three months since I started attending Sunday school and church every Sunday? I began ushering weeks ago, too, and we have even begun saying a prayer at meals now. I feel so much better, too. Don't you think I'm better?"

I smiled and shook my head. "Mr. Parson," I said, "I think it's great that you're going to church and ushering! Just be careful that you're not trying to impress God. You know, if He wants to make you well He certainly can. But you are not going to buy any favors by attending church. God will do what He knows is the best for you and for your wife. I know that you are feeling better, and you certainly seem better, but I can't say whether it's due to your new peace of mind or because your tumor is getting smaller. Let's wait awhile and see, okay?"

Chuck's cancer grew rapidly, and he became progressively weaker. Although his bargain had failed, he was able to avoid a feeling of guilt and personal failure by believing that God was in control. "The failure of the bargain isn't my fault," he said. "It just means that things look different from God's perspective."

The terminally ill individual can often see many ways in which God would be praised and honored by healing him. He can think of people who will at last be "convinced" of God's goodness and power when they examine the evidence that proves God has done the impossible.

When bargaining fails, the terminally ill individual is tempted to blame himself for the failure. Instead of looking at the situation from the point of view that God knows better than he does, the individual may feel personally inadequate. *God has rejected not only my proposal for a bargain,* he thinks, *but me personally.* This feeling causes guilt and depression, the major dangers in a bargain.

In these instances, the individual needs to remember that God's view of the situation is broader than his own. Again, he needs to focus on the power and person of God. He needs to recognize God's sovereignty and right to be sovereign by virture of His unsurpassed wisdom, understanding, mercy, and love.

So, I believe that the preferable response to someone who bargains with God is either a noncommittal "wait and see" attitude or a frank (but gentle) approach, reminding the bargaining individual that God's gifts cannot be bought. This perspective opens the way for acceptance of the situation if the bargain fails and ensures that God will receive the credit if it succeeds.

SECTION FIVE

AS DEATH APPROACHES

16

PREPARING FOR DEATH

Although we all tend to avoid the fact that we will die someday, our responses to death are different. Some people maintain an attitude of complete denial, giving no thought to preparation for eventual, accidental, or sudden death. Others, while not feeling that death is anything they need to worry about, still take care of such practical matters as making a will, buying life insurance, and deciding on the guardianship of their children—just in case.

When we discover that we have a terminal illness, however, each of us experiences what I have chosen to call preparatory grief. As the name implies, preparatory grief consists of two parts—preparation for death ("final arrangements") and mourning. In preparatory grief, we become aware of the fact that our illness will necessitate changes in our life and that we must begin making plans for some of those changes.

The importance of preparatory grief is twofold: it gives the dying individual important and purposeful work to do while he prepares himself and those around him for his death, and it makes the adjustment and arrangements after the funeral easier for those who are left behind. The work allows the dying individual to control the rate of his farewells, to give input regarding funeral preparations, and to help prepare his family to get along without him. As such, it helps him fight off the sense of helplessness and uselessness that often accompanies terminal illness. As the dying individual participates in the preparations his family must make in order to live without him, preparatory grief gives his family the security of his love and concern and minimizes the loneliness of the impending loss.

Characteristics of Preparatory Grief

A very real grief is present in this stage. Dr. Kubler-Ross calls this phase of dying "depression"* because its pervasive sadness and slowing down of physical and mental processes are typical of depression.

---

*Taken from *On Death and Dying*, E. K. Ross (Macmillan, 1969). The thought is found throughout the book.

However, there is usually not the sense of worthlessness and inadequacy that can be seen in other types of depression resulting from anger and guilt. In fact, there may be a sense of completion—of a job well done—as the individual prepares to die. This is particularly true for older adults, who have had time to finish such things as raising children, establishing a business, or paying for a house.

In preparatory grief, the dying individual says farewell, not only to those he loves but also to things, places, seasons of the year, and holidays. There is a need to look at the fall colors and think, *If I never see another fall, Good-by, autumn. You've been lovely.* When winter comes, it may be the last Thanksgiving, Advent, Christmas, or New Year's, and as such it has a new sweetness tinged with the sadness of farewell. There are so many threads in each individual's life. When there is time for farewells, many need to be said. Each individual, place, or thing that has had a part in a terminally ill person's earthly life is something he will lose in death. Many such ties are weakened and severed during the period of preparatory grief. For example, the individual may take a "last trip" to a favorite place, have a last visit with a dear friend, or eat a last meal at a favorite restaurant.

AGE IS AN IMPORTANT FACTOR IN PREPARATORY GRIEF

The mourning aspect of preparatory grief and the necessary preparations for death will, of course, depend on the age of the dying individual. We will divide individuals into the following categories: young children (up to age six); preadolescents (age seven to twelve); adolescents (age thirteen to nineteen); young adults; middle-aged adults; and older adults.

Young Children

A young child will not have to make many external preparations, but he needs to understand what will happen to him when he dies. He needs to realize that he will be "going away" and that no one else can go with him. It is important that the parents take time to answer any questions the child may have and be sensitive to his feelings. The same explanations and descriptions a parent would give if the child were going to visit friends or going to the hospital can be given in the event of impending death. The Bible records enough about heaven for a parent to be able to describe a picture of it to a child.

The most vital preparation a parent can make for his child is to be sure that the child knows Jesus intimately as a friend before he dies—understanding his need to trust in Christ before death. Even a small child can understand the meaning of trusting in Christ and have the comfort of knowing the presence of the Holy Spirit.

A young child's mourning will stem primarily from a sense of loneliness and, to some extent, grief from the pain and discomfort he anticipates in dying. It is qualitatively the same kind of grief the child feels when he must go to the hospital alone, remain with a babysitter at home when he is sick, or go away to stay with friends or relatives.

Preadolescents

As with a young child, it is important for the parents (doctor, or nurse) to give the preadolescent the factual information he requests. Because a preadolescent is a very matter-of-fact young person, he may seem morbid in his requests for details. But his parents should not be afraid to talk with him about such things as dying, illness, pain, funeral arrangements, or possible hospitalization and should help him develop a good idea of God and heaven. A child this age may want some say in the type of funeral service and/or burial planned for him. If he seems to be thinking about such matters and has preferences, his parents should ask him to let them know what he wants. Allowing him to participate in the plans for his own funeral may take some of the uncertainty and fear out of dying.

The preadolescent child should also be encouraged to express his feelings about hospitalization and procedures and, as much as possible, take part in planning for these. For instance, his parents may ask him if he would rather have a certain test done before or after a meal, whether he would like to have a blood transfusion done today or wait until tomorrow, or if he would rather go into the hospital on Sunday night or wait until Monday morning. They must not ask him his preference, however, if he really has no choice in the matter. If he must do something he doesn't want to do, taking time to reason with him and explain the situation will probably be much more help to him than it would be to a younger or older child.

Most preadolescents will not spend much time grieving. Generally speaking, the preadolescent doesn't really understand the final nature of death and doesn't have the future dreams and plans the adolescent has. He has the advantage of living in the present—a state that every terminally ill individual would do well to aim at! Because the preadolescent's ties to the past and future are not strong, he doesn't feel his losses as acutely as others do and copes with the situation by learning facts and gathering information.

Steve Johnson, a nine-year-old boy with acute leukemia, went into remission during his second course of chemotherapy and remained well for the next eight months of treatment. He was cheerful, energetic, and continually optimistic. Although he read widely and was fairly intelligent, he refused to believe that his leukemia was serious and was sure he would recover.

After eight months, Steve relapsed. We admitted him into the hos-

204 • *When Someone You Love Is Dying*

pital again, changed the drugs we were using in his treatment, and he again went into remission after four courses of the new treatment. However, the second remission didn't last long, and Steve soon became very sick. We tried another drug combination, but it was obvious that we could do no more for him. We then decided to let him go home and treat him on an outpatient basis.

During almost every office visit, Steve would ask my husband, "Dr. Kopp, how does it look? Are there any leukemia cells in my blood?"

Jim would answer, "I'm afraid it doesn't look good, Steve. Some leukemia cells are back again."

"But there are just a few, aren't there?" Steve would insist. "There aren't many! I'm getting better, aren't I?"

Recognizing Steve's denial, Jim was reluctant to tell Steve the whole truth. He did, however, have a conference with Mrs. Johnson and told her he had practically given up hope and that Steve would probably die within the next few weeks. After the conference, Steve approached her at home and asked, "Mother, when is Jesus going to make me well?"

Mrs. Johnson sat down with him and replied, "Steve, you know that we have talked about the fact that Jesus might not make you well here on earth. Things look bad now, and I think that Jesus is going to take you to heaven. There you won't be sick or have any pain."

Steve just looked at her intently, saying nothing. "You mean that I'm going to die," he finally said and went to his room. He remained there the rest of the day, even refusing to come down for dinner. The next morning, though, he was his usual cheerful self. "It's okay," he told his mother. "I'm going to heaven, and Jesus will be with me, so I won't be afraid."

Because Mrs. Johnson had prepared herself for losing her son—having worked through some of her mourning and having reached the point where she could "let him go"—she was able to help Steve make his own preparations. Her honesty in facing the fact that her son would die gave him the opportunity to prepare for death.

During the time alone in his room, Steve faced the fact of his death and probably mourned for the things he would lose in dying. Yet, in some way, he was able to prepare himself (with the Lord's help, I'm sure) and accept his death. Shortly afterward, he was hospitalized out of town and we didn't see him again until he died. But we heard from others who visited him that he was a support and encouragement to those who cared for him.

Adolescents

The adolescent individual probably takes dying harder than people of any other age group. He views his life as just beginning and sees infinite possibilities before him. His choices of career or profession, marriage, and lifestyle seem unlimited. It is a very bitter experience, indeed, when he discovers that his life is almost over just when it seems it is beginning. To me, it's like getting to the most exciting place in a novel, only to find that the rest of the book is missing.

Consequently, the adolescent has to make many adjustments as he prepares for death. He must adjust his lifestyle to the treatment schedule and realize that he doesn't have "all the time in the world" ahead of him. His shattered dreams give way to the awareness that every moment must be used well. His parents probably have communicated their expectations of him, and now those, too, cannot be realized.

The adolescent usually has to grow up quickly and work through a lot of mourning in a short period of time. Not only will he lose his actual family (parents, brothers, sisters, aunts, uncles, grandparents), friends, home, present or future occupation, and possessions, he will also lose all his hopes and dreams. Unlike a preadolescent, he has already begun to see some of his dreams materialize but will lose everything he hoped to have. He may mourn the fact that he has no chance to marry, have children, finish his education, or begin his career.

Mark Hanssen was only sixteen when he found out that he had widespread bone cancer. Having already lost an older brother to bone cancer, the news was a double blow to him and he became a difficult and rebellious patient. Alternating between angry rebellion and deep depression, he never felt like cooperating with us in his treatment.

As Mark's disease progressed, though, he changed markedly. He became passive, less angry, and gradually resigned himself to his eventual death. In many ways, he gave up all hope and waited to die. He began to look and act older, and when he died at age seventeen he looked, moved, and talked like an old man.

Before nineteen-year-old Harold James contracted Hodgkin's disease, he anticipated a full life. He bought a beautiful new car and enjoyed showing it off. He started his first job, imagined that he had all the time in the world to make a life for himself, and was looking forward to traveling, meeting people, and having a good time. He had a girl friend (or several—I never really knew) and a large, loving family.

When Harold became ill, he lost his job. With the diagnosis of Hodgkin's disease and the need for time off periodically to come to our offices for chemotherapy treatment, he found it impossible to get another job. Instead of having infinite career and job possibilities before him, he had little chance to find work. Without a job, the car, new clothes, and good times that Harold had enjoyed became harder to support. Suddenly the infinite variety of things Harold thought he had and could do were narrowed down to a strict routine of doctor's appointments, chemotherapy, and laboratory tests. His whole life revolved around his disease and its treatment. It was hard for him, too, because he was the only son in a family of four sisters. As his mother's spoiled darling, he was also "failing" to fulfill her fond hopes and expectations.

As might be expected, Harold at first became extremely rebellious. It was almost a joke in the office when one of us asked when he was due to come in. He managed to get to his appointments, but rarely on the day or at the time for which he was scheduled. Often he would "forget" to get the scheduled chest x-ray or fail to pick up his prescriptions.

Gradually, Harold began to change. He started keeping his appointments regularly, although he insisted on seeing me rather than my husband. (If I wanted Jim to check him over and gave him an appointment for a time when Jim would be in the office, Harold always "forgot" and came when I was there at a time he chose.) Still, he came in at the same time every week for his x-rays and always picked up his medicine, with the firm understanding that he would not go into the hospital under any circumstances whatsoever. "I've developed a life-style that allows me to do what I enjoy doing," he told me one day, "and I want to do as much as my physical condition will allow."

Harold's attitude during the last few months of his life really encouraged me and his family. He came to peace with himself and with God and had a source of inner strength that not only sustained him but also spread to those around him. After coming to terms with his disease, he told me, "I'm confident that God will heal me, and I'm still looking forward to a full and useful life." Yet, he must have faced the fact of his progressive disease because he gave me and his family explicit instructions about the way he wanted his last days to be handled. "I don't want to die in a hospital," he said, "and I want to avoid medication as much as possible, except for the chemotherapy that's necessary." He chose to come to the office for treatment until his last injection—a day before he died—and refused to be helped when walking, even though his progress on his own was painful and slow. In many ways, he was saying, "I'm going to make a go of it as long as I can and fight as long as I have a breath. I'll take the help I need, but I don't want to be pitied or babied."

Occasionally an adolescent will take out his rebellion in a different way, and Mark Timkins is a good example. He began chemotherapy for cancer on his eighteenth birthday, and he is a "good patient." He keeps appointments, follows order, undergoes the tests that are ordered, and generally cooperates. Furthermore, he's brave and uncomplaining, although the treatments make him violently ill for a few days and have given him some pretty rough times. I don't know whether he has faced the fact that his type of cancer is almost always fatal, but I suspect he has and has decided to fight it with everything he has. "So," someone might ask, "what's his problem? He sounds like a model patient."

Although Mark usually comes to his appointments alone or with friends, his mother accompanied him on one occasion. When they entered the examing room, I could sense the tension between them. Mrs. Timkins' first words to me were, "Dr. Kopp, it's important for Mark to get his sleep and eat a balanced diet, isn't it?"

Thinking that there was probably more to the story, I asked, "Could you please explain in a little more detail what's bothering you?"

"Well," she said, "Mark and his friends stay out till all hours of the night, and then he has to get up for work in the morning. And when he's with his friends, he drinks a lot. I would like him home at night so he can get his rest, and I don't think he should be drinking at all."

Mark looked at me sheepishly but didn't give up his position. "We just go out once in a while, usually on weekends," he stated, "and I only have a couple of beers."

"Mrs. Timkins, I can imagine that you're very concerned about Mark and don't want him to do anything that might hurt his chances of getting well," I said, "and that you want to do all you can for him. I'm afraid, however, that his response to treatment will be independent of anything he does or doesn't do in the way of activity. As far as I know, there is no special diet that will improve his condition. Of course, he needs a reasonably well-balanced diet and adequate rest, but I doubt that he needs more rest than he gets. During the week he's on treatment, he will want to eat more lightly than usual and might feel more tired.

"I think that Mark is trying to lead as 'normal' a life as he can and is determined to get all he can out of life. He would like to forget about his disease as much as possible, and I think that's a good attitude as long as he keeps his appointments and takes reasonably good care of himself. Since he hasn't been missing work or losing weight, I suspect that he isn't overdoing it."

"Yeah, I guess that's how I feel," Mark said slowly, looking relieved. "I want to have good times with my friends."

"I think it's important that you understand your mother's concern for you, too, Mark. Perhaps you two can work out some sort of a compromise so that you won't get on each other's nerves."

The discussion seems to have helped. Mark is maintaining a remarkably good balance between living a "normal" life and taking good care of himself (if indeed they can be separated), and his mother has been able to let go of him and allow him to do more of the things that are important to him.

Young Adults

A young, terminally ill adult must do quite a bit of preparation once he learns about and confronts his illness. Provisions may have to be made for a spouse, dependent children, or parents. The young adult must part with the things, people, and places he holds dear and must make financial and legal arrangements concerning the details of his funeral, burial, and redistribution of property. Often, too, he must prepare someone else to take over his responsibilities at work or at home. His mourning is similar to that of the adolescent, except that he has a few more "concrete" losses because his dreams are beginning to come true.

Rita and Roger Baker are an example of two young adults who had to face death. They were the parents of three-year-old Lisa when Rita found out she had leukemia.

Rita responded well to treatment and maintained a good remission for nearly a year. During most of that time, she came into the office once a week and always brought Lisa with her. Roger came most of the time, too. Since her office appointments were scheduled for my working days, I got to know her fairly well. As the year progressed, Rita began preparing herself, Roger, and Lisa for her possible death "just in case."

As Halloween approached, I asked Lisa, "What kind of costume are you going to wear?"

"I'm going to be a witch this year!" she replied, grinning.

"Is your Daddy going to take you trick or treating?"

"No, Mommy's going with me."

Rita looked up at me. "Roger usually does things like that, but this year I want to do it. I'm feeling well now, and who knows about next year?" When Christmas came, Rita made sure that she had time to bake cookies with Lisa, go out and look at the lights in the park, spend quality time with Roger, and sing with the family. Shortly after the new year began, Rita shared with me what she was trying to do. "Maybe that was our last Christmas together, and I wanted us to enjoy it to the fullest. I want Lisa to remember me, and I want her memories of me to be happy ones. But I'm trying hard not to shield her from my illness by bringing her with me to your office and having her visit me when I'm in the hospital."

Rita made the most of her time. Besides taking the opportunity to say "good-by" to Christmas, Halloween, and other happy times of the year, she built a photograph album full of happy memories to leave with Roger and Lisa. Hoping for more time and perhaps a cure, she nevertheless lived day by day, season by season, as if each day might be her last. She allowed herself the pleasure and comfort of Lisa's company in the office and hospital, the care and help her parents offered her, and Roger's love and support. She achieved a remarkably good balance between "acting as if" everything was all right and taking care of her preparatory grief work "just in case."

Middle-aged Adults

A middle-aged adult preparing for death has many of the same tasks to accomplish as the young adult. He usually needs to provide for a spouse and dependent children or parents. He must part from things, places, and people he holds dear and make financial and legal arrangements. Often he must prepare someone else to take over his responsibilities at home and at work.

The difference in preparation between the young adult and the middle-aged adult is in the intensity, rather than in quality. The middle-aged adult has already worked out some legal and financial details. His children are usually grown or nearly grown. He has had the time and opportunity to try out some of his plans and dreams and knows how they worked out. He experiences less of a loss in terms of future hopes and more of a loss in terms of actual possessions. He probably has a home in an established community and has developed a circle of friends and an identity. Although he has had the satisfaction of acquiring many things, his ties to them are stronger than they were in young adulthood. If he's married, the marriage bond is usually deeper, since it has survived much longer.

Jane and John Jones had a rather difficult family situation, for the relations were strained between them and Jane's mother. Prior to Jane's death, she and John and I had gone over in detail the necessity for her to make a will and legally assign guardianship of their three children to her husband. Beyond that, we thought it wise to assign his mother as guardian in case anything happened to John to make him unable to care for the children. Jane was greatly relieved when these practical considerations had been cared for. Her mother-in-law told me several times what a difference the arrangements for her children had made in Jane's peace of mind, her ability to sleep and rest, and even the ability to bear the pain of her illness.

Martha Miller had almost a year to make preparations before her death. Though she often denied that she was unwell, she made sure that her daughter, Sarah, was able to assume her household responsibilities. During the year prior to Martha's death, she was told that Sarah might have to have heart surgery to correct a birth defect. So part of Martha's preparation included getting Sarah to a specialist right away (she could safely have waited, if she had wanted to) and getting the matter cleared up. After careful testing, the specialist determined that Sarah's heart was normal.

Once Martha knew that Sarah was all right, she began to make her own arrangements. She turned over more and more of the household responsibility to Sarah and taught her as well as she could. Shortly before her death, Martha actually asked Sarah to take over the care of the house and her father, and they had a chance to say their "good-bys."

Older Adults

The older adult (a category defined more by attitude, I find, than by actual age) may seem to make few preparations for death. He may, in fact, already have made his preparations and be ready to die anytime. When given the diagnosis of a terminal condition, he will generally say, "We all have to go sometime, and I'm ready to go. I've had many good years, and I'm not complaining."

Many of these individuals have been widows or widowers for years. Their friends have died or grown old and infirm. They have usually sold the family home and moved to a more convenient apartment or rest home. Having disposed of most of their possessions in the move, they find it relatively easy to leave their "things." They have few strong, emotional ties left. They can, if they are Christians, say with the apostle Paul, "I have fought the good fight, I have finished the race, I have kept the faith. Now there is in store for me the crown of righteousness, which the Lord, the righteous judge, will award to me on that day" (2 Tim. 4:7, 8).

Of course, the older adult who is a Christian feels a sadness about having to leave the familiar life and go on to the largely unknown future, but he may also be relieved that he will soon be rid of his weakening body and receive a new one in heaven. He has watched many of his friends and family die and has become somewhat accustomed to and accepting of death.

Mr. Theodore Sanders is such a gentleman. He has just turned eighty-two, although he looks more like sixty-seven, and has a chronic form of leukemia. After being told his diagnosis, he said, "Well, I thank God for every one of the eighty-two years I have had. If it's His time for me to die, leukemia is as good a way as any."

Mr. Sanders is in good remission with his leukemia and can look forward to a fairly long course with it. In fact, I wouldn't be at all surprised if something else causes his death. However, his attitude is one of being ready to go. His earthly affairs are in order, and he spends as much time reading and studying God's Word and in prayer as he possibly can. He has no further preparations to make. In effect, his bags are packed, and all that's left for him now is the departure notice, last good-bys, and his journey to heaven.

Ruth McReynolds was able to prepare for her death by trusting in Christ. She also had to face the fact that she would not be able to train someone to take her place at work before she died. She didn't have time or strength to prepare her husband and daughter to assume her household roles, which caused them much difficulty and inconvenience after her death. She had always handled the financial affairs of the family, and after she died, her husband didn't even know what kind of health and hospitalization insurance she had or how to submit the proper claim forms so that the insurance company would cover the hospital and medical bills.

My friend, Barbara, told me that when her mother-in-law knew she was dying, she sold her house and bought a trailer. Then she invited all her children and in-laws to visit and asked them which of her possessions they wanted.

Barbara said, "I knew she was getting ready to die, but I kept on saying, 'Oh, you won't have room for all these things in the trailer.' I didn't want to face the fact that she was getting ready to die."

Barbara's mother-in-law also illustrated the fact that her preparations were taking place intermittently. During the same visit, while Barbara was talking with her, Mrs. Summers said, "I'm really looking forward to spending time with you next summer so that we can go shopping together. I've gotten too weak and tired to shop by myself now, but by next summer I think I'll be enough better to go with you."

Although she was giving away her things—breaking ties with possessions she loved—Mrs. Summers still clung to the hope that "next summer" she would be strong enough to go shopping, an activity she dearly loved.

PREPARATION CHECKLIST

Now that we have seen how age affects individuals' responses to their preparatory grief, let's review the following checklist, which will help us to understand some of the important preparations that the terminally ill adult (and everyone else as well) must carry out.

(1) Examine his own life and determine if he and/or his family has developed a personal relationship with Jesus Christ and then take the necessary steps to ensure that everyone will meet in heaven.

(2) Develop an up-to-date, valid will that includes guardian provisions for dependent children (if applicable) and provisions for property dispersal. Note: in many states the surviving parent is not automatically made the guardian.

(3) Make any emotional, financial, or legal arrangements necessary for the care of other dependents (parents, aunts, uncles, an invalid husband or wife who cannot care for himself, or assist in the care of dependent children, pets, et al.). If the dying individual is single and has no spouse to assume part or all of the care of his dependents, this business becomes more critical. A guardian should be chosen for de-

212 • *When Someone You Love Is Dying*

pendent children, and they should be informed of the choice. Similarly, arrangements should be made for the care of other dependents.

(4) Once the individual has decided on the arrangements, he must communicate them to his dependents. Although he should take the feelings of the dependents into consideration, he must remember that he is responsible for long-range planning. Unless he meets with violent opposition and is presented with a workable alternative, he should stick with his decisions.

(5) Try to begin transferring responsibilities to his spouse, dependents, or other significant people while he is still able to provide security and reassurance for the individuals involved. For example, he can make arrangements for Aunt Mabel to visit the nursing home into which she will soon be moving or arrange for the children to visit the home of the new guardian to learn the rules, customs, and routines of their new home. In the event that guardianship arrangements will mean moving the children out of town, this may be impossible. However, in such a situation it may be possible to arrange for the guardians to visit in your home. Correspondence with the guardians should cover the essentials (to the children) of their new home: Is there a tree? Can I have a garden? Are there other children in the neighborhood? Will I have my own room? May I keep my dog?

(6) Write out a list of people who need to be contacted at the time of death (lawyer, insurance company, friends, relatives, business associates) and a list of important documents and where they are located.

(7) Discuss what the financial arrangements of the family will be after his death (income from investments, life insurance, need for surviving spouse to work, childcare and household duties) and other related matters that will facilitate the task of the survivor afterward.

(8) Discuss the funeral and burial (or cremation) arrangements —the preacher he would like to have handle the funeral service, the Scripture verses and hymns to be used—and any other matters in this area that he feels strongly about.

This is only a partial list. You should add the particular points that apply to your own particular family to it. Notice that all of the above matters can be taken care of without the urgency of terminal illness and should be updated periodically.

How Can Family and Friends Respond to Preparatory Grief?

When someone close to us is dying, even when we have faced the fact that death is inevitable, we want to put it off as long as possible. This desire is natural, normal, and commendable. However, it often causes us to respond to the individual's preparations for death with reluctance. We want to say, verbally or nonverbally, "Wait awhile. It's not time to get ready yet. Wait!" On the other hand, we at times are able to put aside our desire to procrastinate and actually help the dying individual make his preparations. These two responses to preparatory grief are the most common, and we will examine them in depth.

Responding With a "Wait Awhile" Attitude

Norma Thompson is slowly dying of cancer, but she is still able to live alone and care for herself. While on chemotherapy, she had had a remarkable response. However, she suffered a relapse. As the tumor grew, she became progressively weaker, and she and I had a very frank talk one morning.

"There are no further medical means," I explained, "to halt the growth of your cancer. Although the cancer's growth is not completely predictable and you can look forward to periods of either stabilization or even temporary improvement, your condition will gradually deteriorate." Norma accepted the news easily. She already suspected that things weren't going well and knew that we had exhausted the medical treatments available to her.

The next time Norma came to my office, her son, Dan, and daughter-in-law, Joan, brought her in. Dan, Joan, and their children were very close to Norma. Not only did they live within walking distance of each other, but they also shared many common interests and had a great deal of mutual respect and a close bond of love.

Knowing their close ties, I was a bit surprised at their hostility when they came into my office and sat down. Dan and Joan sat close together on one side of the office, and Norma sat by herself across the room. Norma's face was flushed, as if she had just had an argument, and Joan had tears in her eyes.

The moment I shut the door and sat down, Joan burst out, "Dr. Ruth, Mom has just given up! She said she's going to die. She shouldn't give up hope, should she? Isn't there anything you can do?"

Norma didn't give me a chance to answer. "These kids aren't helping me at all, Dr. Ruth," she complained. "I've been going through my things—sorting them, throwing them out, giving them away. I know that I may not have a long time left, and I want to take care of my things my own way. Besides, I've just helped my sister-in-law, Alice, settle my brother's estate, and it's a mess! He never cleared anything out! He never let anyone know what he had or where it was. It took us months and months just to find out what he had. I'm not going to make my children go through what Alice is going through now."

I turned to Dan and Joan, and Dan spoke. "I guess we just aren't ready to face this, Dr. Ruth. We both know that Mom has cancer, but I, at least, still hope that somehow she'll be cured."

After I talked with the Thompsons a bit longer, we were able to get things sorted out. Norma had been quite depressed, and that worried

Dan and Joan. I pointed out to them that going through her things and making decisions about their disposition was necessarily a depressing activity for Norma. I further explained that Norma's depression didn't seem out of proportion, nor was she obsessively preoccupied with preparing for her death. Her preparation was an intermittent thing that she accomplished when she felt like it.

"I don't spend all my time thinking about dying and funerals," Norma said as our conversation progressed. "I go to get my hair done once a week. I still do as much as I can in the garden. It's just that I know I have all those boxes sitting in the attic, and I'm trying to get them sorted out a little bit at a time. Some of the things I've found are quite beautiful and very useful. Just the other day, I found my grandmother's silver chest with some of her silver in it. I gave it to Joan, and it made her cry!"

Joan smiled a bit sheepishly. "I guess Dan's right. We aren't ready for Mom to start getting things in order. The silver is lovely, though, and I know I'll enjoy having it."

Joan and Dan responded to Norma's preparations for death in a "wait awhile" fashion. This is a normal, initial reaction to the terminally ill person who is beginning to say good-by. Family and friends want to hold onto him and say, "Don't go yet! Not now! There is still plenty of time to take care of things later." At other times, they give the same message by changing the subject or making a break in the conversation by getting up and moving around. They want to believe that there is plenty of time; they may still cling to the hope of a miraculous cure, another remission, or a gift of extra days, months, or years. Sometimes they feel as if they are walking around in a nightmare and that pretty soon they will wake up. To some extent, making preparations for death makes it more real and forces them to face the issue. Indeed, they are almost superstitious about preparing for death. Silly as it is, they seem to believe that preparation invites disaster and that if the individual doesn't prepare it might not happen.

The "wait awhile" response inevitably causes tension. The dying individual feels his time is limited and that he has work he must accomplish in the time remaining. A "wait awhile" response from his loved ones frustrates him, since he feels that he's being kept back from his work while his time is running out.

If the situation is reversed and the dying individual responds in a "wait awhile" fashion to normal preparatory grief in his family, it can cause an even more touchy situation.

When Doris and Clayton Garrett came into my office for help, it was easy to see they weren't getting along. They marched into the office separately and sat down as far apart as they could. Both of them looked directly at me, conspicuously avoiding each other's gazes.

Clayton had been receiving treatment for lymphoma for nearly a year. The disease had been advanced when the diagnosis was made, and he had responded poorly to initial treatment. When he finally had a good response, it lasted only a couple of months and was followed by a relapse. Now he was in remission again, on his third treatment program, and doing fairly well. However, due to the advanced state of his disease and his rather poor response to treatment, we didn't feel that the long-term outlook was very good. We had told the Garretts that Clayton might have a couple of years, but that it was unlikely he would respond much longer than that.

Doris spoke up first. "Clay's being so unreasonable I can't stand it! When I say the least little thing, he nearly bites my head off. We can hardly carry on a civilized discussion any more. I want to know what's wrong with him. If he doesn't change pretty soon, I'm seriously thinking about moving out!" Doris's pretty face was set in angry lines, and she looked as if she might cry.

Clayton was equally angry. "How do you expect me to respond when everything Dory says has to do with my dying? She's after me all the time! 'Why don't you get that will drawn up? Where's your insurance policy? Where do you keep legal documents? What arrangements have you made for the business?' It's a wonder she hasn't dragged me off to pick out a coffin and cemetery lot! I'm not planning to die tomorrow, and I wish she would just lay off!"

As we talked, I discovered that the Garretts had rather extensive financial commitments. They owned and managed a branch of a chain supermarket; Clayton had been investing in real estate in their home town, in Florida, and in Arizona; the supermarket employed a number of people besides the Garretts and owned a couple of trucks and other equipment. Clayton handled all the business and financial matters completely. He alone took care of the payroll, the family checkbook, and the filing of federal, state, and local taxes. Doris didn't have any idea what was involved and was anxious to learn as much as she could from Clay while he was still able to instruct her. Although she had a college degree in business accounting and had even qualified for her C.P.A. license, it had been years since she had even balanced the checkbook! She was terrified that Clayton would die before she had a chance to learn the business and that she would be left with an overwhelming responsibility without the information to handle it.

"There will be plenty of time to make a will later," Clayton told me. "Right now, I'm too busy to bother about it. Besides, with the business the way it is now, I'll probably have to update it within six months. I'd rather wait and see how things go first and then make a will." He felt that Doris's interest in his work and his business showed that she didn't trust him and felt that it threatened his place as "boss." And, underlying everything, was his thinking, *If I don't do anything to prepare for death, maybe it won't happen.*

Clayton didn't want to face the fact that he would have to prepare for his death. He wanted to be able to say, "not yet. There is still time to think about that later." When Doris insisted that he might not have the time later, he began to feel that she was wishing he were already dead. He could see her planning for the time when she would have to get along without him, and it frightened and infuriated him.

In a situation such as this, where the dying individual maintains a "wait awhile" response, a deep rift can form in family relations and make things difficult for everyone. The situation may require outside intervention if it is to have a satisfactory outcome. A doctor, social worker, or counselor may be needed to help the couple (or family) work out a solution that all parties can accept.

Responding With an Attitude of Acceptance

Pam Carter and her husband, Bob, were sitting in my office. I had just explained to them that Pam's breast cancer had become widespread since her surgery three years earlier and that there was no hope of curing it. After we discussed the various drugs used in chemotherapy and their side effects, Pam asked, "How much time do you think I have?"

"That's something I can't predict right now," I replied. "If you respond to treatment, you can probably count on at least one year. If you don't respond, you may not have that long."

"Can you give us some guidelines that will help us in our arrangements?" Bob then asked. "The two of us run a business, and we have to arrange to care for our two children."

Bob and Pam were well aware that Pam's illness would change their way of life, and they were ready to begin making plans. Pam decided to undergo chemotherapy treatment, and she adjusted well to its demands. Later, Pam developed pneumonia, and it was necessary to stop all chemotherapy until the pneumonia cleared up. While visiting her in the hospital one day, we began talking about her condition. "I was impressed by the way you and Bob handled the fact that your tumor has recurred and is now widespread," I shared. "I hope that you respond well to treatment, and I wish there were some way I could give you a more definite idea of your outlook."

Pam began to cry. "I guess Bob and I are used to facing crisis situations," she said. "At least I am. My oldest daughter, Janie, has cerebral palsy, and I have cared for her since she was born. She's thirty-two now, but she still requires much care. The doctors told me when she was born that there was little hope she would ever walk or even feed herself, but I've been able to work with her and now she can pretty well take care of herself. She even takes care of her own room and her clothes.

"When Janie was fifteen, her father was killed in an automobile accident, so I had to face that, too. Bob and I have been married only five years, and I'm afraid that this is harder on him than it is on me." She was crying quietly; tears welled in her eyes. "I feel so sorry for him," she finally continued. "We have been so happy together, and the whole situation just doesn't seem fair."

When I talked with the Carters at other times, they were no longer preoccupied with the arrangements they had to make but were concerned about Pam's response to treatment. They also were busy making plans for the immediate future.

As it became evident that Pam was no longer responding to chemotherapy, she and Bob spent more time getting things in order. They found a home for the mentally retarded and got Janie settled there, transferred the business into Bob's name, and made adjustments so that he could run it alone. They also arranged "final" visits with family and friends while Pam was still well enough to enjoy them. When Pam died, she was at home, and her family was ready because all her preparations had been made.

Pam and Bob, like other individuals dealing with terminal illness, did not remain continually in a stage of preparatory grief. A terminally ill individual (and his family and friends) cannot look steadily at the fact of his own death, no matter how "well" he accepts it. Necessary preparations will come to mind, be taken care of, and the individual will go on living as if nothing were wrong. After all, he (and those close to him) has jobs to do and duties to attend to that demand his immediate attention. He will continue to use denial to give him a "time out" from the hard and serious business of dying and the multitude of time-consuming details that take energy and attention.

In order to prepare adequately for death while still "living life to the fullest," the terminally ill individual (and his family) needs an inner peace and reconciliation that allows him to take things one day at a time. So, as necessary preparations for death come to mind, he cares for them. Meanwhile, he weeds the garden, smells the roses, pays the bills, goes out to dinner, does the laundry, and visits his friends "as if" nothing was wrong. Although he knows he is dying, he also is decidedly alive as yet and intends to *live* as fully as possible until he dies!

How Family and Friends Can Assist During Preparatory Grief

How, then, can we (as family and friends of a dying individual) accept the need for preparation and permit the dying individual to prepare for his death? Is there anything we can do to help him make preparations when he is reluctant to do so? The following suggestions may help in dealing with preparatory grief.

(1) Be aware that the dying individual may want to prepare himself and his family for his death. Look for signs of preparation. This response may occur at any time after initial denial has been dropped. It is likely to be intermittent and appear inconsistent because the dying individual will devote time to preparing for his death in-between other activities. A switch in conversation from "When I'm gone, I'd like Amy to have my good china" to "Let's try to go to Florida for Christmas this year" can be hard to follow, but it should not be totally unexpected.

(2) Try not to make his work harder for him by putting him off or not taking him seriously. Remember that an individual in the process of dying has work he wants to accomplish, and he has a limited amount of time. He may have added handicaps of physical weakness, discomfort, or impairment of sight, hearing, or muscle control. Don't add to his handicap(s) by appealing to him to "wait" or by adding the burden of your grief to his own.

(3) Find something you can *do* to help. There may be letters to write, appointments to make, or people to see. Offer your services as secretary, chauffeur, or research assistant. Focusing on practical, physical work will help both you and the dying individual deal with your emotions during this stage of terminal illness. Try not to ask, "What can I do?" Rather, look for things that need to be done and ask if you can help with them. ("May I help you get things up from the basement to sort through?" "Do you have anything you want me to drop off at Goodwill?" "Do you need a ride to the bank?")

(4) Take notes. The information the dying individual is giving you now is mostly for future reference. When you have written something down, you can afford to forget about it. This will prevent you from dwelling on details of wills, insurance, funerals, and other depressing matters while still assuring you that you will have the information when you need it. It also will relieve the mind of the dying individual to know that his wishes, requests, information, and instructions have been written down in an easily accessible place and that he no longer needs to worry about these matters.

(5) Don't push for more preparation than the individual is willing to give. The state of preparatory grief is intermittent. You may want to help him sort through one more box, but he may be tired. If so, put things away and wait until he's ready. Keep a notebook and pencil handy to write things down when the dying person is ready to talk; put them away when he has had enough.

(6) If you, as a member of the family, feel that the dying individual is not giving enough time or thought to preparing for his death, approach the subject as a service that he can do for you. Let him know

that this is an important matter that he alone can take care of. Dwell on the help he will give his family by preparing them and the peace of mind he will have in knowing that he's done everything he could for them. If this approach still causes him to resist angrily, drop the subject and do what you can on your own to prepare for his death without involving him.

(7) Finally, don't expect too much from yourself. Your own involvement will make it hard for you to analyze the situation properly at times. You may find yourself doing the very things you vowed never to do. The different stages are difficult to recognize at times. Your participation as an emotional, interested, and involved individual makes you act and react in ways you might not always choose intellectually. Remember that there are people around who can help—your minister, doctor, nurse(s), friends, family. Don't be afraid to ask for help when you need it. Recognizing the emotional states surrounding terminal illness doesn't immunize us against the emotions; it can, however, help us in coping with them and hopefully smooth the way in the difficult journey between fatal diagnosis and death.

THE INDIVIDUAL'S FINAL SPIRITUAL PREPARATION

Once the terminally ill individual begins to make definite plans for death, he is ready to examine what Scripture has to say about his condition. The Bible's message is for him and for his friends and family. First, it promises him the glorious reality of a future hope, the assurance of heaven, and the promise of reunion. Second, it gives him the opportunity to turn over his concerns and those of his loved ones to his capable, loving, and kind heavenly Father.

The Comfort of Christ's Resurrection and Presence

Edna Peters was dying. For many years she had lived one day at a time, knowing that her death was approaching but not yet ready to prepare for it. One day, when I began to examine her, she was filled with anxiety. "What's the matter?" I asked. "Is there anything I can help you with?"

"Dr. Ruth, I'm so afraid of pain! What if I reach the point when there's nothing to relieve my pain? What would I do? I just know I couldn't face that. I don't mind dying, but I can't stand the thought of having to go through weeks or months of suffering!"

"Edna," I asked quietly, "do you know Jesus?"

"Oh, yes!" she exclaimed. "In fact, I've been getting to know Him better and better lately. This past week, the pastor at our church came out to the house and baptized me. He's been visiting me regularly, and he's always such a help."

"Well, then, you know that Jesus cares for you, don't you?" I said, and Edna agreed that this was so. We then talked about God's wonderful knowledge of each of us, discussing the way He had created each of us alike and yet uniquely different. We talked, too, about Jesus' suffering and death on the cross.

"Edna," I said, leaning forward in my chair, "can you believe that God can help you? Can you believe that He won't let you have any more pain that you can take? He knows what you can stand and what you can't stand, doesn't He?"

Edna nodded, and tears began flowing down her cheeks. I took her hand, and we prayed a simple prayer together, telling the Lord about Edna's great fear of pain. We then asked Him to either spare her the pain or provide her with the strength to bear it.

The next week, Edna's daughter, Julie, telephoned. "You can't believe the change in Mom! She's much less nervous. She's eating better, too, and sleeping through the night."

The next time I treated Edna, she reminded me of our conversation. "You know," she said slowly, "now when I start to hurt, I remember that Jesus is with me and that He won't let me hurt any more than I can stand. It sure helps."

"I've got some more good news for you," I answered. "What does Easter mean to you?"

"Why, it means that Jesus died for my sins so that I could become a Christian!"

"That's part of it," I agreed, "but the most marvelous part of Easter is the fact that Jesus rose from the dead. You know, when He came back to life, He had a new body. Something about His body helped people recognize Him, because His disciples knew who He was. But He didn't have to eat anymore, although He could and did. Traveling a great distance wasn't a problem for Him, and closed doors weren't any obstacle. Best of all," I added, "now that He has risen from the dead, He never has to die again. Do you know that God has promised to give us bodies like that? We won't have any more sickness or pain, and we won't have to wear glasses, wigs, or dentures. No more dying! Isn't that a wonderful hope to look forward to?"

Edna stared at me, and she began to smile. "I never really thought about that before," she stated. "I'm going to go home and read all I can about my new body."

When Edna died several months later, she was calm and peaceful. She had been able to remain at home until her last four days, when she became too weak for her family to care for her. She never had the severe pain she had feared so much, and she died knowing that her future included receiving a resurrection body like Jesus' and being in heaven with Him.

The joy of the Christian message centers around the fact of the

Resurrection. At one time, I felt that the apostle Paul was exaggerating when he wrote, "If only for this life we have hope in Christ, we are to be pitied more than all men" (1 Cor. 15:19). *After all,* I thought, *we have the joy of knowing God in this life, the satisfaction of doing His will.* However, this was before I had the close contact with death I have had during the past few years. Now I can agree with Paul. For me, the fact of Christ's resurrection brings with it the hope of a resurrection body, the hope of a new heaven and a new earth, and an end to the "law of sin and death" (Rom. 8). The entire created world will be affected. Pain, sickness, suffering, and tears will be things of the past.

The fact of Christ's resurrection forms the basis of our hope. Since Christ has risen from the dead, death is not a final parting from those we love but only a temporary separation until we meet again in far better circumstances. This reunion is not automatic, however, for it is contingent on our belonging to God's family. If we want to be reunited with those we love, we must become children of God. The apostle Paul clearly teaches in 1 Thessalonians 4:16, 17, that this reunion will take place. "The Lord himself will come down from heaven, with a loud command, with the voice of the archangel and with the trumpet call of God, and the dead in Christ will rise first. After that, we who are still alive and are left will be caught up with them in the clouds to meet the Lord in the air." When we are prepared spiritually for the future, the futility and vulnerability that we feel in the face of terminal illness become less threatening and easier to bear.

Arranging a Meeting in Heaven

Ron and Barbara Molleck were faced with a difficult situation. Barbara's mother, Mrs. Eiler, had a highly malignant form of cancer. It was growing rapidly, and there was no successful treatment available. Ron and Barbara were reconciled to her impending death but were concerned about her relationship with God. "Mom doesn't know the Lord," Barb told me. "Each time I'm with her, I feel that I may never have another chance to talk to her, but I just can't discuss the subject. She has always resisted the message of faith in Christ. I'm scared to bring it up now—and scared not to."

Ron and Barbara had three adorable girls who were Mrs. Eiler's only grandchildren. She loved them, and Barbara knew that the children returned their grandmother's affection. "How will I ever be able to face my girls and explain to them why Mom died without accepting Christ?" she asked me. I advised her to ask her mother that same question. Since Mrs. Eiler had already begun to dispose of her belongings, had attended to her will, and was taking practical steps to prepare for her death, the time was obviously right for this approach.

Barbara described the situation to me later. "I was like a kid about to give her first speech! My mouth was dry, my heart was pounding, and my knees were weak. All this, just to tell my own mother about the Lord! I started several times and didn't know how to say it. Finally, I just blurted out, 'Mom, I don't want you to die without knowing Jesus. I want to be able to tell Mary Sue, Jenny, and Alice that Grandma's in heaven after you are gone. Do you believe in Christ? Can you let me know that we'll see you again in heaven?'

"Mom was quiet at first, but she didn't get angry. She told me she would like to be sure that she was going to heaven, too. Then the telephone rang, and we didn't get a chance to talk anymore. Do you think I did the right thing?"

Barbara, Ron, and I continued to pray for Barb's mother, as did many others. Little by little, she began to ask about Christ. Finally, one day when she and Ron were talking, she looked straight at him. "Ron, tell Barbara that I'll meet her in heaven. Tell her to tell the girls that Grandma's waiting for them with Jesus."

That was the last time Ron or Barbara were able to talk with Mrs. Eiler. Barbara later told me about the relief and joy she experienced when she got the message. "And now I have an even better way to talk with my girls about the Lord! They love Grandma, and if Grandma's in heaven they will want to get ready for heaven so that they can see her again. Isn't it neat the way the Lord works?"

Trusting in God's Resources

Walter Henry, at age thirty-seven, was dying of leukemia. He had a young wife, Anna, and two little girls. Tending to be fearful and timid, Anna had never worked outside the house and the thought of facing life without Walter terrified her. The last time I saw Walter, he was in critical condition and quite despondent. "Mr. Henry, how's it going?" I asked. "Can I do anything to help?"

Walter replied so softly that I could hardly hear him. "I'm tired now," he said, as tears filled his eyes. "I'm ready to go. It's just Anna and the girls."

I nodded and sat down on the edge of the bed. "It's hard to say 'good-by,' isn't it? When you love people very much, it's hard to leave them."

We were quiet for a while. Then Walter spoke. His voice was urgent and stronger. "How's she going to manage? She will be all alone, now, and the girls are so little. How will they get along? Anna's needed me so much; I can't understand why this has happened."

"Walter, can you believe that God loves them?"

He nodded.

"As much as you love them?"

Again, he nodded.

"More than you love them?"

He smiled. "Yes, God loves them much more than I do."

"Can God take care of them?"

Walter though a moment, understanding what I was getting at. "Yes, He can take care of them."

"Then let us just commit them into His care. You know, He created them. He loves them. He has resources to care for them that you never had. Let us ask Him to teach Anna to depend on Him, to teach the girls what a loving Father He is, and to take care of them for you."

Walter and I prayed, committing his family to God's care and protection. When we finished praying, his arrangements were complete. He had done everything he needed to do and was free of worry and responsibility. Later that day, Walter went peacefully to his home in heaven.

17

WAITING FOR DEATH

I HAVE NEVER gone into a room where an individual was in the "waiting" stage of dying and found the television on, the radio blaring, or family members carrying on active, lively discussions. The room is always quiet. Family members may be sitting by the bedside, talking in hushed voices or reading quietly. The patient is usually "resting," often with his eyes closed. No longer interested in national, local, or even neighborhood news, he doesn't seem to have the energy or the inclination to reminisce about the past. In a very real sense, he has completed his preparation and now is merely waiting for the inevitable.

The waiting state is the only state of a terminal illness that is not interspersed with periods of denial. In this sense, it is the only continual state in which the individual completely accepts the nature of his illness and the inevitability of death.

WHAT IS THE BEST WAY TO RESPOND TO DEATH?

Some people believe that quiet waiting is the ultimate goal in "successful" dying and that the failure to achieve it indicates that the terminally ill individual has failed to accomplish all he might have during the dying process. I don't believe this. I have seen people die after short and long periods of "waiting." I have seen people die who have fought death to the very end. I have seen death overtake individuals who seemed to still be in a state of initial denial. It is impossible to describe an "ideal" psychological state in which to die that applies to everyone. We can, however, examine individual responses to impending death by characterizing basic age groups, for age is a primary factor governing the way an individual faces his own death.

GENERAL CHARACTERISTICS IN BASIC AGE GROUPS

Young Children

Young children basically live in the present and are not likely to go through a waiting period. Even the projected departure of visiting grandparents or a proposed family trip, for example, doesn't hold the same meaning for young children that it does for adults. Until Grandma and Grandpa have actually gotten into the car and driven away, children do not really accept the fact they are leaving. The same principle applies to children's views of death. Until death actually comes, they do not realize its reality.

Pre-teens

Pre-teens deal in a much more factual world than younger children do and are perhaps the most rational (in terms of demanding that strict rules of reason be followed) of all human beings. They are most apt to face death with the attitude, "It's coming, we can't avoid it, but why cry over that *now?*" Steve Johnson, whose bout with acute leukemia we examined in chapter 16, typifies this age group with his face-to-face confrontation and struggle with death. The apparent, matter-of-fact acceptance of death and the final "let's get on with the business of living" attitude were prevalent during his illness.

Adolescents

From adolescence to old age, the waiting period is likely to be brief if it occurs at all. Recall for a moment the cases of Harold James and Mark Timkins. I, for one, would have been disappointed if those young men had "given up" and spent time waiting for death. Although both of them did come to terms with the fatal nature of their disease and Harold obviously was aware of the shortness of his time as death approached, they were determined to savor every minute they had left. To me, this position was not only appropriate; it was admirable. They had so much living to squeeze into such a short time!

Mark Hanssen's acceptance of his condition, on the other hand, seemed to demonstrate more of a defeat, for Mark failed to discover a solution to the dilemma of his disastrous illness that would be acceptable to him and allow him to make the most of the rest of his life. However, Mark did not have the five or six years of adolescence, with its learning and maturing, that Harold had. Perhaps the only "acceptable solution" for Mark as an early teen was to rather rebelliously acknowledge defeat.

Adults

Any adult may or may not experience a waiting period. The young and/or middle-aged adult, however, generally has more details to take care of before he dies than an adolescent or older adult and will often continue making arrangements almost until his death. Few aspects of his life have concluded, so he often doesn't have time to even take care of the important arrangements, much less all of them.

When there isn't a noticeable waiting period before the young or middle-aged adult dies, it in no way indicates a failure on his (or his family's, doctor's, or anyone else's) part. It doesn't mean that he has failed to accept the fact of death or to adjust to it. It may be merely a reflection of his age and the stage of life he's in.

The older adult's response to death is also dependent on many factors. If he has just remarried, is active in business, or in some other way is still in the "middle" of life, he may be so busy with preparations for death that there is little or no perceptible time of waiting.

On the other hand, the older adult may demonstrate the waiting period in an obvious manner. The individual who greets the diagnosis of a terminal illness with the attitude, *I've lived my life, and now I'm ready to die,* will most likely spend time waiting for death. This type of person has few "loose ends" in life. He is unlikely to have small children or other dependents to arrange for and may already have retired from his occupation. He may have sold his family home and disposed of or distributed his possessions. His friends may have moved away or died. In short, he has less business to attend to and more time, relatively speaking, to attend to it. As a result, he has time for "waiting."

Fleur O'Brian had had a long, stormy battle with breast cancer and had spent many months expressing both constructive and irritating anger. Now, hospitalized with pneumonia at age sixty-seven, for what turned out to be the last time, she talked to me about beginning physical therapy so that she could get back on her feet. "I want to get a walker and learn to use it," she said to me, "so that I can be steadier at home." She asked for changes in her medications and once in a while needed a sleeping pill. Gradually the pneumonia cleared up, and I wrote the physical therapy request. Fleur, however, was getting weaker.

"Let's wait a few days for the therapy, until you feel stronger," I said, and that was the last time either of us mentioned it. From that point on, Fleur began slipping away, a little at a time, day by day. For several days, I went into her room and greeted her by saying, "How are you today? Can I do anything for you?"

Each time, she took my hand and said, "Hello. I'm all right. No, I have no complaints, and there is nothing I need."

Then came the day when I went into the room with my usual greeting and Fleur merely opened her eyes, took my hand, and said, "Nothing, thank you." After that, she spent much of her time sleeping. She would talk with members of her family for a few minutes at a time, then close her eyes and sleep again. She stopped asking for medication and never complained. Toward the end of her life, when I went into her room she would merely open her eyes to see that I was there and then close them again. I, too, stopped talking, and our visits consisted of my coming into her room, sitting down on or beside the bed, and holding her hand for a moment or two. I did check with the members of her family who were with her constantly to see if she needed anything, and they, too, told me that she seemed to want and need nothing and spent most of her time sleeping. Finally she failed to waken.

Martha Miller's lung cancer made it hard for her to breathe. As the condition worsened, fluid accumulated in her chest and made breathing even more difficult. Having to struggle so hard for each breath, she was constantly near panic. She also suffered severe pain, aggravated by her anxiety and inability to rest. Narcotics helped to dull the pain; oxygen made breathing easier. All in all, though, she was in the middle of a terrific struggle merely to take one breath after another.

Having settled all her family business, Martha had time to say her "good-bys," particularly to her husband and daughter. Fighting for each breath she took until the end, she never enjoyed a period of peaceful sleeping similar to Fleur's. Yet, I fail to see that there was anything lacking in Martha, in her family situation, or in the care she received. She might well have gone into a peaceful waiting period if the physical demands of her bodily functions hadn't prevented it. Perhaps it would have been better if she had died the way Fleur did. However, their final causes of death were markedly different and contributed significantly to the manner of death.

Jean Babbingdon underwent a long terminal course, hanging onto a mere thread of life for weeks longer than anyone thought was possible. She seemed to fade almost imperceptibly from day to day. Yet, I think that she and her immediate family entered the preparatory phase of dying more completely than I have seen it in any other case. By the time she died, her family had worked through all the final arrangements and almost completed their mourning. She slipped into a brief waiting period at the end of her life, after severing her emotional ties and family bonds, and then died.

All three of these women had raised children to adulthood, accomplished set goals in their careers or community, and had seen many of their dreams and plans fulfilled.

There is no particular virtue in "progressing" from one stage in the dying process to another. Orderly progress is rarely observed, and some stages are so brief that they go unnoticed or are absent altogether. There is no reason to suppose that it is necessarily "better" to die after going through a period of waiting than to be a fighter and not give up at all until the end.

The various stages we have examined are, therefore, useful mainly as a general description that seems to hold true over a wide range of diseases and ages, both for patients and their immediate family and friends. Having a uniform understanding of possible states of mind in the dying process, it is easier for us to discuss the actions and reactions that these states of mind provoke and to talk intelligently about ways to approach the dying individuals and those closely involved with them. The following section shows the important role of the family in understanding and responding to someone during the waiting period.

HEALTHY RESPONSES DURING THE WAITING PERIOD

It is important for the husband, wife, or other family members to be present during the waiting period. The dying individual is much more at ease with his spouse or other family members present, and those present will later have the comfort of knowing they were there at the end.

The presence of the family member(s) not only eases the departure of the dying individual; it also forms a bridge to the beginning of the survivors' new lives by providing protection against guilt and regret.

Mary Jenson was jointly under my care and the care of another doctor. When she was hospitalized for the last time, I didn't actually see her or her family until she had been in the hospital for a day. When I entered the floor where her room was, her husband and son walked up to me. Obviously upset, they wanted to talk with me. We went to a visitors' waiting area and sat down.

"Dr. Kopp, how is Mary? Is this the end?" her husband asked.

"Mr. Jenson, I think this is it. Of course, I can't tell you how long she has, but if you have anything you want to say to her, now is the time."

"Do you really think it's all right to talk to her?"

"Of course! If you don't tell her the things you want to say now, you may never have a chance. Besides, she may want to say some things to you."

"Dr. Jordan told us that she was going, and I have a feeling she knows, but he said not to say anything to her so that she wouldn't lose her spirit and give up. You know, during the last several days, Mary seemed to want to tell us some things, but then she didn't." I then told the Jensens that in my opinion discussing death with her wouldn't do her any harm and that it might give her a chance to talk about things she wanted to say.

"Can we stay with her?" Jim, her son, asked. "We have tried everything."

His father then explained that Mary was in a two-bed ward and that the head nurse on her floor insisted on adhering rigidly to hospital visiting hours. "We want to spend the night and, if necessary, several nights," he told me, "so that we can be with her until she dies. The nurse won't make an exception, and I have spent much of the day going from one authority to another to see if there is any way we can be allowed to stay the night." Now, after a frustrating and fruitless half-hour with the hospital administration, he appealed to me. "Dr. Kopp, can you do anything about this?"

First I went to the nurse. "Miss Hill, I have never had this happen to one of my patients. We have terminal patients in the hospital all the time, and it has always been understood that the immediate family has unrestricted visiting privileges, except in the case of emergency situations in the room, when they might be requested to leave briefly."

Miss Hill remained adamant. "The presence of the family will interfere with nursing duties and is absolutely unallowable."

"Okay," I stated. "Please find me another bed in the hospital right now and transfer Mrs. Jensen there. I know that if we move her to the third floor, there will be no further problem with the family's staying all night." I had to leave the floor at that point, as soon as I found out Mary's new room number.

About a week later, Mr. Jensen came to see me to let me know what had happened. "They got her to another room almost as soon as you left, Dr. Kopp. Jim, Jim's wife, Lois, and I were with her. She talked quite a bit, even telling Lois how she wanted her hair fixed after she died and what dress she wanted to be buried in. Mary also told Lois what to do with some of her things, and I don't know what all they talked about. After Jim and and Lois left, I took her in my arms and we talked. I can't remember everything we said, but she told me many things and I told her many things. Then, while I was holding her, she was gone! It was so quick and peaceful. I'm so glad I was there and that we had that last chance to talk." During the remainder of our conversation, he repeated the fact that he "was holding her in his arms when she died."

Although medically we were expecting Mary Jensen's death, she hadn't been "ready to die" until she had a chance to make final arrangements with her family. At that point, she was at peace and died. There was no pain, discomfort, or fuss of any kind.

Milly Harris, another older woman, went through a well-defined waiting period before she died. When we admitted her to the hospital for the final time, we discussed the fact that there was no longer any treatment for her. We agreed to keep her as comfortable as possible, and I specifically asked her husband whether they wanted to try to get her home for one "last time." Neither one of them felt she would be able to go home or that Mr. Harris could care for her. In effect, when she entered the hospital, we all understood that she was ready to die and was waiting for the end.

I noticed when I visited her that Milly had brought some special things from home. She had photographs of her son and two grandchildren, a lovely, cut-glass vase supplied with fresh flowers, her family

Bible, and one or two other small mementoes. My visits with her were restful (at least for me). She seldom said much or asked for anything.

One day I changed my pattern when I walked into her room. Milly opened her eyes, saw me, and closed them. I sat down for a minute on her bed and held her hand. She didn't respond at all. Since her husband was spending most of his days and nights with her, I asked whether she might not rather be left alone with him. "Milly, if you'd rather not have me stop by every day, just say so. I enjoy seeing you, but I don't want to be a bother."

Milly's eyes flew open, and she was suddenly very alert. "Oh, it's no bother having you stop in! I'll see you tomorrow." With that, she closed her eyes decidedly and went back to sleep.

Later on in the week, Mr. Harris asked me if I thought it would be all right for him to go home. "I've got to get the corn in, and this is the last week I can do it. I've let things go as long as I dare."

"Don't you have a neighbor who owes you a favor or one you could ask to get the corn in?" I asked. "I don't think you'll need to be here much longer, but it's important for you to be here now." He was able to make arrangements to stay another week, but as it turned out, he only needed to be there three more days. Milly died in her sleep, with him beside her holding her hand.

George Parish came to my office a day or so after his wife, Esther, had died. "Dr. Ruth, I just wanted to tell you how it was. You know, she died almost two months to the minute she was admitted. I was there with her, and she began gagging. I called the nurse for help, and together we suctioned her out. Esther stopped breathing for a minute, but then she was stronger and even said that she felt better. As I was holding her in my arms, suddenly, without warning, she gagged again. The nurse suctioned her again, and I gave her artificial respiration for a few breaths. I knew better, but I couldn't help myself! She took a couple of breaths on her own and then she was gone."

George's eyes filled with tears (my own weren't perfectly dry), and then he repeated, "She was in my arms, and I was holding her when she died." Esther had spent the last six weeks of her eight-week hospitalization in a waiting stage; George had been with her the entire time. His presence with her had been important, because whenever he had left her room, Esther had been restless and uneasy. I'm sure that, in the future, George will be greatly comforted by the fact that he did all he could for his wife and that he was actually holding her when she died.

HINDRANCES TO A HEALTHY WAITING PERIOD

In some ways, the period of waiting is one of the most difficult times to face during the course of a terminal illness. All the preparations have been completed and close friends and family of the dying individual can easily become impatient waiting for him to finish dying. On the other extreme, people have the tendency to carry over the "wait awhile" response to preparatory grief into the waiting period, clinging to the dying individual and refusing to let him die. It is difficult for friends and loved ones to match the pace of their own separation from the dying individual to the rate at which he is dying.

Jane White was an attractive, vivacious woman in early middle age. Her husband, Ed, was devoted to her. Their youngest child had just graduated from college. Business was good, and for the first time in their lives they were free to travel and enjoy their lives together without being concerned about children and finances.

Then Jane developed cancer. Surgery could only remove the most painful area of tumor, since Jane hadn't discovered it until it had spread. After surgery, she experienced a period of good chemotherapy response, followed by a dramatic remission during which she felt better than she had before surgery. This was followed by the inevitable relapse, and we had to tell Jane and Ed that there was no further treatment and that the disease would be progressive until eventual death.

Jane and Ed faced the situation well. Together they fought for each good hour she had left. When Jane reached the terminal phase of her illness, Ed promised to keep her at home and care for her himself. During the first month of her home confinement, Jane and Ed took care of all the necessary arrangements.

The period of waiting began. One week, two weeks, three weeks passed. Jane became steadily weaker. Every time I saw her, I noticed a slight change for the worse.

About a month after Jane had gone home, Ed began asking me, "How much longer can this go on?"

The only truthful answer I had was, "I don't know."

The weeks dragged on through late winter and into early spring, but Jane still hung onto life. One day she told me, "I don't see why I can't just die. I'm ready. Ed's ready. This is so hard on him, and I just wish I could go."

Finally, several months after she had gone home "to die," Jane died. When I saw Ed that morning, he told me, "Dr. Ruth, I don't know if it's wrong, but last night I prayed that there would be an end soon. I couldn't stand to see Jane getting weaker and weaker. I can almost say that I'm thankful it's over now."

Mark, the White's son, had the opposite response, however. I had told him, too, that there was almost no chance whatsoever for his mother to recover. When she first arrived home, he seemed reconciled to her condition. As time went on, however, and she was still alive, he began to look for signs of recovery. He urged her to try and get up, convinced that she was getting stronger. He became violently upset when she was unable to eat and would sit with her for hours, feeding her slowly and patiently, determined to help her regain her strength.

When Jane finally died, Mark took it hard. In some ways, it was like a personal insult! After all he had done to try to help her recover, she had died. For awhile, he interpreted his father's acceptance of his mother's death as evidence that "Dad didn't really love her." He asked me, "How could he love her and take her death so calmly?"

Mark eventually was able to realize that his mother's death had been inevitable and that his father's acceptance of it was normal and natural. As Mark worked through his own grief, he was able to see his father's deep grief, and father and son were able to become close again.

Clinging to a dying individual makes it very hard for him to die. It puts the responsibility on him to live and often makes him feel guilty for not being able to live. It implies to the dying individual, "After all I've done for you, don't you dare die! That would be the height of ingratitude. I deserve better treatment than that." It adds stress to the process of dying and can do much to prevent peace and acceptance at the time of death.

SUGGESTIONS TO MAKE THE WAITING TIME EASIER

Don't Put a Time Limit on the Dying Process

Dying is a highly individualized matter, and even doctors who have seen many patients die cannot accurately predict when death will occur. It is best to live each day as it comes and try not to plan too far in advance. Of course, decisions need to be made during critical periods in the course of illness, expecially the decision to call family members "home" to the dying individual. But it is impossible to know when "this is it." I've gone through more than one "deathbed" with several of my patients.

Be Around

There comes a time when talking almost stops. There is nothing left to do or to say to the dying individual. At this time, family members are tempted to feel useless. Unless the dying individual has said "good-by" to them and indicated that he doesn't want to see them again, family members should still manage to be by his side. At this point, almost all meaningful communication is nonverbal, and their presence—the act of holding his hand, stroking his forehead, holding him in your arms—means more than anything else.

During the waiting period, the dying individual is often literally in the middle of the family—in the middle of the hospital room, in the middle of the living room at home—and family life goes on around him. Other members of the family carry on their studies, their work, their hobbies, but often make an effort to do as much as they can within sight and sound of the dying person. This is perhaps symbolic, because the dying person is still part of the family but no longer has an active part in family life.

Adjust to the Dying Individual's State

Remember that during the individual's final days of life, he will have little energy left while waiting for the end. New ideas and concepts will be hard for him to grasp, while old and familiar subjects will be reassuring.

Once an individual has reached this point, there is little he needs or wants. He has completed his work and is now ready to go. This is the time to repeat childhood prayers, well-known hymns, and such favorite passsages of Scripture as Psalm 23, John 14, or the Lord's Prayer.

If the work of preparation has been completed, waiting can be a peaceful time of rest for all concerned. Plans don't need to be made. There is no further business to attend to. Most of the communication between the dying individual and his friends and family will be simple, since much of it will be nonverbal. As we have seen, family members and friends support the individual primarily by their presence and their touch. Consequently, if there is a waiting period, it can be a time of quiet and renewal between the ordeal of fighting a fatal illness and the adjustment of bereavement.

---- 18 ----

FACING DEATH AS A CHRISTIAN

IN FACING DEATH and coping with terminal illness as patients, family members, or friends, we have many resources available to help us. We are not at sea in a rudderless ship, nor are we totally alone. We need not be helplessly dependent on the whims and inclinations of doctors or nurses in their care of us or in the care of our loved ones. Using the guidelines and descriptions found in previous chapters, let me summarize briefly what we can do to effectively deal with terminal illness and death.

COMMUNICATE OPENLY AND HONESTLY

With Others

Open, honest communication, coupled with an emphasis on the expression of love, is the basis for maintaining ties with family members and friends. It also forms the foundation for a satisfactory relationship with those who care for us (or our loved ones). Although this type of communication is not automatic, it can be learned and is one area where we can prepare for the possibility of a family crisis before it occurs. Basically, it consists of sharing honestly with others the feelings we have and allowing them to do the same. It means asking our questions in as clear a way as we can to our doctors, nurses, family, friends, and so on. It also means answering their questions honestly and without blame.

With God

Open, honest communication with God is also the key to availing ourselves of His resources and love in the face of illness and death. Instead of hiding behind "spiritual" prayers and attitudes, we need to admit to Him (and ourselves) that we are angry, feeling helpless, in despair, or in need. Then we must wait on Him for His answers, trusting that He will answer. We need to avoid both the temptation to turn away from Him and the tendency to speak for Him.

Use the Available Tools

Many practical, common-sense tools are available to help us constructively handle our feelings and reactions to illness and death. Our awareness of the common reactions to terminal illness can, for example, help us and our loved ones prepare to meet them. If we can be honest about our feelings with ourselves, our family, our friends, and with God, then we can effectively use these tools.

Write Things Down

One of the major tools I use and recommend is the simple exercise of writing things down. In the case of a potential or actual response of denial, for example, the act of writing down symptoms and problems can help us avoid some of the detrimental delay often experienced during this state. Writing down information about the illness—diagnosis, names of medications, treatment plans, appointments—can also help us communicate more accurately with others involved in the illness and circumvent selective hearing and forgetfulness.

Become Aware of and Recognize Feelings

Feelings such as anger that surface during the course of terminal illness can be difficult to handle. Yet anger, for example, can be instrumental in providing us with the vital impetus to fight illness to the best of our ability and wrest the fullest amount of living possible out of each day. Again, awareness of our anger is the first step toward coping with the situation. Then, our honest recognition of the anger-producing situation will allow feelings of fear, frustration, and helplessness to surface and will go a long way toward helping us accept our anger. Furthermore, our recognition of accompanying feelings of helplessness and frustration may point to realistic ways of alleviating these feelings and reducing our anger.

Anger, as we have seen, is often revealed in blaming, accusatory communication. Learning to see our hostility and defensiveness when we are being blamed or accused, to stop before responding, and to answer the feeling underlying the accusation rather than the accusation itself will go a long way toward protecting us and our loved ones from the divisive, alienating effects of anger. The same principle can be applied to other feelings.

Express Love and Appreciation

Expressions of love and appreciation are often simple and are profoundly important during the course of terminal illness. Love is the best antidote to fear and the best protection against loneliness. Physical expressions of love and nearness are almost always possible, regardless of how ill the individual is, and they say as much (or more) than words. Holding someone's hand, putting an arm around his shoulder, rubbing his back or neck, or just sitting with your hand resting lightly on his hand are all effective ways of saying, "I'm here, and I care."

Realize That Good Can Come From Terminal Illness

In all the stress and strain surrounding terminal illness, I have been impressed with the overwhelming number of "good" family situations that I have seen. There are more uncomplaining, supportive, and loving husbands, wives, parents, children, aunts, uncles, and so on than I had imagined. In the midst of a crisis, it is amazing the way so many family members unite and help one another over the rough spots. I don't for a minute suppose that these family members are perfect; I am sure that they experience angry outbursts, resentment, irritability, and general difficulties. What is so surprising, then, is the way so many people are able to endure the crisis of a terminal illness in their families without undue stress and strain on the family ties. Often, the families emerge intact or even stronger after the crisis has passed. This fact makes me believe that with God's help and increased understanding, most family members can use the crisis of terminal illness and death as a means of growing in the knowledge of God and in love for one another.

Recognize the Strain of Terminal Illness

Each of us who is involved in the course of terminal illness must make allowances for the physical and emotional fatigue occasioned by the illness by budgeting time and energy—making time in a busy schedule for naps, quiet moments, and relaxing recreation. We need to be realistic in our expectations of ourselves, taking a good, long look at the physical and emotional strain present during terminal illness.

Admit Mistakes and Continue On

Finally, we must remember to take it easy! One person doesn't have to do everything, all at once. There is room for us to make mistakes—and correct them. There is time to learn by trial and error. There is time to enjoy life, enjoy the family, and enjoy other loved ones. Few, if any, errors are completely irrevocable. The words, "I'm sorry," can go a long way toward repairing breaks in relationships caused by our ignorance, fatigue, and inability to cope.

THE FINAL CHALLENGE

How do I, as a terminally ill individual, reconcile the fact of my mortality with my rich spiritual heritage as a child of God? How do I come to terms with sickness and death in my own human body? How do I face the awfulness of parting, not only from those I love or from my earthly treasures of things and places but also from the physical body that I so closely identify with my self? How do I look through pain and see purpose, look through the chaos and disruption of death to see order, look through decay and deterioration with eyes dimmed by tears to see the glory of God?

The Bible speaks of a day in which God Himself will wipe away our tears. In Revelation 21:4, we read, "He will wipe every tear from their eyes. There will be no more death or sorrow or crying or pain." As a child of God, I have been promised a part in that day. Though the laws of death and decay govern my present body, when Christ returns He will exchange my body for one that is fit to live in that new world. "The bodies we have now embarrass us for they become sick and die; but they will be full of glory when we come back to life again. Yes, they are weak, dying bodies now, but when we live again they will be full of strength. They are just human bodies at death, but when they come back to life they will be superhuman bodies. For just as there are natural, human bodies, there are also supernatural, spiritual bodies" (1 Cor. 15:42–44 LB). Paul summed up my wonderful hope, my glorious future, when he wrote in 1 Corinthians 15:49, "Just as each of us now has a body like Adam's, so we shall some day have a body like Christ's" (LB).

My hope is based on the historical fact of the Incarnation; it is ratified by the triumph of Easter Sunday when Christ rose in victory over sin and death. God almighty, in the person of Christ, voluntarily chose to take on Himself the limitations of fallen humanity. He humbled Himself so that, as a result of His humiliation as a man, I might be exalted to the status of a child of God. That glory before Him which gave Him strength to endure the cross is set before me as well. He bought my entrance into glory. Although this does not negate my tribulations and suffering, it gives me a goal toward which to press. A reward ahead will transform my mourning into rejoicing and my tears into shouts of gladness.

No wonder Christians refer to "our blessed hope." I can look forward to participation in the kingdom of God, to the end of sin and death, to the freeing of the natural world from the laws of deterioration and decay imposed on it by sin, and to an end of sickness, pain, sorrow, and tears.

Before I die, I want to learn to live, starting now, in a real expectation of this hope. I want to order my life in light of the fact of my eternal future. I want to learn to look at trials in terms of the glory that lies ahead, valuing them for the lessons of submission and obedience they can teach. I want to grow in spiritual maturity, realizing that God is not only teaching me to live on this earth but also preparing me for service and a place in His future kingdom.

Before I die, I would like to grow in understanding. I want to learn what it means to be fully human and to find God's abundant provision for my physical, emotional, and spiritual needs. I want to learn the secret of harmony within myself, between my humanity and my spiritual nature.

I am glad that my hope as a Christian is not limited to my future glory. I have a high priest, Jesus Christ the righteous One, who intercedes for me before God (Heb. 7:24, 25). Before I die, I would like to see in myself the fruits of His intercession, increasing in personal likeness to Him. I would like to know His comfort in my trials and see, in turn, how this helps me to comfort others during their hour of need (2 Cor. 1:4). I would like to understand more fully the mystery of the human-divine nature of Christ and appreciate more and more His complete adequacy to help me in the present because of His acquaintance with grief, pain, suffering, and death.

Most important of all, I want to live before I die! I want to live fully, taking each day as a precious gift. I want to live wisely, following God's daily leading, without regrets. I want to live freely, taking each situation of my life as it comes from the hand of my loving Father without anxiety or fear. Then, when I face my own death, I believe that I will be able to see my Father's house beyond the valley of the shadow, and death will be, not the end, but merely the passageway to a new beginning.

२